D0290553

MR. JUSTICE BLACK:
THE MAN AND HIS OPINIONS

JOHN P. FRANK

MR. JUSTICE BLACK

The Man and His Opinions

Introduction by
CHARLES A. BEARD

Alfred A. Knopf: *New York*

1949

THIS IS A BORZOI BOOK,
PUBLISHED BY ALFRED A. KNOPF, INC.

Copyright 1948 by Alfred A. Knopf, Inc. All rights reserved. No part of this book may be reproduced in any form without permission in writing from the publisher, except by a reviewer who may quote brief passages in a review to be printed in a magazine or newspaper. Manufactured in the United States of America. Published simultaneously in Canada by McClelland & Stewart Limited.

FIRST EDITION

To

WALTON HALE HAMILTON

Source of Ideas

INTRODUCTION
by Charles A. Beard

The precise and temperate representations of John P. Frank's volume on the life and work of Hugo Black offer inducements to many reflections, widening out into the shadowy limits of human analysis. To citizens who cherish the Jeffersonian tradition or recognize its force in American history, they may serve as an invitation to review partisan conflicts. Choosing the plane surface of personal inquiry, inveterate foes of Justice Black may be inclined to regard the moderation of Mr. Frank's statement as designed to undermine their resentments and inveterate friends to undervaluate it as lacking in warmth and voltage. If pondered, however, under the admonition that history has ways of its own in dealing with the ephemeral, the pages of this book may be otherwise construed. So deliberated, they may be taken, first of all, as a solicitation to consider anew, in our time of turbulence and groping, the greatest of the political issues that confront citizens of the United States, namely the underlying tenets of the Constitution, which, by the duties of his office, Justice Black is bound to interpret and sustain with all the powers of his mind, whatever may befall him.

This issue, defined by statesmen and publicists in various formulas, may be briefly described as follows: How to maintain a government strong enough to defend society against external and internal foes and yet so organized as to protect, by supreme law and its administration, the liberties of the people against oppressive actions by public agents or popular tumults. Although, by its terms, a paradox, the prescription is inescapable, if, as the dilemma has been phrased, society is to depend, even during the gravest crises in human affairs, on reflection and choice rather than on force and accident in the conduct of its government.

"To protect, by supreme law and its administration, the liberties of the people." This crux in the formula of the American constitutional system puzzles ingenuity and, subjected to a process of meditation, elicits a major inquiry: How are the lawyers and the judges, on whom a heavy obligation for administration is imposed by the supreme law, to be educated and become experienced for the effective discharge of their responsibilities? Believing that Mr. Frank's volume deserves an accredited place in the literature of constitutional law for use in legal instruction, formal and informal, I shall dwell upon its significance in this general, yet living, relation before turning to the life and work of Justice Black in particular.

It is difficult for me to imagine any book better adapted to kindling the interest of law students in the presuppositions of knowledge, certainty, probability, possibility, and conviction which enter into the making of judicial decisions and opinions. Even students bent on learning how to win cases in the courts of law may sharpen their wits for such achievements by mastering the record here assembled by Mr. Frank. All the more, if it be remembered that an opinion is a "judgment resting on grounds insufficient for complete demonstration."

With regard to the utility of Mr. Frank's volume for education in constitutional law and its administration, I can perhaps best explain what I deem its import by avoiding the abstractions common to educational theories and resorting to a few items of personal experience; for, in some ways, I have been in and of the stream of tendency which has marked the course of thought about constitutional law and government through many years. At least I have watched the development of this thought and the changes in it now coming to effective expression, clearly, in the pages of the book before us. After all, have we not been well advised to consider law in terms of life?

At the opening of this century, when I began the systematic study of constitutional law at Columbia University, as directed by the case method then prevailing, I had undergone no little discipline in the study of general history — the concreteness of personalities and events — and in the methods of historical research and exposition. Ever revolving in my mind as I confronted successive cases in constitutional law were three questions which, among others, my distinguished instructor in history at Oxford University, Frederick York Powell, had reiterated as his students sought a knowledge and understanding of situations and movements in history: What are the relevant documents available to us — papers, letters, and other memorials? Who is the author of each document? What can be known about the author's life and work which will help us to analyze, evaluate, interpret, and understand the document with the highest possible degree of assurance?

These questions, I had supposed, would be asked about the documents in each case of constitutional law as it was taken up for discussion and exposition in the classroom. To my surprise nothing of the kind happened. Law students seemed to have little interest in inquiries of this nature. To them a case was adequately presented or represented by the documents printed in the particular report of the Supreme Court or in the case book. Cogitation centered on three primary concerns: What are the facts in the case, as disclosed in the mere record before the class? What is the decision of the Court? What is the line of reasoning in the opinion deemed necessary to the support of the decision?

If, in the classroom discussion of the case, objections to a decision or an opinion of the Court were raised, special con-

sideration was sometimes given to dissenting judgments or
to conflicts with one or more earlier precedents. As to the
briefs and arguments of the counsel in the case, they were
occasionally mentioned but, as I remember, only occasionally when fragments from the briefs happened to be printed
in the law book before the class. As to the historical circumstances that formed a context for the case, they too received
little if any consideration.

By what intellectual processes did the justices who read
the briefs, heard the arguments, and passed on the case
arrive at the decision and the "necessary reasoning" of
their opinion or opinions? In the time of my apprenticeship, justices of the Court appeared in the cases as if dis-
embodied spirits speaking the unsubstantial language of
logic. Justice Holmes had not yet delivered the memorable
dictum: "General propositions do not decide concrete cases.
The decision will depend upon a judgment or intuition
more subtle than any articulate major premise."

In 1902 a justice of the Supreme Court, in the theory of
the classroom, seemed to be a kind of master mechanic. Indeed, as I heard the budding lawyers and judges talk, I was
often reminded of a machine once used in the Bank of England to test the coins deposited day by day. When a coin
was gently placed on its delicately balanced receptacle, the
machine trembled for a second or two and then dropped the
coin, right or left, into the proper chest as sound or spuri-
ous according to its monetary merits. To me, fresh from
seminars on historical methods, the weighing, measuring,
and logistical method of "learning" constitutional law
seemed in 1902 a strange way of searching for the meaning
and upshot of cases.

Four years earlier, Professor Powell had asked me to
make, as an exercise in critical historiography, a study of
the memorials of Saint Dunstan (A.D. 909–988) and report

on the man and his work, with a view to arriving at a judgment respecting the qualities and predilections of the saint and the authenticity of the writings ascribed to him. But in 1902 our class in constitutional law at Columbia went through the income-tax case of *Pollock* v. *Farmers Loan and Trust Company* (1895) as if it had been an adventure in deductions drawn from a major premise grounded in the ineluctable nature of things. Nobody proposed to devote several days to examining the life history of Chief Justice Melville Fuller or, for that matter, Justice John M. Harlan. In truth, had this exploration been ordered by the instructor, no biographical materials, such as Mr. Frank supplies for Justice Black, would have been available to the explorers. It was not then the fashion of authors who wrote biographies of Supreme Court justices to go far, if at all, into their social and economic backgrounds or presuppositions.

Nor in my student days did it ever occur to me that I should attend a session of the Supreme Court in Washington to hear the arguments of counsel in a case of momentous national interest or the oral delivery of the opinions rendered by the justices in such a case. Certainly this enlightening experience was no part of my formal education and constituted no requirement for the degree of doctor of philosophy in public law. Moreover, not until long after I had won this degree did I visit the musty record room of the Supreme Court, untie the tape that bound together the documents of a historic case, blow the dust from the crumbling papers, and discover the mass, variety, and animus of the materials presented to the learned justices for the purpose of bending their minds one way or another.

However, in the study of American constitutional history, as distinguished from constitutional law, I learned a number of things which ran counter to the mechanical fictions employed in the teaching of public law. I traced in that history the long and ever recurring political conflicts over the exercise of powers by the Supreme Court — conflicts subsequently described with scholarly skill in the writings of Charles Grove Haines. I discovered that many of the most distinguished justices had been politicians before their elevation to the bench, had been selected by politician Presidents, and had been confirmed by politician Senators, more than occasionally and accidentally with reference to matters of large public policy over which the country was sharply divided. My studies in constitutional history were supplemented by personal experiences. For instance, in 1916 I heard lawyers of the highest social standing denounce, in the violent language of the stump, Louis D. Brandeis when he was nominated by President Wilson for a place on the Court and I lived to see Justice Brandeis, by demonstrations of wisdom and learning, put to shame the very men who had so mercilessly and abusively condemned him.

If fifty years ago students of constitutional law could have had at their command volumes on the life and work of all the justices who appeared in the law books, such as Mr. Frank now provides for Justice Black, they might have been spared many grave misunderstandings in their practice and pleadings and, indeed, the Court might not have wounded itself so often by ill-considered and arbitrary actions. This is not to say that Mr. Frank tells or pretends to tell what lawyers call "the whole truth." He undertakes no such adventure in omniscience, but he does present a discriminating and well-documented memorandum on the life of Justice Black and a collection of his opinions so ordered that readers may draw their own conclusions as to the nature of his views respecting crucial points in the law of the land.

Having followed for several years Mr. Frank's articles as they appeared in various law journals, I acquired, quite independently, before I met him in person, a firm respect for his capacity to conduct painstaking explorations in the field of public law and to embody his findings of fact and his opinions in clear statements. Like all mortals, even those who claim to be "above the battle," Mr. Frank has his sympathies, but, constantly aware of them, he strives in his expositions to keep well within the limits of the relevant evidence and to observe faithfully the canons of critical scholarship. Hence I have confidence in the integrity of thought and labor that went into the making of this volume.

Although Mr. Frank's acquaintance with Justice Black and his work as a member of the Supreme Court has been far more intimate than mine, I can confirm out of my own knowledge many of the judgments pronounced in these pages. As I have related elsewhere (*The Republic*), I first met Hugo Black at a small dinner gathering in Washington late in 1934, as I recall the time, and did not catch his name at the moment of the introduction. He was my nameless companion during the dinner and we engaged in a lively conversation about matters ordinary and extraordinary.

In the course of our exchanges I discovered that the gentleman by my side had read widely in history, American and European, had made scholarly excursions on his own account, was eager to get to the bottom of things, and dealt in a most judicial temper with all the dissents and objections I filed with him. He was a good listener and a good talker. When we disagreed on a point in argument, it was a pleasure to note the catholicity of views he manifested in examining all phases of our contention. I concluded with delight that my anonymous interlocutor was a man imbued with a sense of history and more eager to explore than to dogmatize. Not until after the dinner party had dissolved did I learn from my host that the guest on whom I had passed a wholly impersonal judgment was Senator Hugo Black of Alabama.

With various views of Senator Black as reported in the *Congressional Record* I had acquired some acquaintance before I met him. He had in 1930 vigorously supported my friend Senator Bronson Cutting in the espousal of a bill involving liberty of the human spirit — a bill to impose restraints on the "censorship of imported literature" then freely and wonderfully exercised by customs agents. In that struggle with bureaucrats and self-constituted guardians of the people against "impure" and "dangerous" thoughts I had long been interested; and in fact I had helped to draft the petition which Senator Cutting placed in the *Record* of March 30, 1930, with the names of many distinguished scholars attached to it.

As Mr. Frank indicates, Senator Black, speaking on the issue presented by this bill, said: "I have an inherent opposition — I presume it comes, perhaps, from reading a great deal of Thomas Jefferson's philosophy — I have an inherent, well-grounded opposition to investing in the hands of an individual [customs officer] judicial powers on matters of supreme importance with reference to the dissemination of human knowledge."

Memory of this service to liberty rendered by Senator Black confirmed the judgment I had reached on the occasion of our first conversation. Subsequent exchanges with him strengthened my belief that in an hour of some ultimate test he would say with his mentor, Thomas Jefferson, from whom I too have learned lessons of liberty: "I have sworn on the altar of God, eternal hostility against every form of tyranny over the mind of man."

Despite the storm that broke about Mr. Black's head

after his nomination to the bench by President Franklin D. Roosevelt, I was yet of the opinion that in coming years of stress and strain he would as a justice of the Supreme Court stand foursquare, to the best of his abilities, on the personal and political liberties guaranteed by the Constitution of the United States. Some of these liberties, to be sure, are indefinite in nature and citizens may legitimately differ about applications in particulars. For example, I find myself dissenting from Justice Black's opinion in *Everson* v. *Board of Education of Ewing Township*. But, having followed the cases on civil liberty decided during Justice Black's tenure, I think it may be truly said that he has consistently labored to sustain and enlarge the precious rights of persons to every privilege encompassed by the term "fair trial" and has valiantly upheld liberty of expression — these guarantees of guarantees.

This Justice Black has done with a force, firmness, and daring that place him, in my opinion, even above Justice Holmes and Justice Brandeis in the record of judicial resistance to governmental encroachments on the liberties of press and speech. Born and reared in the tradition of states' rights, he has none the less, with a courage and cogency worthy of John Marshall, declared void acts of state authorities in violation of these fundamental liberties. When hearing the claims of the humblest and meanest person to that "equal justice under law" proclaimed by the very stones of the Supreme Court building, Hugo Black remembers that "the poor" as well as "the rich" are specifically mentioned in his oath of office. Personally familiar with the straitened circumstances of men and women who labor with their hands for a living, he has a vivid sense of the perplexities confronting them when they become involved in the toils of the law, unprotected by the wit and learning of able counsel. In all the annals of the Court it would be difficult, if not impossible, to find another justice so intimately acquainted with the disadvantages they encounter in the struggle for existence, and the meaning of judicial decisions in terms of life and equity for them.

Although the Supreme Court, taking advantage of technicalities, has recently sidestepped some of the most glaring cases involving civil liberty, it is difficult for me to believe that, given his open record, Justice Black has been a regular party to these contrivances. At all events, in our age of war and renewed slavery for war prisoners, it is well that he has a voice and a vote in the secret sessions of the Court at which petitions for the writ of certiorari are reviewed and granted or denied.

In his volume *The Growth of American Constitutional Law* Professor Benjamin F. Wright, of Harvard University, says: "The history of judicial review does not furnish the evidence to indicate that the Supreme Court will, in periods of intense feeling or hysteria, afford a sanctuary to those whose views run counter to the popular will" — that is, in the very periods when courage is most needed. Professor Wright's prediction may come true; but, if so, unless I mistake the nature of the man, Justice Hugo Black will strive until the last hour to keep open the refuge established by the Constitution against the passions of rulers and multitudes. For this reason, apart from all others and despite all the counterblasts blown and to be blown, it is my verdict that Mr. Frank's volume should be judicially received and thoughtfully examined by every citizen concerned with the fortunes and fate of the Republic.

New Milford, Connecticut
Midsummer, 1948

AUTHOR'S PREFACE

Hugo Black is one of the most controversial figures of the public life of the last two decades. The biographical sketch and the collection of opinions presented here are intended to acquaint those readers who do not closely follow the Supreme Court of the United States with the part played by President Roosevelt's first appointee to that Court. The opinions are chosen from those written in Black's first ten years on the Court.

Few men not candidates for national office have been the object of either as much hatred or as much praise as Black. The biographical sketch makes very little attempt to estimate the validity of the hatred or the praise. It is far too early to attempt Black's critical biography, and this sketch makes no such pretense. It is offered as a short account of salient events in a full life. My own relationship with the Justice as a former law clerk may lessen objectivity though it increases knowledge.

To promote ease of reading, this sketch has not been footnoted. The quotations come from interviews with many persons, from newspapers, and from public records. The quotations in section 2 dealing with particular cases are, except as noted, taken from the Birmingham papers.

I hope one day many years hence to do a comprehensive biography of the Justice, and would appreciate letters from persons who may read this volume who can add information.

Thanks are due to the many persons who contributed

material to this sketch, to friends who have given much editorial advice, to Dr. Beard for his foreword, and to my wife for her considerable labors in completing the manuscript.

JOHN P. FRANK

Indiana University
Bloomington, Indiana

CONTENTS

THE MAN

THE OPINIONS

I. *Control of the Economy*

Contents

II. *Civil Rights*

Contents

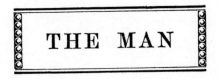

THE MAN

Chapter I

CLAY COUNTY

It was poor country, very poor country, in which Hugo Black was born, but his family was, by poor country standards, a well-to-do family indeed. Clay County was an east-central Alabama county, hardly part of the traditional South at all. It had few pillared homes in classic lines on sloping hills. It was not even good cotton country, for corn took more of the acreage, and beans did almost as well. Though cotton was the cash crop, it was "bumblebee cotton," so low that people said a bee could pollenate the blossoms while he sat on the ground. It was poor man's country, with Negroes of course, but only a few; the white men farmed for themselves in Clay County, and in the 1880's and '90's they sometimes had not enough to eat, and especially not enough meat.

These people were mostly Scotch-Irish, who had settled in the South a hundred years before. Martha Toland Black, Hugo's mother, was something of a newcomer, for her ancestors the Tolands came to the United States as fugitives from a suppressed Irish rebellion about 1800, but the Streets, her maternal ancestors, and the Blacks had come earlier. William Black was born in Clay County in 1848 and became a farmer and storekeeper there. He was following in the footsteps of his father, George Walker Black, who had been born in Georgia but had become an Alabama storekeeper.

William Black was storekeeping and farming in Harlan, in Clay County, next to the Tallapoosa border, when his eighth and last child, Hugo La Fayette, was born on February 27, 1886. The "La Fayette" had been William's middle name, and the first name came from Hugh, often used in the family and adapted to Hugo because Martha had been reading Victor Hugo before the baby was born.

Martha was an unusual person in a poverty-stricken and ignorant land. She was postmistress at Harlan, which was all the officialdom Harlan had since it was only a postal address to mark William Black's farm and his store and the cabins of two tenant farmers who helped till his land. Martha Black was a small woman, of one hundred and ten pounds, who did her own housekeeping and her own cooking and frequently milked her own cows. She worked her daughters hard, prayed nightly and devoutly, and kept a firm discipline over her sons. This was normal routine for a Clay County mother. What was unusual was that, in an area that gave little attention to girls' education, Martha had been sent to an academy. Throughout her life she enjoyed reading, and valued education for her children.

The Black farm, on which Hugo was to live only until he was three years old, was a large farm with a small house. The central portion of the house had once been a log cabin, but William Black was a prosperous man, and he covered his log cabin with clapboard made from timber on his farm. Then he added to his one room four small bedrooms, and next to the house, a few feet away, joined by a walk of three planks on the ground, he built a kitchen. This home was big enough not to be a shack, or a cabin, like the neighbors', but a house. It had a barn and a privy in the rear. Hugo was not to become accustomed to the luxury of indoor plumbing until he moved to Birmingham twenty years later. It was a self-contained life, with a stock of horses, cows, pigs, and sheep furnishing labor and food, and with Martha Black to weave the cloth and make the clothes for the children.

But even a self-contained farm lacked a school, although it tried to supply the need. Robert Lee Black, Hugo's eldest brother, taught school in one of the cabins at Harlan, and Hugo at the age of three toddled to class until he became bored and ran out to play; but the other children could no longer manage with such a makeshift device. The family moved a few miles to Ashland, where the storekeeping opportunities were good and the schooling opportunities led all the way to a glorified private high school with the impressive name of Ashland College. William set up the store of Black & Manning in this town of three hundred and fifty people, and his wife made ready their home.

The Blacks' five-room house on Church Street and a later home of similar size were so nearly the same that they can be described together. They were five-room houses, with large grass, garden, and wood "patches" and space to keep a cow, a horse, and chickens. Scuppernong grapes, which Hugo loved and later tried unsuccessfully to transplant to Washington, grew in the garden. The rooming arrangements were simple: a kitchen, a parlor, the parents' room, a room for the girls, and a room for the boys. Each room had a fireplace, and occasionally a blocked chimney sent smoke pouring into a room. All this was undistinguished. The most unusual feature of any home of Martha Black's was the flower-beds. In her home Burpee's seed catalogue was used more than any other book but the Bible. Honeysuckle covered the porch, and two small cedars on each side of a walk to the house were surrounded by phlox, roses, and violets.

Life in Ashland had few horizons broader than Clay County. When a man became excited about politics, it was usually local politics. William Black, as befitted a business-man who left a forty-thousand-dollar estate wrung out of nothing and who owned farms and financed sharecroppers, was a conservative Democrat who refused to support William Jennings Bryan in 1896; but he never grew as really excited about politics as the time he took the startling step of supporting a Populist for probate judge. It was the fore-most act of political independence of his life, but in Ash-land men grew excited about the office of probate judge.

At the same time the Blacks had a little more contact with a world outside Clay County than many of the County's residents. William Black was a man of some reading, and he subscribed to the *Montgomery Advertiser*, which by itself gave him a small distinction. His own library included not only the inevitable Scott novels, all of which Hugo read as a boy, but also a little of other writers, and of poetry.

For Hugo it was an easy boyhood, with work in the gar-den and the earning of a little spending money the principal chores. The daughters of the house carried most of its bur-dens. Hugo had close friendship with his oldest sister, Le-ora. She made many of his clothes, but their affection sur-vived even a little Lord Fauntleroy suit. The two children owned a tiger cat named Dandy Jim, Leora owning the body and Hugo the tail. It was never necessary to divide their interests.

Much of Hugo's time went to play. The favorite games of the community were pitching dollars or horseshoes. Neither was a gambling game, for gambling of any sort would have been considered the grossest form of sin, and Hugo never played cards, even for pleasure without gambling, until he was twenty years old. Silver dollars were pitched at a hole in the ground in much the fashion that horseshoes are pitched at a stake, and both horseshoes and dollars in this poor community remained the property of whoever was fortunate enough to own them. Other sports were baseball, fishing, and croquet. Contributions among neighborhood children raised a dollar and a quarter for a communal croquet set; Hugo contributed a dime.

Romance comes young in Alabama, and shortly after the age of twelve Hugo could join the other children at basket suppers. A dime or fifteen cents, paid after appropriate secret revelations of the ownership of the basket, permitted the buyer to share supper with the girl of his choice. But in these and later years there is no record that any romance was serious enough to be noteworthy. Occasional companions of young Hugo are mentioned, but old-timers of Clay County do not suggest either that he left any broken hearts or that he took one with him.

The dime for a basket supper was not lightly obtained. William Black believed that his children should earn their spending money, and Hugo never had a regular allowance. Wages were low, cotton-picking or odd jobs paid very little money, and Hugo was never a fast cotton-picker. He learned to set type for the weekly paper, for which he was paid thirty cents a column. It took all day, however, to set two and one half columns; and this was no source of frequent wealth, for the work was so lucrative that only on rare occasions was it given to a youngster. A more likely job was folding newspapers. He could earn seven cents by folding three hundred. Yet typesetting was fun because the typesetter was allowed to make up "locals" to fill the columns. Hugo's first published literary composition, as he later recalled it, was: "Bill Jones has been seen on the streets of Ashland. Bill is looking fine."

7

Hugo was the son of a storekeeper and the grandson of a storekeeper, and he sought his pocket money in trade. He once had a thriving business in selling used dime novels of the Nick Carter variety, and he worked up a flourishing trade in soft drinks. His one really big financial killing came on a Fourth of July when at a picnic he made thirteen dollars selling soda pop.

Ashland was twenty-two miles from the nearest railroad, a day's trip each way, and there was money to be made in the hauling trade. Frequently Hugo drove a wagon to the railhead and brought back a load of supplies. He carried his own blankets with him and slept curled up on the floor in the wagon yard. This two-day chore, besides rich pay in pleasant adventure, carried a cash reward of one dollar.

The Blacks had moved to Ashland so that the children might go to school, and school was the first obligation for Hugo. He went to school from the beginning grades through Ashland College, at best roughly equivalent to completing the freshman year of a modern college. In the elementary grades one teacher had several classes. For the first four years, for example, Hugo had as his teacher Miss Lizzie Patterson. Miss Lizzie let Hugo finish all four of the first four readers in the first year, with the result that reading was both a little simple and a little tedious for the next three. Most of the teaching was of the most obvious sort of country school training in fundamentals. The occasional declamatory contest was an exciting extracurricular activity. Under Leora's training, Hugo came in second in declamation to Lee Miller, later a street-car conductor and farmer.

Since Clay County was outside the Black Belt, a comparatively small proportion of the population was colored. The relations of the white and Negro population were gov-

erned by convention, and the conventions were accepted
without question. For example, Old Hamp, a Negro occasional helper in the Black garden, would never have
dreamed of eating with the Black family; yet Leora Black
frequently did sewing for the children of Hamp's family.
Though the Negro and white children as youngsters might
play together, these relations traditionally became less close
as they grew older.

Only one serious racial incident occurred during Black's
youth. A white boy shot and killed Eli Sims, a seventeen-
year-old Negro boy, in an argument. The white boy was
tried and acquitted, though everyone in Ashland knew he
was guilty; and he was found not guilty in part because
witnesses were bribed and in part because his father was
a thoroughly respected man. Another murder later sent
the boy to the penitentiary.

The Sims murder was a profoundly disturbing emotional
incident for the white population of Ashland. Nothing of
the sort had happened in the memory of the inhabitants,
and it was a wrong with a deeply disturbing wrongness.
For the Black family it was particularly disturbing. Hugo
was thirteen at the time. He could remember days when Eli
had pushed him about in his wheelbarrow. Hugo's father
disapproved of the culprit's release, and the subject was
frequently discussed at the family dinner table. For William Black this was no question of relations of the races.
Rather, it was an elemental matter of right and wrong. "If
one murderer can escape, none of us will be safe," he said
worriedly to his wife and children.

The murderer did escape, but the incident had rippling
effects. It increased the dissatisfaction of William Black
with the local Democratic Party and was one of the factors
contributing to his momentary bolt to the Populists. It

gave cause for some first thoughts of fairness to Negroes. It left a guilty feeling in the minds of many of the white residents of Ashland.

In Clay County, local politics was lively stuff. Unlike the richer cotton counties, here the Democrats had no strangle hold. The Republicans and the Populists were strong enough to capture occasional county offices. Hence, in a state of real doubt as to the outcome, Hugo went to the meetings called in behalf of the candidates for the county offices. Politics and law were a controlling interest with him from boyhood, for jury speeches and stump speeches were the best entertainment Ashland had to offer.

The Populist program in Alabama was popular essentially because it appealed to low-income white farmers, and it had its strongest hold in Clay and adjacent counties. The few Negroes in Ashland, for example, were in some respects better off than many whites. As Joseph Manning, a Populist leader from Ashland, has written in his biography: "Many of them [the colored population] had their white folks to whom they could look. They could get by through service and had 'the pan' to rely upon and the cast off clothing of the white folk. The poor white was white and too proud for this." The notion was expressed in a song: "I'd Rather Be a Negro than a Poor White Man." The program of the Populists was aimed at overthrowing the domination of the bosses from the sixteen Black Belt Democratic counties. It was a program for the revision of the laws on crop mortgages, for the protection of tenant farmers, and for the general betterment of farm labor. The white farmers for whom this program was devised were in truth at the very bottom of the ill-clad, ill-housed, and ill-fed one third.

It was among these people that Hugo learned his politics. He was ten years old when in 1896 William Jennings Bryan carried the Populist program into the Democratic Party.

The lines between Populists and Democrats thinned to
personalities in areas such as Clay County, where it was
necessary for all three parties to offer very much the same
program to the dominant farmer voters, and it was very
easy for most of these Democrats to endorse Bryan as the
Democratic-Populist candidate. They could accept not only
the program of free silver, but also the program for a federal income tax, control of banks and trusts, and the abolition of the labor injunction.

At some time in the course of these years Hugo Black's
political philosophy took on its fixed objectives. His economic views between childhood and young manhood were
of course nebulous, and he did not begin serious reading on
such subjects until, as a law student, he began to audit
courses in political economy at the university. But the public speeches he attended — practically all the speeches made
in Ashland during his boyhood — were a great influence.
What the political speakers said was re-emphasized by the
ministers, for the ministers of Clay County had economic
views that much of Alabama would have considered advanced. The churches of Ashland taught a simple religion,
and while now and then an evangelist would preach the doctrine of hell-fire, the main theme of Ashland sermons was
love, kindness, and treating one's neighbor as oneself.

As his own philosophy took form, Black departed from
the philosophy of his home and of his father, for in the
1890's in Alabama the well-to-do storekeeper was at the
local summit of the capitalist class. At some time in these
years Black came into basic agreement with the majority
of the poor white population of Clay County. The general
objectives of the Populists and of the liberal Democrats of
the nineties became his objectives. The issue of free silver
soon disappeared, but certain deep convictions about antitrust laws, control of financial institutions, regulation of

11

THE MAN

wealth through the income tax, and opposition to the intervention of courts in labor disputes became Black's fixed principles of political action. Of even deeper importance, Black drew from the agitation in Clay County strong sympathy based on the most intimate acquaintance with the very poor, and he became absolutely saturated with the essential conception of the Populist philosophy, that the people had the right through their government to improve the condition of their daily lives. When Black left Clay County to go on to professional school, he took with him virtually nothing in the way of wealth and education; but he carried the general purpose of those who in later decades were called New Dealers.

At the age of seventeen Hugo Black enrolled in the Birmingham Medical College. His reason was a little vague; he preferred law and had attended every trial he could in Ashland. But his brother was a doctor and his mother wanted him to be one too. Besides, he was very young, and the medical school was closer to home than the law school. He stayed for one year — long enough to pick up a job lot of odds and ends of physical facts, which later were of some use in his personal-injury cases — and spent the following summer apprenticed as a medical student to his brother. By the end of the summer, however, he and his brother had decided that medicine was not the profession for him, and in the fall he went to the University of Alabama, at Tuscaloosa.

At Tuscaloosa, Black's first choice was a liberal-arts education and he proudly presented his credits from Ashland College as evidence that he was entitled to entrance in at least the sophomore year. The university authorities took another view of it and said that he could only be a freshman. Since it was easier to get into law school at the university than to get into the sophomore class, he decided to short-cut formal education and enroll directly in the law school.

Hence in 1904 Black undertook the two-year program of the University of Alabama Law School. It was a small school, with forty students in the entering class and three faculty members. He was probably the least-qualified student in his class, both because he had had no appreciable pre-law college training at all, and because he was so young. As Professor Somerville of the faculty once put it, "I won't say whether Black is the best student in school or not. I will say he has learned the most of any student in school. He had the most to learn."

If Black had the most to learn, he was determined to try to learn it. The school used the textbook method of teaching, with lectures, rather than the modern system of class discussion of cases, and it had no law review. Black spent most of his time for two years in the library and was on the honors list of the school.

In 1906, at the age of twenty, came graduation and admission to the bar. At that early date Black had pretty much the same general plan of most law students graduating from most law schools for many decades before and since — he would practice law, he would enter politics, he would acquire some wealth and more fame. With a headful of dreams he returned to Ashland, spent substantially all the remaining cash of his inheritance on books, and opened his office.

As with most young lawyers who hang out their own shingles, there was little to give substance to the dreams. In the first year Black had almost no clients. He collected a few bills and checked on a few applicants for a mail-order insurance house at a fee of fifty cents a person. Happily, he lived with a brother, and his expenses were even lower than his low income.

And then in September 1907 came calamity. The store building containing the office burned down and Black's entire library went with it. He was without insurance and virtually penniless except for a five-hundred-dollar interest — highly unliquid — in his father's old store. With his total liquid capital in his pocket, Black headed for Birmingham to begin anew in the practice of law.

Chapter II

CRIMINAL LAW

Black arrived in Birmingham, twenty-one years old, with no acquaintances except a few other transplanted Ashlanders. Without money, without friends, and without more polish and sophistication than could be acquired around the Ashland general store, he had only his energy and his determination with which to get started.

Black's first need was the acquisition of an office and a place to sleep. He found a bedroom, which he shared with three other men, and took space in a small office, which he occupied with no noticeable success for about two months. The next move was to an office across the street from the courthouse, where he was able to rent a desk in an attorney's office for seven dollars a month.

Meanwhile he set forth to get acquainted with Birmingham. Here his fraternal organizations were of assistance. In Ashland it had been customary for young men to join both a church and one or more lodges. As a youngster Black had been much impressed with both the Masons and the Knights of Pythias and had been admitted to the Masons and taken his first degree in Ashland within a few days of his twenty-first birthday. He was also a member of the Knights of Pythias there, and had been clerk of the Baptist congregation. These affiliations he transferred to Birmingham, and both church and lodge activities — later including the Odd Fellows — made it easy for him to make friends. For twenty years he taught a Sunday-school class.

Black kept the business for the mail-order insurance company and, at fifty cents an investigation of proposed policyholders, he was soon earning fifty dollars a month. The fifty dollars was helpful and so was the opportunity, for in the course of the investigations of the credit rating and standing of the applicants he met many of their friends.

Such potboiling was, of course, hardly the practice of law, and the few bill collections that supplemented Black's income gave no great sense of professional accomplishment or profit. Eventually he was given his first real case by the attorney in whose office he was renting a desk. In the 1900's in Alabama it was the practice not to keep convicts in jail but to lease them as contract laborers to industrial concerns. A Negro convict who had been leased to a steel company had been held fifteen days overtime by the company. Black sued for damages. He prepared the case as exhaustively as any case in his life and it was tried before Judge Lane of the local circuit court. The defendant's counsel was a leading Birmingham lawyer, William Grubb, later a federal district judge. Grubb began the defense with various motions to dismiss, each of which Black combated with well-prepared arguments. Judge Lane finally addressed Grubb: "Billy, I don't think you are going to be able to scare this young fellow or talk him out of it. Let's get down to the case." The trial proceeded, and Black got his first verdict, $137.50.

Far more important than the fee was the impression made on Judge Lane and on Judge Grubb. Even after Grubb had become federal district judge he gave Black material help in his campaign for prosecuting attorney. Lane eventually became one of the four city commissioners. He consolidated several police-court judgeships and substituted one judge for the city of Birmingham. Black was appointed to the position and held it during 1911 and 1912.

The police-court judgeship was not very important and no one, including Black, thought that it was. The court was one ugly room with a cage at one end in which the petty offenders of the city were held during the disposition of the docket. The court sat for as many mornings a week as was necessary to dispose of business, and the rest of the time Black was free to practice law. The duties were those handled in some smaller communities today by justices of the peace and in some of the larger communities by the municipal courts of the lowest jurisdiction. The defendants were the petty criminals, vagrants, drunkards, dope-users. Most often they were the unhappy dregs of the Negro population.

But though the work was of no great significance, it was at least a mark of recognition. A Birmingham reporter who had been in Ashland on the day the appointment was made reported that "it was but a few minutes until every man, woman and child in the town and community had heard the news and was talking about it. . . . The appointment is considered as a mark of recognition that raises him at least one rung along his career." More important, the business of the petty offenders' court was interesting. It was good newspaper copy, and the Birmingham police court was covered by the local press with a detail far greater than was given to the proceedings of the state Supreme Court. There were few residents of Birmingham who had not heard of "Judge" Hugo Black by the time he left the police court in October 1912.

The position called largely for common-sense judgment. When Joe and Lindy Jackson, a Negro couple, had a fight and Lindy had Joe arrested, Judge Black (a young bachelor) dismissed the case with some observations on happy marriages. Jim Williams, arrested in a crap game for carrying a gun, pleaded that the gun was not his, and Black ruled: "I am inclined to believe you and you can go." When three white men were charged with opium-smoking, one of whom had lung trouble, the other two were fined fifty dollars each and were jailed, while the sick man was allowed to leave town. When Mose Roden, a Negro, was charged with carrying a concealed weapon, which was a rusty gun, Judge Black tried the gun, found it unusable, and dismissed the case. On the other hand, Napoleon Watkins was fined twenty-five dollars for striking his wife with a knife.

The cases came in great volume. There were over a hundred on many a Monday morning after a riotous weekend. Most of them were instances of petty violence. Others gave some variation. Thus, Nancy Little, a Negro, had Mary Bryant, also a Negro, arrested for slander for having said that Nancy had given testimony leading to the arrest of Mary's Uncle Jasper. Black dismissed the complaint, lecturing the parties on taking trifling disputes to court.

The leniency with which Judge Black treated the Negro offenders caused some surprise to residents of Birmingham who were not used to such kindliness. When eleven Negroes were charged by a police officer with disorderly conduct at a dance and were found not guilty by Judge Black, a Birmingham newspaper commented in surprise that Judge Black had discharged the defendants despite the fact that usually in the lower courts "A negro's testimony does not go very far against that of a white man, especially if he happens to be an officer." On another occasion twenty-two Negroes were charged with disorderly conduct at a dance broken up by the police. In finding the defendants not guilty, the Birmingham papers recorded, "Black told the arresting officer he had no more right to break up that dance than any other."

On March 14, 1912 Virgil Mickens, a Negro, came up for trial charged with disorderly conduct for assaulting the white agent of a Birmingham loan shark. Mickens had borrowed fifty dollars and the first year he paid twenty-five cents a month interest for each dollar — 300 per cent; during the second year he paid 240 per cent. Judge Black figured up the interest, looked hard at the agent, and turned to the prisoner. "You can go," he told the prisoner. "You don't owe this man anything." And then to the courtroom Black said of the defendant: he "needs no punishment here. He has been punished enough."

Yet when the Negro population insisted on victimizing themselves, there was nothing the police-court judge felt he could do to help them. In September 1912 George White, a Negro faith healer, was charged with having obtained money under false pretenses by selling cures to the Negro population. One hundred and fifty-three Negroes appeared in court to testify in behalf of alleged cures. After a dozen had testified, Black said to the remainder: "All who have been saved from some terrible disease or calamity by George White, hold up your hands." Every hand went up, and Black said: "If you Negroes want to be flim-flammed out of your money by this faith healer, it suits me. He is discharged." However, when "Dr. Frenchy," white, was charged with selling three-cent charms to Negroes for seven dollars and a half, Black said: "I am satisfied you sold this trash to these ignorant Negroes," and gave a sentence of ninety days and a seventy-five-dollar fine.

Black's administration was not without criticism. He had undertaken the work of several judges under the consolidation, and he handled it quickly. In May 1912 a critic complained that Black had disposed of 150 cases in about 150 minutes, and that it was impossible to give fair disposition in that time. The *Birmingham Age-Herald* replied that on the particular day 118 cases had in fact been disposed of in about 150 minutes. Of the 118 cases, 80 were pleas of guilty, 8 were discharged, 15 were continued or otherwise disposed of, and 15 were tried and resulted in conviction. The editorial writer commented that there were two methods of dealing with minor offenders. One was to hold them in jail for up to a month pending trial and then send them to the mines to work off the costs of their pre-trial incarceration. The other was the Black method of disposing of every case within twenty-four hours so that there would be no costs for the defendant to have to work off. Between the two devices, neither of which were thought very satisfactory, the *Age-Herald* preferred the latter.

The local prohibition law received vigorous enforcement from Black, an ardent prohibitionist. When the question arose, however, whether the excise commission of Birmingham could revoke the license of wholesalers selling to illegal liquor dealers, Black held that under the statutes they could not. The question was a serious one, and he filed his first formal written opinion on the subject.

The serious question of liquor control received no more public attention than the case of the kiss in a public park. A young man was fined five dollars by Black on a charge of kissing his girl in the park, and the girl was fined one dollar. The disparity was later explained on the ground that it had been worth more to kiss the girl. The papers had a carnival of ponderous humor with the case during August and September 1912. One editorial writer said: "In the dales and along the hilltops of Clay County, which reared Hugo L. Black and sent him to Birmingham to be one of its most able and most promising young men, there are no public parks, but there are public roads." So long as sweethearts could kiss in a horse-drawn buggy, thought the editorial writer, the rights of man and of woman were still adequately protected.

Such almost countless newspaper stories of Black gave him real standing in the community. Late in 1911 a visiting student of police-court administration was quoted by the *Birmingham News* as saying that he had visited almost every police court in the United States and that Black was handling his work with "a greater degree of perfection" than the visitor had ever seen. He continued: "Judge Black has one of the most analytical minds of which I have ever known and he comes more nearly dealing out real justice than any police court judge I have ever seen." In retrospect this may be a small compliment; but it was typical of the tone of the Birmingham press in 1911 and 1912, a press proud of the town's promising twenty-five-year-old judge.

From 1910 to 1914 Black also carried on the practice of law in the Farley Building, first with Barney Whatley, later Democratic national committeeman from Colorado, and then with David J. Davis, later a Federal district judge. In the latter firm Black handled a general tort, labor, and contract practice, while Davis did the real-estate work for the firm. For Black every part of the practice was genuinely fun. He liked to draft pleadings, he liked research, he liked briefing, and above everything else he liked trying cases. He was developing a skill at the examination of witnesses that was to be his foremost talent in practice. Slowly he was beginning to make a good living. Toward the end of these four years he was earning close to seventy-five hundred dollars a year.

His income then, as later, came almost wholly without the aid of any sizable corporate retainers. With the exception of one Swiss insurance company, his entire practice was either for small business, such as the Herman Beck Candy and Grocery Company, or for individuals, and it always remained so.

In 1914 Black decided to run for the position of county solicitor, or prosecuting attorney. He had three opponents, the foremost of whom was Harrington Heflin, Senator Tom Heflin's brother, who had held the office of prosecutor for sixteen years. Black campaigned intensively for eight months, reaching every voter and attending every meeting he could. He was elected, and became prosecutor in December 1914.

Hugo Black remembers the three years as prosecutor as the hottest years of his life — more pressure and more hostility poured on him than during the lobby investigation, or during his senatorial campaigns, or even during the attack after the Court appointment. For Black was a young man out to make a reputation for handling a job well. He knew only one way to do a job well, and that was to do it diligently. And in Jefferson County there were vested interests in a sluggish administration of the prosecutor's office.

In the first place, there was the fee system. Everyone profited by keeping Negro crapshooters in jail as long as possible, for the state paid fees and the prisoners paid costs, which made tidy incomes for jailers and sheriffs. Black began by canceling five hundred such cases, and the result was talk of impeachment.

When Black went into office, there were 3,238 criminal cases pending, 92 of them being capital cases such as murder, violent robbery, and rape. There were 35 pending murder cases alone. Black's principal campaign pledge had been that he would clean up the docket, and he and his two assistants set out to do it. In his first week they tried twelve of the capital cases, resulting in eleven convictions and one acquittal. The first case Black tried himself. It was a murder charge against Robert Todd, who was sentenced to life imprisonment.

After a fast start the pace kept increasing. Speed was as important to the criminals as to the prosecutor, for as soon as the sentence began, costs stopped running against the defendant. The evils of the fee system began to be freely discussed in the Birmingham press as the citizens came to realize that it was expensive to everyone but the sheriff and the clerk of court to keep prisoners in jail unnecessarily. On March 6, 1915 twenty-two criminals pleaded guilty in one day, a new record for the county; and the *Birmingham Age-Herald* reported with relief that "Judge Fort and the solicitor [Black] investigated each case and they were sentenced at once and will begin serving out the sentences at once."

Finally, when an adequate foundation had been laid, Black appealed to the Governor for a special temporary judge for Birmingham and to the legislature for an extra five thousand dollars for assistants in his office. The gist of his plea was a larger economy: he could save the state more than salaries would cost were he to clean up the docket completely. Both legislature and Governor were convinced, and his pleas were granted. With the aid of extra judges to hear the cases and an energetic staff to help try them, Black had the Jefferson County docket up to date by the time he left office.

Frequently Black found himself unpopular with the respectables. For one example, he prosecuted some coal companies for short-weighting their employees. For another, when asked by the insurance companies to force a stop to ambulance-chasing, Black replied that he would do so on one condition: the insurance companies should use their enormous power in the legislature for the passage of a statute permitting the courts to set aside settlements obtained by insurance companies with injured workers before the workmen were fully aware of what their injuries were. That ended the discussion.

In the three years of service as prosecutor Black tried more murder cases than he could ever count from memory. Not only was the docket loaded with old cases, but new ones of course occurred. He convicted Jim Colias, a restaurant-keeper, of murder in the second degree. He tried the town marshal of Pinckney City for the cold-blooded murder of Gus Goolsby. But undoubtedly the most sensational trial in those three years was the case of Louis Walton.

Louis Walton was a respected merchant of Birmingham, described by a friendly press as a man of "birth and breeding." He was the dominant shareholder in the Walton Trading Company, the other two nominal shareholders being his wife and an employee, M. O. Barton. Each had a thirty-thousand-dollar insurance policy in favor of the firm. On or about April 15, 1915 someone killed Barton with a bullet through the head on the Mulga road not far from Birmingham.

Prosecutor Black had very little on Walton except suspicion. Walton's story was simple: He and a friend had driven Barton to a point near Mulga, where Barton got out to call on a girl. Barton was supposed to rejoin Walton for the return ride, but didn't, and after a considerable wait Walton returned without him. Walton's time was well accounted for, and it appeared that the guilty person might never be found. An indictment of Walton was bound to be unpopular, for it was almost impossible for the business community of Birmingham to believe that one of their number might commit a murder solely for money. A "Unique Problem in Psychology," the press headlined: could such a man "strike down a friend of many years simply for money

— where no question of fear, hatred, or jealousy" was involved?

Black indicted Walton and at the conclusion of his affirmative evidence he had only a good circumstantial case. The defense put Walton on the stand and opened him up to cross-examination.[1]

Black began on the alibi, but could not dent it. He then turned to the corporation. How much money had Walton actually invested in the Walton Trading Company? Five thousand dollars. How had he paid that sum? By check. On what bank? The Birmingham Trust. Black turned to the judge: "Your honor, I ask that an instanter subpœna be issued to the cashier of the Birmingham Trust Company to bring in the books showing this transaction." Interruption from Walton: "I misspoke; it was the First National Bank." "The same request, your honor," said Black.

Walton's confidence was visibly going. "On mature consideration," said he, "it was cash I put into the company." And where had the cash come from? His pocket. And how long had it been there? The upshot, as question followed question, was that Walton had been carrying five thousand dollars around in his pocket since his mother had died and left it to him some years before. Then came questions on a new tack, questions which revealed that while each of the three shareholders in the company were equally insured for the benefit of the company, the arrangement was that should Walton or his wife have died, Barton would have received only one per cent of the total insurance, while when Barton died, Walton and his wife controlled ninety-nine per cent of the resultant payments.

Then came the vital question from a prosecutor calling on his entire and considerable forensic skill, from a prose-

[1] The Walton cross-examination has been reconstructed from newspaper and eyewitness accounts and is not word-for-word accurate.

cutor who could make each word sound like impending doom: "Mr. Walton, isn't it true that you never invested any money in the corporation? And that the whole corporation was arranged to take out accident insurance on this young man? And that the accident insurance was so arranged that if you died, your wife got ninety-nine per cent of the total insurance, and that if this young man died, you got ninety-nine per cent of the total insurance? And isn't it true that you murdered this young man to get that insurance money?"

The tension in the courtroom was more than men could bear. Oddly enough, it was the judge who broke first. As Walton sat silent and then began to flounder into "Well, ah, well, ah . . ." the judge leaned over the bench and said with excitement: "Answer him, Mr. Walton, answer him!" The interruption broke the tension, and Walton recovered sufficient poise to make lame denial. The jury divided, ten for conviction and two for acquittal. Before the case could be retried, Walton went to Atlanta, took out accident insurance, and on the return trip blew himself to death with dynamite in the men's room of the train, killing not only himself but some adjacent passengers.

Black was a personal and political dry, and he enforced the liquor laws stringently. A statute regulating liquor advertisements in newspapers had largely been honored in the breach. The press contended that it was unconstitutional, and when Black threatened enforcement, suggested a test case. Black would hear none of it. The newspapers could make a test if they desired, he said, and of course were free to litigate as fully as they desired; but if they did, they would have plenty of test cases to choose from. For beginning with the following Sunday, said the prosecutor, there would be a separate prosecution for each liquor ad appearing in violation of the statute. On Sunday the ads stopped.

As Black's first year as prosecutor turned the halfway mark, he began to notice an inordinately large number of confessions, particularly of Negroes, from the town of Bessemer, a suburb of Birmingham. Investigation gave Black the explanation — the Bessemer police were running their own private torture chamber and were obtaining confessions by as brutal a third degree as existed in America.

Black as county prosecutor had no very clear jurisdiction over the Bessemer police since their conduct was a matter for control by Bessemer itself rather than by a county official. Yet the Bessemer horror stories could not be borne without some remonstrance. Black formed his plan of action and consulted with his grand jury. It was a good grand jury, typical of the community from which it was drawn: John Powell, merchant; Bert Lytle, yardmaster; William Salter, farmer; Uranus Prickett, bookkeeper; Manly Massey, clerk; and Walter Lawrence, trunk-maker, were some who served on it in the course of Black's term. Black drafted a report to the judges of the criminal court, informing them of the situation. The grand jury approved, and the report was published on September 18, 1915. It was a sensation:

> We find that, according to their own statements, Officers —— and —— have repeatedly been guilty of the practice of the "third degree" in a manner so cruel that it would bring discredit and shame upon the most uncivilized and barbarous community. We find that a uniform practice has been made of taking helpless prisoners, in the late hours of the night, into a secluded room in the presence of these two officers, and others whose names we have not been able to obtain, and there beat them until they were red with their own blood, in an effort to obtain confessions. We find that this cowardly practice, in which four big officers with pistols safely strapped on their bodies, would thus take advantage of ignorance and helplessness, has been continuously in operation for a number of years. A leather strap with a buckle on one

end, and a big flap on the other was invented for the purpose of assisting the officers in this heinous practice, contrary to the letter and spirit of the constitution of the United States, the constitution of Alabama, the universal sympathy of the human heart. . . .

The defense of those who use the third degree is always that the victim is guilty. In Bessemer it was apparent that some of the victims were innocent, but Black's answer went to broader grounds. A man did not forfeit

> his right to be treated as a human being by reason of the fact that he is charged with — or an officer suspects that — he is guilty of a crime. Instead of being ready and waiting to strike a prisoner in his custody, an officer should protect him . . . such practices are dishonorable, tyrannical, and despotic, and such rights must not be surrendered to any officer or set of officers, so long as human life is held sacred and human liberty and human safety of paramount importance.

The report also charged drunk and disorderly conduct by the police, as well as stealing of prisoners' property. It concluded with the request that three officers be removed from the police force.

The first impulse of the Bessemer aldermen was to refer the matter to their own police committee for investigation. But Black refused to present his data to that committee. It was the nepotism of that committee, as well as the council, that had permitted the situation to arise, and one of the members of the committee was a brother of one of the officers accused. It was finally agreed that an impartial committee of citizens should be appointed, one by Black, one by the council, and one by the two appointees, and that the committee thus created should have public hearings.

The hearings continued in late September and early October 1915. Bessemer, as the press reported it, was a "city at fever heat." It was necessary to move the hearings to the courthouse to accommodate the crowd. Many of the Negroes, afraid to appear, filed affidavits recounting their tortures; but some did appear. It was established without question, for example, that four officers had strapped John Westbrook, a seventy-year-old Negro, to a door and had beaten him almost to death. (Black later indicted the four for the attempted murder of Westbrook, but was unable to convict them.) The actual presentation of the charges Black assigned to Assistant Solicitor Perry, his aide from Bessemer, and Perry examined a former officer as follows:

Q. Did you ever see officer —— beating Negro prisoners?
A. Yes.
Q. How did he beat them?
A. Sometimes there were three or four of us on a prisoner at once.
Q. What did you beat them with?
A. Fist, stick, chair — anything we could get hold of.
Q. Where did you beat them?
A. No particular place; sometimes in the warden's office.
Q. Did you know Westbrook?
A. Yes.
Q. What was his condition after being beaten?
A. Looked like he had been hammered up a bit; like some of the police had had hold of him.

On October 19 the Citizens' Committee reported. It asked the resignation of two members of the city council, scored the Mayor, and recommended the removal of four police officers. Slowly the situation was worked out by the people of Bessemer. Meanwhile the rest of Jefferson County was taking its stand. Some praised Black, but some were annoyed because such conditions were not respectably buried and ignored. The *Birmingham Age-Herald* minimized the significance of the investigation, saying: "as a matter of fact conditions such as are prevalent in every other city have been brought to light."

Black's surprise election to the office of prosecutor as an independent Democrat and his vigorous conduct of his office thereafter had made him enemies who were determined to embarrass his administration. The device was ready at hand in the legislature's haphazard distribution of the prosecutor's functions. Under the then existing state of the Alabama law, there were technically *two* prosecutors for the Birmingham area. One was the county solicitor, an official with prosecuting functions for Jefferson County, which included Birmingham. This position Black held. The other was the circuit solicitor. The circuit solicitor also had prosecutor's duties in Jefferson County. In practice the circuit solicitor's post had been a sinecure, with no substantial duties; and the legislature had never been compelled to decide what the boundaries of each office were. The then current circuit solicitor, however, had been elected on a program of action.

The anti-Black faction determined to take advantage of the situation. When the criminal case of Trent Abernethy was called for trial in Judge Fort's court, Black rose to say: "The State is ready for trial." The circuit solicitor also rose, and declared: "The State is not ready." Fort, after extensive argument, decided that Black was the representative of the state, and the circuit solicitor merely his assistant.

There followed a comedy of judicial politics. The Supreme Court of Alabama affirmed Fort in February 1917, but Black's opponents were undaunted and still ingenious. The circuit solicitor declared that he had the right to name Black's other assistants, and he thereupon named three aides of considerable political strength. Forney Johnson, Black's political adversary and counsel to the county treasurer, advised that only these assistants could be paid. Appropriate actions to test the point were instituted, and this time the Supreme Court decided against Black.

Meanwhile World War I had begun. Black had been a supporter of the Bryan peace program before American entry, and believed the war unnecessary; but after the declaration of war he felt there was nothing for it but to swallow his opinions and do what he could. Though over draft age, he was still a bachelor and anxious to serve.

The court decision thus provided an excellent solution for his personal problems. He was ready to resign and go into service; and it would have been useless to carry on as prosecutor if his worst political enemies were to control his staff. Black volunteered for the army.

Some were pleased and some were sorry. The *Birmingham Ledger* was one of the latter. It said: "Mr. Black has served Jefferson County well. He has kept the county jail empty, he has lopped the payroll of the county, and he has called attention to slack methods in the county affairs."

Chapter III

EDUCATION OF A SENATOR

Black's year in the army was a drab experience. In due course he became an artillery captain, and his promotion to major was pending when he was discharged; but he never served outside the United States, and he had no experiences of any particular value. He formed an unswerving conviction that the veteran is entitled to the most abundant possible reward from his government when he comes home. He was delighted to be out and home again by the end of 1918.

"Captain Black has resumed practice and has opened his office on the ninth floor of the First National Bank Building," said the *Birmingham Age-Herald,* and for a short time he practiced alone. There followed a series of partnership associations and at various times there were firms of Allen & Black; Black, Altman & Harris; Black, Foster & Harris, Black & Harris, and Black & Fort.

Black was able to buy himself an auto on the profits of his first three postwar months, and his practice continued to boom in the years following. Meanwhile he was almost entirely out of politics. He made a few speeches for John W. Davis in 1924, remaining a good Democrat in the face of the lure of the LaFollette-Wheeler Progressive ticket. But politics was receding as a primary interest. Black was establishing a home.

Upon his re-entry into practice, Black, though highly eligible, showed some signs of becoming a confirmed bachelor. He was without many family attachments — his father had died in 1899 and his mother in 1905, and three brothers died between 1897 and 1915. Only two sisters and one brother remained of the once large family, and they had their own ties. Black was living in bachelor quarters with a group of young men and was completely footloose when he met Josephine Foster at a Birmingham dance.

Miss Foster was very young. She had left Sweet Briar College to join the Yeomanettes, the World War I women's naval auxiliary, and she had spent the war in New York. She was still in uniform when she met Black. The resultant courtship had obstacles. There was the usual period of demure no before flustered yes, and there was a family rumbling in the background, occasioned by Black's working-man practice, about "that young Bolshevik." But in February 1921, a few days away from Black's thirty-fifth birthday, he and Josephine Foster were married.

The marriage gave Black an asset that in the next twenty-five years he was to need badly. His wife was interested in politics, as she became interested later in the work of the Court; but she was never obsessed with either. She was interested both in writing and in painting, for example, and enjoyed being a mother and a hostess. She showed little taste for campaigning, but much for laughter. A different woman would have molded a more strident husband, for Black's tendency was always to become totally preoccupied with the political issue or the case of the moment. It has been Josephine Foster Black's peculiar contribution that, no matter how violent the attacks on her husband, no matter whether ninety per cent of the press from coast to coast was screaming for his scalp, she has always been able to find something to make her husband smile.

The peculiar quality of balance that Mrs. Black has given to their marriage is hard to define, and is perhaps most easily described by its result: Black, like most American liberals of prominence, has been overwhelmingly and frequently denounced by the press. So were Bob LaFollette, Sr., and George Norris. That denunciation, that burning blast of what the individual must consider the wildest misrepresentation, turns many men bitter. Black, with his wife's help, has been able to receive that denunciation in good spirit, or in indifference.

From 1920 to 1925 Black's practice boomed. His practice took the usual shape of that of the liberal lawyer with some labor clientele. He represented the United Mine Workers and some other unions in their not very plentiful business. Thereby he forfeited, deliberately and cheerfully, the corporation cases; but when the working men of Birmingham suffered accidents, they regularly brought their cases to Black. He was fabulously successful as a jury lawyer; he and his partners were dissatisfied if they did not win ninety per cent of their cases.

After the fashion of most lawyers, Black asked large verdicts, and his amazingly flexible voice and his dramatic abilities induced juries to give his clients enormous amounts of defendants' money. It became necessary not only to win his cases but to protect the verdicts from reduction in the higher courts. A $3,000 verdict for a hernia victim and a $10,000 judgment for a fireman whose leg was injured were upheld; but the Alabama Supreme Court scaled down from $50,000 to $30,000 an award for an injured railroad worker who spent a year and a half in bed and was crippled for life. When a fifteen-year-old girl was awarded $10,000 for a sprained arm and some dubious internal injuries, the Alabama Supreme Court said: "We cannot avoid the sus-

picion that the jury in this case has been rather too liberal
with the money of the defendant"; but the verdict was allowed to stand. In a case involving an eye injury coupled
with alleged discharge of the employee for refusal to settle
the claim, Black's jury verdict of $25,000 was reduced to
$6,000 by the court. The court, in concluding that "passion
and not reason dictated the amount of the verdict," said:
"Indeed, counsel for appellant [Black] demonstrated, upon
the submission of this cause in oral argument, his ability to
eloquently present the cause in the most forcible manner."

During the years 1919 through 1925 Black's firm handled 108 cases in the appellate courts of Alabama, an average of fifteen a year. Excluding eight memorandum decisions, the distribution of the remaining hundred cases gives
a clear picture of the nature of Black's practice.

TABLE OF 100 CASES

Tort (largely injuries)	53
Insurance (largely fire, life)	11
Domestic relations	9
Criminal	9
Contracts	8
Property	4
Wills	3
Agency	2
Bills and notes	1
	100

The most sensational case in these years was the defense
of Edward R. Stephenson, a Methodist minister, for the
murder of a Catholic priest, Father James E. Coyle. The
shooting took place on the steps of the Catholic rectory on
August 12, 1921. Father Coyle had previously performed a
marriage ceremony between Stephenson's minor daughter
and Pedro Gussman, a swarthy Puerto Rican. Stephenson

had strongly opposed the marriage, and had also strongly opposed his daughter's earlier inclination to accept Catholicism.

Stephenson's plea was self-defense, and with Black as his attorney he made it stick. His story was substantially that he had been searching for his missing daughter when he went to the rectory, that he had quarreled bitterly with Father Coyle over the marriage ceremony, that Father Coyle had assaulted him, and that he had shot in self-defense. Because of the unusual standing of the parties the case attracted wide attention, and Black's participation in the defense cost him the sympathy of many of Father Coyle's adherents. It was subsequently charged that Black exploited the prejudices of the community in his defense, but Black himself believed that he won because the prosecution handled the case ineptly and relied on evidence easily proved untrustworthy.

As Black's practice grew, he slowly became a respectable himself. The local papers considered it worth reporting when Judge Black endorsed the five-million-dollar school bond issue. The Birmingham Bar Association made him a director and chairman of its committee to control ambulance-chasing. He taught Sunday school regularly at the Baptist church, kept up his lodge activities, and became Grand Chancellor of the Knights of Pythias. He was not in politics, but he was keeping an eye open for the main chance.

Oddly enough, a boost toward that chance was given him by the Republican national administration. The Department of Justice, under the general direction of Assistant Attorney General Mabel Walker Willebrandt, wanted to prosecute a number of persons, including prominent Democrats, in Mobile for conspiracy to violate the Prohibition Act and was unable to find a Republican in Alabama of sufficient standing to take the case. Finally the Department retained Black, who agreed to take on the case at the request of a number of Alabamans, without government compensation.

Meanwhile Black had been campaigning for Davis in the 1924 election and had roundly denounced Daugherty, President Harding's highly vulnerable Attorney General. Alabama Republicans complained to the new Coolidge Attorney General, Harlan Stone, and Mrs. Willebrandt asked Black to come to Washington to discuss the matter.

As Black sat in Mrs. Willebrandt's office, their visit was constantly interrupted by phone calls from politicians asking her to cancel prosecutions in their states — requests that she rejected politely but firmly. Hence by the time the conversation turned to the business at hand, Black had gained a real respect for his Republican superior and had begun a friendship that has lasted since. Black explained that he had vigorously attacked Daugherty, and Mrs. Willebrandt agreed that this was fair political tactics. "But," she said, "you will have to see the Attorney General."

The visit with Stone was equally pleasant. It was the first meeting of the two, and Stone said in substance: "My position is clear. I would rather have a competent Republican doing this job; but if I can't get a competent Republican, I want a competent Democrat. You go back and do the job. I will make only one request, that you accept a salary for your services. Our salaries are not large and will not be fair compensation for you, but I cannot approve of anyone working for the government without compensation." In later years, when Black was a Senator, Mrs. Willebrandt occasionally entertained the Blacks and the Stones at dinner, and it was one of Stone's favorite small jokes that he had given Black his start with the government.

The publicity value of the conspiracy trials had some

political advantage. So did Black's membership in the Ku Klux Klan.

On September 11, 1923 Black joined the Birmingham chapter of the Klan. He had deliberated for almost a year before doing so. The reasons for staying out were the obvious ones — he had very close friends among the groups that some Klansmen condemned; he had consistently and publicly upheld fair play for Negroes; he had never in his life given evidence to anyone of a belief that Nordics had a right to rule the world. The reasons for joining were also simple: he was a poor man's lawyer, and thousands of Birmingham workmen were in the Klan; and he was ambitious for political advancement. The rationalizations were threefold: first, that very few Klan members either practiced or approved of racial violence; second, that perhaps there was a chance to bore for decency from within; and third, that the Southern liberal in politics must do a certain amount of pretending if he is to stay in politics at all.

In 1925 Black resigned from the Klan at the beginning of his senatorial campaign. It was a friendly resignation, its timing motivated by the fact that it was considered by many Klansmen undesirable and improper for a member to be a candidate for office. He had attended few meetings while a member, but thereafter he spoke at Klan meetings perhaps eight or ten times in the course of his campaign.

It was a long campaign; for on June 10, 1925 Black announced that he would run for the Senate in the 1926 election. The decision to run had origins old and recent. Black's political interests reached back to boyhood, and his resolve that he would one day actively be engaged in politics was made in law school. Since in America politics is usually a lawyer's game, such a resolve for a law student is almost routine. Black differed from the typical law student only in that he daydreamed his major sortie into politics as an event to occur after he was successful as a lawyer. By 1925 he had saved a sufficient sum so that, with a senatorial salary to supplement his own resources, he would be financially independent.

The immediate decision that his major effort was to be for the Senate and that the time had come to make the attempt was reached about two months before the 1925 announcement. Black then determined to seek the Senate seat for the same reason that many other lawyers relinquish lucrative practices for public office: he had a real desire to perform a public service, and a real idea that he could do it.

Oscar W. Underwood, the incumbent Senator, was an economic conservative of the most conservative type, and he was an idol of Alabama politics; but he had opposed both the Klan and prohibition, which meant that his next campaign would be uphill work, and he was an old man. For whatever composite of reasons, Underwood announced about three weeks after the Black announcement that he would not be a candidate to succeed himself, and the field was thrown wide open.

In the campaign that followed, there were four candidates in addition to Black. Thomas E. Kilby, a former Governor, had inaugurated the first bone-dry law in Alabama but was widely regarded as personally a wet. John Bankhead, a representative of the leading political family in Alabama, was a conservative representative of the agricultural interests; four years later he became Senator with Black's support. Judge J. J. Mayfield, formerly of the state Supreme Court, was a distinguished lawyer and Black's good friend then and later. L. Breckenridge Musgrove was a prosperous businessman who had the militant support of the national Klan. Of the five, Black was the youngest, the least experienced in the larger affairs of government, and the least known outside his own county. He also had the least money and the most energy.

The first step was to make virtues of necessity. He was young — he stressed that he could "give to the State the best years of his life if elected." He couldn't match dollars with Bankhead, or Musgrove, or Kilby, and in any case he was running as the poor man's candidate: a major platform plank was the call for the enforcement of the ten-thousand-dollar campaign limitation.

Early in the campaign Black prepared a large handbill stressing what he thought would be most appealing in his record to the voters of Alabama. The most emphasized portion of the handbill was the following section, printed in bold type:

> BORN ON A FARM IN CLAY COUNTY
> GRADUATED LAW UNIVERSITY OF ALABAMA
> GENERAL PRACTICE OF LAW TWENTY YEARS
> HAD BEEN JUDGE CITY COURT, BIRMINGHAM, AND SO-
> LICITOR, JEFFERSON COUNTY
> RESIGNED AS SOLICITOR AND SERVED AS VOLUNTEER IN
> FIELD ARTILLERY WORLD WAR
> REPRESENTED STATE PROSECUTION GIRARD LIQUOR CASES
> 1916
> SERVED ASSISTANT ATTORNEY GENERAL UNITED STATES
> PROSECUTION MOBILE LIQUOR CONSPIRACY CASES
> IF ELECTED WILL TAKE OFFICE AT AGE 41 YEARS
> CAN GIVE TO STATE BEST YEARS OF HIS LIFE IF ELECTED.

The basic principles of his platform were veterans' aid, farm relief, prohibition enforcement, restricted campaign expenditures, and immigration restrictions. More important, he opposed use of the Muscle Shoals Dam, left idle from World War I, for private power development, and pledged instead his support of a cheap fertilizer program with the Shoals as the source of production. The principal endorsements were by W. M. Wood, of the Alabama Baptist

State Convention, and L. D. Patterson, pastor of the Avondale Methodist Church of Birmingham, who said: "He is the kind of prohibitionist to go to the United States Senate now."

Black's prohibitionism represented a deep-seated personal conviction held with emotional fervor. As police-court judge and as prosecutor he had witnessed the consequences of drunkenness with sickening frequency, and his support of prohibition was buttressed by more personal causes. There had been drunkenness in his own family, and his favorite brother had driven a horse and buggy into a stream and had drowned while under the influence of liquor. Black himself never drank at all and today takes only an occasional glass of sherry, though time has sufficiently moderated his feeling to permit liquor to be served in his home to those guests who may want it.

But the platforms scarcely distinguished among the candidates. There was no avowed wet in the race; and Bankhead, who had no Klan connections, cried: "America for Americans" frequently and loudly. In so far as there were distinguishing issues, they were essentially issues of personality and spirit. The real and effective element in Black's platform was the sheer statement of fact: he was born in Clay County, notoriously poor man's country. He could declare: "I am not now, and have never been, a railroad, power company, or corporation lawyer." His circulars proclaimed him "The Candidate of the Masses," and even among those eligible to vote, there were more poor people in Alabama than there were people with sizable numbers of dollars in their pockets. The reaction that elected Black was typified by the *Opp Weekly News:* "He knows better how to sympathize with the common people."

Compared with his four opponents, Black was virtually unknown. He was running against an ex-Governor, a former Supreme Court Justice, a millionaire businessman, and the best political name in the state, and at the beginning no one seriously thought Black had a chance. His response was a determination to speak to, or shake the hand of, as nearly as possible every voter in Alabama. He began the campaign early, and had been in fifty-seven counties before Kilby got started. As the *Birmingham Post* put it, "For rapidity of movement and territory covered, Hugo L. Black, a newcomer to state politics, is setting a pace that other candidates for the U.S. Senate are finding hard to equal. Black, a Birmingham attorney, has been continuously on the road for the last 30 days and his headquarters here announced that he has been in every county in the state and in some of them twice. He has delivered more than 60 speeches in the last 30 days and has travelled more than 2,000 miles. Black travels alone in an Overland automobile and apparently expects to wear out the car before the primary in August." The statement was wrong in only one respect — Black wore out two cars before the primary in August.

Thus on May 19 the readers of the *Tri-Cities Daily* could read an ad calling them to hear "Sensational! The Evil Power Scheme Revealed — Hear Hugo Black, candidate of the masses." Next day he was on to other towns.

On May 26 at ten o'clock in the morning he spoke in Coffeeville, at three o'clock in the afternoon he spoke in Jackson, and at eight o'clock in the evening at Thomasville. Next morning at ten o'clock he spoke at Morvin, and so on into another round of three-a-day stands.

Black's organized support came from the Women's Christian Temperance Union, many of the labor unions, and a portion of the Klan. On the other hand Klan Imperial Wizard Hiram Evans supported Musgrove, and Alabama's senior Senator, Tom Heflin, the most avowed anti-Catholic ranter in the history of the Senate, was thought to be secretly backing Kilby. Bankhead had a good share of respectable conservative support. Of Bankhead's platform the *Birmingham News* managed to say: "It is a conservative platform, and yet progressive, in that it is forward looking, without radicalism."

By the end of the campaign the discussion had moved far from the issues of the day. The anti-Black forces began to proclaim that Black was not really the poor man's candidate, because he was wealthy, too; and Bankhead made a statement that Black's Birmingham real-estate holdings were worth $278,000. Black responded with an offer to sell his property to Bankhead for half that amount. If comparative poverty was the issue, the voters must have believed Black was the poorer man, for at the August primary he was nominated handily, receiving forty per cent of the first-place votes in a field of five and enough second-place votes to make him the candidate.

Three weeks later, on September 2, 1926, there was a gathering of the Birmingham Klan to consider miscellaneous business for the "Realm of Alabama." Imperial Wizard Evans, Atlanta dentist and chief Klansman, was present and gave a ripsnorting Klan speech.

The chairman, Alabama's Grand Dragon James Esdale of Birmingham, called Governor Graves to the stand and said: "Judge Black, you come up here too, please." Esdale turned to Dr. A. D. Ellis of Tuscalloosa and called him to perform "a little task." Ellis thereupon awarded to Graves and Black Grand Passports, or honorary Klan memberships. Said Ellis: "They are good as long as you are good."

The crowd called for speeches from Graves and Black. Graves spoke first, concluding with a pledge to make a better Alabama not only for Klansmen but for every citizen of the state. Black's turn came next.

It was a difficult moment. Black had spoken all over Alabama in the preceding months, and if hundreds of news clippings are evidence, he had never mentioned white supremacy, Catholics, or Jews. The closest he had come to the Klan line was his anti-immigration stand, and there he had followed the position of the American Federation of Labor. The particular occasion was difficult because Ellis talked like a man who thought the Klan was going to collect a debt from the new junior Senator.

Black began by thanking the members for their support. He declared that he had been elected "by men who believe in the principles that I have sought to advocate and which are the principles of this organization." Wizard Evans had also been brought up in Ashland, Alabama, but had left before Black was old enough to know him. His father, Judge Evans, had stayed on, and Black told an anecdote about Judge Evans's habit of saying: "If you can't say something good about a man, don't say it." Black declared that the phrase had "been written into my heart and into my conscience."

As a Senator, he said, he would need counsel from the people of Alabama, and he hoped that those present would let him know what they thought about affairs. Yet he could not let the Ellis implied threat stand without response: if his hearers ever disagreed with his position on any matter, he said, tell him about it; but "There will be, and there is now, but one way, and if my heart remains true to the God of my father and my mother, there will never be another to secure conduct from me, and that is to convince me that the thing that is wanted is right." He would rather abandon his office at the end of a year than yield to popular clamor "by pandering to the things that are wrong and contrary to American tradition and instincts."

He thanked Esdale for his support and acknowledged that there were some present who had not supported him:

"There may be some who did not. That is all right. That is your privilege and prerogative as an American citizen. I would not take away from it in the slightest degree. The great thing I like about this organization is not the burning of crosses, it is not attempting to regulate anybody — I don't know, some may do that — but, my friends, I see a bigger vision." The vision was America "as it remains true to the principles of human liberty." He concluded with a note of gratitude to those Anglo-Saxon patriots, fathers of the "principles of liberty which were written in the Constitution of this country and in the great historical documents," and dramatically thanked his hearers.

It was Black's last Klan meeting. A few years later Mrs. Black found the Grand Passport in a drawer and disposed of it.

In a post-election interview the new Senator declared that he planned to close his law practice entirely and that "I expect to occupy an inconspicuous place in the Senate for some time." Black was fully aware that in a real sense he was largely uneducated. He had little more than a high-school education plus his law training, and most of his learning had come from unsystematized reading, particularly of Jefferson, during the years of practice. His first step upon arriving in Washington was to settle down to systematic reading, particularly in government and history, and he spoke very little in his first several sessions. He was sworn in as a Senator on December 5, 1927, and in January the *Birmingham Post* reported him as saying: "I have done more reading since I came to Washington than ever before." The *Mobile Register* observed that "Alabama makes a good Senatorial average, with one Senator [Heflin] talking incessantly, and one not at all."

The reading program Black undertook after he went to

the Senate was a broad education, a continuation on a broader scale of the reading program he began on graduation from law school. The first book he read after his election was Adam Smith's *Wealth of Nations,* and from it he wandered on to other works in economics and government. Similarly in other fields his method often was to begin with a good book and follow its leads. For example, in Birmingham he had read John Draper's *History of the Intellectual Development of Europe,* which led him on to the general study of history.

This general reading was not specialized in any particular view or doctrine, but much of it gave substance to the existing trends of Black's own philosophy. Draper is an example, with his theme that the object of our civilization should be "to secure intellectual freedom as completely as the rights of property and personal liberty have already been secured. Philosophical opinions and scientific discoveries are entitled to be judged by their truth, not by their relation to existing interests."

An offhand listing by Black of books he had read, largely between 1926 and 1937, included several hundred volumes. Among the historical works were extended excerpts from the writings of Franklin, Hamilton, and John Adams and all of Jefferson's voluminous writings; the records of the federal Constitutional Convention and of the state ratifying conventions, numerous biographies of Revolutionary and nineteenth-century American political leaders, Warren's and Myers's Supreme Court histories, most of the writings of Charles Beard, and numerous other historical works. His reading in Greek, Roman, and European history, though less comprehensive, was extended and included translations of Herodotus, Thucydides, Plutarch, Suetonius, Seneca, and Cicero.

His reading in other fields was more than a sampling. He

read Shakespeare frequently, and Milton, and the romantic English poets of the nineteenth century. He read nineteenth-century American writers such as Hawthorne, Thoreau, and Twain. In government and economics he read, among others, Montesquieu, Rousseau, Locke, Brice, Mill, Marx, and Spencer and particularly cherished Veblen. In philosophy he read Aristotle, Spinoza, and some of St. Thomas Aquinas and St. Augustine. His thorough reading of William James and John Dewey awaited a summer after his appointment to the Court which he devoted to modern legal philosophy and the American philosophers in whom that legal philosophy originates.

The distribution of bulk in his reading shows what would be deduced independently from his opinions: Black has comfortable acquaintance with the social sciences and the humanities, but primarily he is a historian.

The transition from quiet Birmingham to busy Washington was also a great adjustment for Mrs. Black. She was twenty-seven, the youngest hostess in the Senate, suddenly thrust into a far more elaborate set of social customs than she had ever known before. The cards of Paul Claudel, Katsuji Debuchi, and von Prittwitz-Gaffron, the French, Japanese, and German Ambassadors, looked far more impressive than any cards circulating in Birmingham. Hugo junior and Sterling got a card too; theirs was obtained through less formal social channels and was a genuine autograph of Amos and Andy.

The Senate into which Black came was divided into three fairly well-defined blocs: the conservative Republicans, headed by such men as Smoot of Utah and Fess of Ohio; the Democrats; and the liberal Republicans such as Norris, LaFollette, Cutting, and sometimes Borah. Black was to find himself eventually in the Norris camp, along with such Democrats as Walsh and Wheeler of Montana and Costigan of Colorado, but there was a period of sparring and making acquaintances before the lines could be crossed.

The Seventieth Congress had its quota of strong men, weak men, and fools, and foremost of the fools was Alabama's senior Senator, Heflin. Heflin was the national idol of the Klan, and his favorite amusement was denunciation of Catholics. Black had no intimate acquaintance with Heflin before the election, and it was not necessary to work closely with a minority colleague afterward. The first sharp break came in February 1928, when Senator Walsh introduced a resolution for the investigation of the power industry. Walsh, a Democrat, was the Senate's prize investigator and had exposed the Teapot Dome scandal. Heflin opposed the resolution, supporting instead a resolution for an investigation by the Federal Trade Commission. His stated reason was simple: that Walsh was a dry Catholic, that the Catholics realized that Smith, a wet, could not be nominated in 1928, and that the fame of this investigation would make Walsh the Democratic nominee. Black on the other hand, as the *Montgomery Journal* noted with pleasure, "stands stalwartly for the inquiry and supported Senator Walsh at all times during the committee controversy."

Congress adjourned for the national political conventions of 1928, at which Black was not a delegate, and the Democratic Party nominated Al Smith. Smith was pure poison to many Alabama voters. He was a dripping wet and a Catholic. Heflin announced that he would support Hoover, and the Klan climbed on the Republican bandwagon. Black immediately announced that he would support Smith, but the problem of the Democratic leaders in Alabama was serious. It was obvious that there would be a substantial "Republican" vote in Alabama for the first time since Reconstruction. Democrats feared that unless the rebellion was handled delicately, a real Republican

Party in Alabama might be the result, while if the erring sisters were allowed a graceful departure and return, the breach would quickly be healed.

Black assured Senator Swanson of Virginia, the senatorial campaign manager, that the Alabama electoral votes would go to Smith, but he and most other Democrats campaigned very quietly. After his original announcement Black sent a great many letters all over the state, each saying in substance that he certainly would not have chosen a wet candidate for the party, but that he would certainly support the party choice once it was made. He repeatedly declared, in flat contrast with Heflin, that he would feel obligated to resign his seat in the Senate if he did not support the party; and without formal speeches he campaigned for a straight ticket through one Congressional district as the supporter of the one Congressman thought menaced by the Republican upsurge. When the votes were counted, Smith carried Alabama by seven thousand votes.

In 1930 came real war with Heflin. The better components of the Alabama Democratic Party had had enough of Heflin, who had been making the state a laughing-stock, by 1930. Yet his strength with the rank and file was strong enough to make his nomination virtually certain. The controllers of the party committee hit upon the device of excluding from eligibility for the Democratic nomination all who could not take an oath that they had supported the whole party ticket in 1928. In other words, Heflin, who had supported Hoover, would be ineligible to run as a Democrat.

Black had no real strength in the party committee. As a minority Senator he had no patronage, and he had been elected as an almost unknown independent Democrat. Hence he neither caused the eligibility rule nor approved of it; it was, in his most outspoken opinion, totally illegal for the committee to exclude anyone from running as a Democrat.

The voters, rather than the committee, were entitled to make such a choice.

But once the party decision was made, Black felt bound to support it. Heflin declared that he would run as an independent, and as the election impended, there was real likelihood that his strength with the Klan voters and anti-Catholic elements in the state might carry him to victory. Black spoke all over the state, making fifty or sixty speeches in behalf of Bankhead, the regular party nominee. Bankhead was easily elected.

But the fight was not quite over. Under the pre-twentieth-amendment system Heflin returned to the Senate for his Lame Duck session from December 1930 to March 1931; while Bankhead was not actually sworn in as a Senator until December 1931, thirteen months after the election and only seven months ahead of the primary in 1932, at which Black would have to stand for re-election. Heflin meanwhile unsuccessfully fought his exclusion from the party ticket in the Alabama courts and had secured a recount, which showed that he was badly beaten. He then transferred his fight to the Senate itself, contending that Bankhead should not be seated because of Heflin's exclusion from the primary. In the months that followed, from December 1931 to the final vote on April 28, 1932, Black upheld the right of Bankhead to be sworn, on one occasion making the longest and one of the most powerful addresses he ever offered to the Senate on any issue. He explained that both Bankhead and he had opposed the order of the committee as illegal, but that the question was one finally to be decided by the Alabama Supreme Court, which had decided it. Bankhead was finally seated by a vote of 64 to 18, with Senators Norris, Frazier, McNary, and Cutting among the minority group. Norris, for example, was able to support Heflin as a token of his own resistance to control of political offices by party organizations.

Black offered few bills of note and participated only slightly in debate for the first few sessions. He offered a bill to suspend immigration, he opposed a redistricting that would have cost Alabama a seat in Congress, and supported Norris's campaign for open executive sessions, but for the most part he was reading and listening. He took an early interest in the loose financing of the United States Shipping Board, which he was later to investigate thoroughly; and he successfully carried an amendment to the Board's appropriation limiting the salaries of its staff attorneys to ten thousand dollars a year. His other principal early turns on the floor were in his debate with Senator Bruce of Maryland and in the discussion of Muscle Shoals.

Bruce was a wet Democrat who delighted in taunting the Southern states on the claimed hypocrisy of their demands for law enforcement. After one such attack Black became genuinely annoyed and rose to make impassioned answer. It was a florid reply, sprinkled through with "the calm sunshine of Dixie," "the South, a land composed of noble and brave and patriotic and loyal law-abiding citizens," the "Stars and Stripes."

The peculiar aspect of the reply to Bruce was that Black never in ten years in the Senate attempted anything like it again, despite the fact that for home consumption it was enormously effective. Southern Senators were pleased, and the home folks were delighted. It was an easy and harmless way to gain both publicity and popularity. Yet Black on only one other occasion, in his reply to Senator Byrnes in support of the Wage-Hour Act, spoke as a sentimental Southerner, and he never again spoke with the sentimentality of the reply to Bruce.

Muscle Shoals was Black's primary interest in the Senate until the New Deal made the Tennessee Valley Authority a reality. His participation in the Muscle Shoals debates was his one important exception to his general non-participation in Senate debates in his early years as a Senator. A program for development of Muscle Shoals had been part of his campaign platform, and he tried to make it effective.

The Muscle Shoals Dam on the Tennessee River in Alabama had been built during World War I to supply nitrates for munitions. After the war it stood idle for years, while Senator Norris attempted to prevent its cut-rate sale to private interests and to reserve it for government production of power. The only power being produced was going to the Alabama Power Company.

There were three basically different views of a desirable future for Muscle Shoals in 1927 and 1928. One was the Norris view that the dam should be part of a project for the government production and distribution of electric power, particularly to municipalities. A second was the view which Black early represented in the Senate, that the project should be leased to private companies, the power to be used for the manufacture of fertilizer. A third was the view either that the project should be sold outright to private power interests or that the power produced should be sold exclusively to private interests.

The program on which Black was elected was a fertilizer program, and he clashed squarely with Norris. A Norris Shoals bill was about to pass the Senate when Black came into office, and as Alfred Lief, able Norris biographer, has said, "A newcomer from Alabama, Hugo L. Black, successor of Underwood, raised hob." [1]

Black and Norris were equally "anti-Power Trust,"

---

[1] Lief: *Democracy's Norris* (Harrisburg, Pa.: Stackpole Sons; 1939), p. 312.

though at first each may have suspected the good faith of the other. The Black position was that the Southeast was the greatest fertilizer-consuming section of America, and that a reduction in the fertilizer bill would mean a direct monetary benefit to farmers. At the same time he felt that the sole beneficiary of a government power-production program would be the private power companies, for, he contended, the municipalities were already committed to power purchases from the Alabama Power Company on long-term contracts, and hence that company would be the only big customer for government power. Black therefore was generally sympathetic to the fertilizer bid of the American Cyanamid Company.

The Norris position, on the other hand, was that for technical reasons the Shoals properties were not suitable for fertilizer production, and that in any case the offers of the fertilizer exponents were not bona fide, but were really attempts to tie up the power for the benefit of private power interests.

It took Norris and Black approximately a year to come to an understanding, and each then substantially modified the position he had held before. Black gained from Norris a sense he had not previously had of the potentialities of public power for the welfare of the people of the South. Black in part convinced Norris, who came from a state which used almost no fertilizer, that the plowed-out lands of the Southeast needed fertilizer as much as rain.

A central element of the Black education on Muscle Shoals was the discovery that Norris was exactly right in his charge that private fertilizer was a cover for private power. Senator Caraway's Committee on Lobbying asked Black to undertake the portion of the investigation relating to Muscle Shoals, and Black thereby obtained his first intimate insight into large-scale political corruption. The

report on May 21, 1930 declared that the American Cyanamid Company was combining its efforts with those of the
Union Carbide Company, which by secret agreement was
to obtain a great share of the Muscle Shoals power for non-
fertilizer purposes if Cyanamid ever obtained the lease it
sought. The report showed that out of $45,000 spent for
lobbying activities jointly by the two companies, $34,634
came from Carbide, which had no fertilizer objectives at all.
The report showed further that a legislative representative
of one of the largest farm organizations had been bribed
to make it appear that the farmers of his organization were
opposed to public power and supported the private bid.

In the course of discussion of the Shoals project in 1928
and 1930 Norris adopted three of Black's proposals, and
Black became a zealous supporter of the Norris plan as thus
amended. The three modifications were: (1) that a portion
of Shoals power should go for fertilizer; (2) that Alabama
and Tennessee should receive some payment in lieu of the
potential taxes lost if the project were operated by the government; and (3) that municipalities should be given
thirty-year contracts for power purchases from the government instead of the fifteen-year contracts originally proposed by Norris. The purpose of the latter amendment was
to assure the municipalities of power for a long enough
time to permit them to build their own transmission lines.

In 1928 the Norris proposal passed and was pocket-
vetoed by President Coolidge. In 1931 it passed Congress
again, and was vetoed by President Hoover. By 1930 Black
had become one of the most energetic supporters of the Norris plan as modified by the suggestions listed, and on April
3, 1930 Senator Norris said to the Senate:

> I want to commend the Senator from Alabama for the
> interest he has taken in this legislation. He has been of
> almost invaluable assistance. I know that when the

Lobby Committee commenced to investigate, a request was made of me to meet with the Committee and question witnesses, inasmuch as it was supposed that I had a considerable general knowledge on the subject. It was a physical impossibility for me to do that, on account of other work that I had. The Senator from Alabama was importuned to do it. I myself requested him to do it. He has been of great service to the Lobby Committee — almost invaluable service. I think they will all agree to that; and I know, as a student of this subject and of this particular investigation of this subject, that we cannot praise the Senator from Alabama too highly.

In 1929 the Congress began its consideration of the bill that was to become the Smoot-Hawley Tariff Act, the highest tariff in the history of the country. Black opposed most of its provisions, including increases for cement and iron, which were produced heavily in Alabama. He did support vigorously an increase for graphite, the product of Clay County, though his amendment was abandoned by the Senate conferees.

One tariff provision provoked a vigorous discussion of civil rights. The bill as the Finance Committee sponsored it permitted customs officials from whom there was no practical appeal to exclude books as either obscene or subversive. Senator Cutting of New Mexico proposed an amendment limiting the power of the customs inspectors as to such works and providing review. Black energetically supported Cutting, while Heflin opposed. Black declared that the right of free expression was too valuable to be so lightly restricted, that schools and churches rather than censorship must counteract offensive literature. The American citizen should be "persuaded in no way except by logic and reason." Black emphasized that one man might think a book offensive while another might not, and said: "I have an inherent opposition — I presume it comes, perhaps,

from reading a great deal of Thomas Jefferson's philosophy — I have an inherent, well-grounded opposition
against investing in the hands of an individual judicial
powers on matters of supreme importance with reference to
the dissemination of human knowledge."

The second session of the Seventy-first Congress, which
sat from December 2, 1929 to July 3, 1930, met shortly
after the great stock-market collapse of 1929 and the beginning of the depression. Black had been a Senator for
two years, and the new session marked the end of his self-
imposed and unofficial apprenticeship. For the next eight
years he was to take a fully active part in the deliberations
of the Senate. He was a member of the Judiciary Committee and studied closely the operations of the federal courts.
Occasional comments show that he was developing doubts
about the comprehensive wisdom of the Supreme Court,
and he joined Norris and Borah in opposing the Supreme
Court nominations of Parker and Hughes because of their
anticipated conservatism. Black also began to exhibit interest in problems of minimum wages and the hours of labor.

If interest was stirring on wages and hours, it was already full-formed on the first principle of Clay County notions of a sound government, the enforcement of the antitrust laws. Understanding that the Attorney General was
being urged to relax a consent decree obtained eight years
earlier against the meat packers, Black appealed to him
not to do so. To Black, the militant enforcement of the antitrust laws was the only antidote that could save a free capitalist system:

> If huge mergers and stupendous monopolies are to
> be granted the privilege of supplying the necessities of
> the people, it cannot but lead to an extended govern-
> mental supervision of business and general regulation
> and restriction of profits. Business profits must be con-

trolled, either by the method of enforcing competition
or by strict governmental regulation of profits, which
few desire.

By 1932 the nation's major question was what to do
about the depression. Senators LaFollette, a Republican,
and Costigan, a Democrat, had a proposal, a $275,000,000
federal relief measure. The proposal marked the first long
step toward abandonment of the century old notion that the
federal government should remain largely indifferent to the
distress of the poor in time of depression. Black opposed the
LaFollette-Costigan measure and contributed largely to
its defeat. He and Senators Walsh of Montana and Bulkley
of Ohio offered an amendment to permit state control of the
relief program, with a large appropriation. The amendment lost, 31 to 48, and thereupon Walsh and Bulkley supported the bill while Black opposed it. Said Black, the bill
"is wrong in principle. It would tend to destroy the last
vestige of independence on the part of the people of the
United States. It is establishing a Federal bureau with
powers unequalled since the days when the Roman prole-
tariat looked for and accepted the crumbs as they fell from
the table of the rich." The bill lost, 35 to 48.

By the time of the 1932 elections the Alabama legislature
had changed the election laws to provide that there should
be two primaries if necessary; a first to select the two top
candidates and a run-off to determine the majority winner
if there was no majority on the first election. The first primary was held in May, the second on June 10.

Once again Black had to face four candidates. They
were Kilby, whom he had defeated before; Anderton, a dry;
Burns, a wet; and Charlie McCall, a former state attorney
general who had spectacularly resigned from the Klan a
few years before.

Before the first primary Black did substantially no campaigning, staying in Washington, where the Senate was in session, and devoting himself primarily to protecting Bankhead's Senate seat against Heflin. Theoretically he was doing nothing in his own behalf. He said not a word about the election, about his opponents, or about the issues that concerned his opponents. He did not have to. Two of his official acts as Senator had been on the front pages of the newspapers, and they seemed well designed for home consumption. The first was a bill he successfully carried through for a five-million-dollar fund for loans to persons who had suffered great damage by a tornado that swept Alabama in 1929. The second was his defense of the Alabama primary system, under which Bankhead had been elected, despite the attacks of Delaware's Republican Senator Hastings. Both stands put him at the forefront of public attention in Alabama far more favorably than any amount of campaigning could have done.

Meanwhile his opponents kept up a vigorous attack and attempted to force him into debate. They tried throughout the period of the first primary to obtain some statement on prohibition in the hope that he would thus alienate either the wet or the dry vote; while Kilby, the original bone-dry Governor, himself took the stand that he supported resubmission of the eighteenth amendment to a national referendum.

The Heflin defeat in 1930 had showed that Klan support in Alabama had become something of a liability, and Kilby, who had taken no part in the elections of 1928 and 1930, attacked Black vigorously for allegedly having been a Klan candidate in 1926 and then having deserted the Klan in 1928 without being a militant Smith supporter. The Klan membership charge was thoroughly and completely aired by Kilby and by his strong supporter, Congressman Sam Hobbs. In late April Birmingham was circularized by

Black's opponents with a facsimile copy of the Klan Grand
Passport that had been granted to Black on September 2,
1926, and on April 29, 1932, on the third column of page
one, the *Montgomery Advertiser* printed the entire language of the Grand Passport. This document was doubtless released by the Klan itself, for the Klan had been
anti-Black since his 1928 support of Smith and his large
part in defeating Heflin in 1930, and in the 1932 election
Heflin publicly bent all of his power in support of Kilby
and against Black. This was politics gone utterly topsy-
turvy, for here in 1932 was Kilby, with Klan backing, attacking Black for his Klan membership of 1926.

With the exception of prohibition and Muscle Shoals,
no large public issue was discussed in the 1932 campaign.
On Muscle Shoals, Black's opponents charged that he had
tied himself to Norris's coattails and was no longer representing Alabama interests. Since Black was largely credited
by the press with having materially aided Norris in the passage of the 1931 Shoals bill, which President Hoover had
vetoed, the charge was of little effect. Prior to the first primary Black said nothing about prohibition, though he had
a bone-dry record. The opposition was hard put to it to
make an issue.

Kilby charged Black with nepotism, since Black had appointed his wife as his secretary for a portion of one summer and had two other relatives on his clerical staff. The
charge at least to some extent boomeranged, since Southern
courtesy rebelled, in the words of the *Ozark Southern Star*
against one who would "drag Southern womanhood into
the mire of politics." Black in the campaign before the second primary declared that Mrs. Black had been a good
secretary, and that if he ever again needed summer help he
would reappoint her.

The other charges were of similar proportion. The *State*

Press, a Kilby organ, charged that Black had supported the right of a Negro, R. R. Moton of Tuskeegee Institute, to vote. McCall charged that Black had trapped innocent Alabama farmers into defrauding the government by making the tornado relief bill too complex for them to understand. Black's critics asserted that in 1928 he had planned to desert Smith, that at a secret meeting in Wisconsin with Norris and the Democratic vice-presidential candidate, Joe Robinson, he agreed to support Smith in return for preferred committee assignments, but that he then fled first to Battle Creek and then to Canada to avoid taking a stand. The facts were that Black was in Wisconsin at a Knights of Pythias convention when Smith was nominated and immediately announced his support; that he did not see either Robinson or Norris there; and that he was not in either Battle Creek or Canada within many years of the 1928 election.

On May 3 the voters of Alabama went to the polls and Black received forty-nine per cent of the total vote, only a handful short of the required majority. Kilby was a bad second, but all the other candidates and Heflin lined up behind him, and the run-off race began.

Black came back to the state for ten days of speech-making in late May and early June, and then returned to Washington. He was back in Alabama for three days before the June 14 election. Kilby was campaigning so diligently that, according to the *Montgomery Advertiser,* Black's friends were convinced "that the silver tongue of Black himself is needed to stem the tide of his opposition." The *Advertiser,* never a warm Black supporter, observed:

> Senator Black is one of the best campaign speakers produced in Alabama in two decades. He proved his mettle in this regard in 1926 when he spoke all over Alabama and led a field of strong men. And again in Ala-

bama recently he showed his mettle as a public speaker. His Montgomery speech demonstrated that he is an even more finished orator now than he was six years ago, when he made hundreds of speeches in the interest of his candidacy.

In the run-off campaign Black announced his stand on prohibition. Six years had not changed his conviction that liquor was a foremost source of evil, but it had changed his convictions in two other respects. He no longer thought that in the midst of terrible depression prohibition was a paramount issue; and he no longer thought, if he ever had, that it was possible for the drys to enforce prohibition against a people who did not want it. Kilby he dealt with in a burst of annoyance, declaring in Kilby's home town of Anniston: "I have no patience with a man who will ride into office on the dry issue and proceed to try to keep the state dry by drinking up all the liquor in existence." For himself, he declared, he remained both a personal and a political dry; but the time had come to resubmit the matter to popular vote. As a Senator, he would vote to submit a repeal amendment to the people; as a voter in Alabama, he would vote against it.

Black's total active campaign time was perhaps two weeks. But in preceding summers he had assiduously canvassed the state, and both the American Federation of Labor and the Railroad Brotherhoods, old clients, energetically supported him in 1932 on his record. He was renominated on June 14, receiving about sixty per cent of the total vote.

The six years since he had begun his first campaign had been the period of the education of Hugo Black. Had he been defeated at the end of the first term, his name would have been long since forgotten and his accomplishments in his Senate career could have been assessed as mine-run. He had been a fairly consistent liberal **Senator and** had become a good member of the Norris team.

But the six years had not been lost. They had given Black the education he had been missing. He came to the Senate a well-meaning Southern liberal. He finished his term with a grasp of facts and of method and a grasp of the national, rather than regional, liberal spirit. From Bob LaFollette he had learned much of the technical aspects of tax law. From Cutting he had gained much of the spirit of the liberal tradition. From Norris he had gained knowledge of the power industry and of the potentialities of his own home river, as well as patience and legislative craftsmanship. From his own constant application he had learned much of government and of history and of constitutional law.

In sum, by 1932 Black was in many respects a changed man. His larger purposes and articles of faith remained largely what they were when he left Clay County, but in six years he had completely broken with the Klan, he had seen prohibition sink to a minor place in his hierarchy of issues, he had materially changed his mind on the potential of Muscle Shoals. In his second term if he were to speak of labor, or taxation, or power, or fertilizer, or transportation, or the judiciary, he was to be an expert on his subject.

Chapter IV

THE NEW DEAL

When Black returned to the Senate for the last Hoover session of the Congress in December 1932, he came with a new confidence. He had been resoundingly re-elected by the people of Alabama, and a Democratic President and Congress would take office in four months. Black was shortly to become a majority Senator instead of a minority Senator, with all the new opportunities for action which that status gave.

The next five years were full, so full that no short sketch can even review the high spots. Black was consistently active, both in committees and on the floor. Yet even in those crowded years a few deeds stand out above the others. One was the five-year fight for the legislation that eventually became the Fair Labor Standards, or Wage-Hour, Act, the first federal statute to ensure even a small day's pay for a full day's work. Another was the group of investigations, for it was as an investigator that Black performed his greatest service to the New Deal. In the years from 1930 to 1936 he conducted a series of major investigations, one into Muscle Shoals lobbying in 1930 as an aid to another committee; one into ship subsidies, which extended into air-mail subsidies; and one into lobbying activities against the

Public Utilities Holding Company Act of 1935, which developed into a general lobbying investigation in 1936. Some of the investigations and the Wage-Hour Act are considered here.

Such a selection requires many omissions. It ignores the successful legislative struggle to block a ten-million-dollar subsidy to the International Mercantile Marine that Postmaster General Brown planned to allow only forty-eight hours before he went out of office. It overlooks Black's many veterans' bills and his efforts to liberalize the laws relating to injuries to railroad workers. Excluded is Black's vigorous opposition to the Wagner-Costigan antilynching bill in 1935 on the stated ground that the bill as drafted would be as applicable to labor union disturbances as to the few lynchings in the South. Excluded also are Black's vigorous fights in support of the President's Court plan in 1937 and his campaigning activities all over the country in support of Roosevelt's re-election in 1936. In the 1936 election Black was one of his party's principal speakers throughout New England and the Middle West, and with LaFollette, La Guardia, Norris, and other Progressives he formed the Progressives for Roosevelt Group, which wooed the votes of independents and Republicans for the President.

The new confidence engendered by a new administration made Black far more outspoken than he had been in earlier years. A good example is his attitude in the debate over the confirmation of Rex Tugwell as Under Secretary of Agriculture in 1934. Tugwell was one of the favorite objects of the antiadministration attack, for he not only was a professor but had written books. Many who supported Tugwell in the Senate as a matter of loyalty to the President were very careful to disavow the books. Black listened to the qualified words of praise from some of his colleagues and finally got to his feet to say:

It is my intention to vote for Dr. Tugwell, because I am for him. I am for the views he has expressed, as I understand those views to be written in his books. I am for him because I believe that he is one man who is not content with looking backward, who for every thought he has in mind is not bowed down by slavish precedents. I am for him because he dared to express his unbelief in some of the theories which have been announced by theorists of the past, and because he does not accept a principle of political economy which has been announced and which has been organized and which has been accepted in the past merely because it has been accepted in the past.

In these five years Black departed from the President's program on major matters only five times, once only slightly. He pushed his thirty-hour-week bill before the administration was ready to undertake maximum hour legislation; he voted to override the President's veto of the bonus and he strenuously opposed the NRA because it amended the Sherman Antitrust Act to permit price-fixing by business groups. He also successfully fought portions of the Economy Act of 1933 limiting the availability of veterans' hospitals. His sharpest personal clash with the President came when Black supported an amendment by Senator McCarran to provide a prevailing wage for certain relief workers. For the larger part, Black had found in Franklin D. Roosevelt a leader he could follow.

In 1934 the airplane business was booming, with plenty of government money for everybody on the inside. The industry was almost entirely controlled by three large holding companies. Plane production, motor production, transportation, and even insurance were tied together by interlocking companies. The government financed the industry in two ways. It bought planes for military purposes, and it subsidized air transport by paying large sums nominally for the carriage of mail but actually for the purpose of developing the industry. Between 1926 and 1933 the United States paid $87,564, 988 in subsidies.

Entire power and responsibility for the allocation of airline routes to the various companies, and hence entire control of subsidies, lay with the Postmaster General. He was Walter F. Brown during the Coolidge-Hoover years, and he was also the chairman of the Republican National Committee. Charges of favoritism, fraud, and corruption were certain to result from such a system, and in 1934 the Black committee on ocean and air-mail subsidies began its probe.

Hearings began with testimony that two days before going out of office Brown had burned large quantities of Post Office files relating to ocean and air-mail contracts. Brown later returned to Postmaster General Farley papers that he said he had taken by mistake. There followed a series of charges and denials from which a clear picture of a promotors' and politicians' holiday began to emerge.

Black determined to discover what sort of profits were being made in this government-subsidized industry. He revealed an astonishing story to an interested country. Indeed, the spectacular pyramiding by which financiers had developed Pratt & Whitney Aircraft into the United Aircraft holding company was as sensational as any episode in the history of business buccaneering. For example, in 1926 Charles W. Deeds, then a lad of twenty-three, sank the sum of $40 into Pratt & Whitney stock at 20 cents a share for 200 shares. Two years later he received a stock dividend of 16,000 shares. This he exchanged for 34,720 shares of United. At the time of the transfer his stock had a value of $3,367,000, and in 1929 it had grown to $5,624,000. He had actually cashed in $1,600,000, and had a substantial number of shares left. Prior to 1927 he had no experience in the aircraft business, but in the seven years before 1934, when he was thirty-one years old, he received $142,000 in salary and $151,000 in bonuses from Pratt & Whitney and its successors.

Black showed that the fortunate Mr. Deeds was far from being the only beneficiary of these arrangements. Fred B. Rentschler, brother of the president of the National City Bank of New York, invested $253, which he ran up to a 1929 paper profit of $35,575,848 and a liquid profit of $11,000,000. He had also received $5,585,000 in salary and bonuses between 1924 and 1933. Rentschler did not care to answer Black's inevitable question: "Do you think it is right for the United States government to subsidize any companies when the officers draw salaries and bonuses of several hundred thousand dollars?" The inquiry went on to discover that George J. Mead, until recently vice-president of United, had turned a $207 investment into $7,796,293. The City Company of New York, which had arranged the consolidation of Boeing Aircraft, Pratt & Whitney, and the Chance Vought Company into United, had made $5,895,000, and had issued stock to a preferred list of insiders at $30 a share while the public was paying $97 a share. In a short period of time Boeing made $5,332,-284 on an investment of $259.14. When asked by Black what the public was paying for shares at the same time, Boeing replied: "I don't see where the public came in on this." Black responded: "The public came in between $87 and $160."

Black also discovered that there had been glowing opportunities for politicians in aeronautics and in shipping, as collectors both for the party coffers and for their own. William B. Robertson, of St. Louis, testified that William Sacks, a leading Republican politician, had guaranteed to get Robertson a contract from Postmaster General Brown if Robertson would pay Sacks a handsome sum and give liberally to a St. Louis Republican campaign fund. Sacks testified that he had acted as an attorney only. More important, it was established that Brown had a secret joint stock-market account involving $1,000,000, part of the collateral for which was 3,000 shares of International Mercantile Marine stock. I.M.M. was one of the concerns receiving ship subsidies. The joint account was held by Brown with a friend, Joseph H. Bagley, Washington representative of Bruce & Co., flooring manufacturers, and Brown had instructed that Bruce flooring be exclusively used in many federal post offices.

Brown replied that I.M.M. had been given no postal contracts while he was in office; but Black showed that two other companies had been given postal subsidy contracts shortly before being absorbed by I.M.M.

The kin of the mighty picked up the comparatively small change. An official of Western Air Express testified that his firm hired Ernest Smoot, son of the powerful Republican chairman of the Senate Finance Committee, to attempt to induce Comptroller General McCarl to withdraw a ruling expensive to Western. Black revealed that Ernest Smoot proceeded to do his job for Western, and soon wrote back to his client: "If nothing happens first of next week, my father and I will see McCarl again." Smoot charged $15,000 for his services, but Western was unwilling to pay so much. Colonel Paul Henderson, United official, testified that he paid either $3,000 or $5,000 to Lehr Fess, son of the influential Republican Senator from Ohio, for two days' work expediting the passage of legislation desired by his company. Henderson was very helpful to high-ranking Post Office officials. He lent $10,000 to Chase Gove, Assistant Postmaster General Glover's principal assistant; and he sent a wire to an associate as follows: "I should like to be able to tell Glover on Monday that his

nephew is fixed up some place on the western division. . . .
I think this is extremely important. Glover will have more
to do with the mail subsidy allocations than any other man."

All this was juicy scandal, but it was not fundamental.
What was fundamental was that the entire system of air
contracts had been made in violation of the statutes requiring competitive bidding. Black's most important evidence
showed two meetings in the Post Office Department in a conference room adjacent to Brown's office on May 19 and
June 4, 1930. Those present were the air-line insiders, and
excluded were those aspirants for air routes not on friendly
terms with the Postmaster General. These meetings, under
the chairmanship of William P. MacCracken, former Assistant Secretary of Commerce for Aeronautics, divided up
the air-mail map of the United States in accordance with
suggestions from the Postmaster General. As one carrier
representative put it, they were "willing to do anything
within reason to work out the plan rather than have to have
competitive bidding."

This little group, by a process of agreement among themselves, effectively eliminated the competitive bidding required by statute. The program thus formulated was carried out. For example, on one transcontinental route there
was thereafter only one bidder. On another Brown awarded
the route to the *highest* rather than the lowest bidder. He
also used a power to "extend" routes without competitive
bidding to add 5,983 miles to the air-mail system, a one-
fifth increase in the whole mail-mileage system.

On January 26, 1934 Black lunched with the President
to discuss the work of his committee. In Black's view, the
whole system of air-mail contracts emanating from the
1930 secret split was fraudulent and completely illegal. He
reminded the President that it was within the Chief Executive's power to cancel fraudulent contracts.

Meanwhile the Justice Department and the Post Office Department of the new administration were making their own inquiries. On February 9, 1934 the President announced that all air-mail contracts would be canceled as of February 19 and that the army would begin to carry the mail until a new system of contracts was devised.

But Black had one bit of real excitement before the cancellation. The Brown administration had apparently left the Post Office in a blaze of burning papers. Glover's secretary testified that before leaving office he had burned four packages of mail for Glover. Though all were in official government files marked "air mail contracts," the witness gravely assured the committee that they consisted of personal letters about stamp-collecting.

The wave of destruction was not over. Assistant Commerce Secretary MacCracken, who had presided at the 1930 meetings, had become a Washington attorney for many air lines when he left the sub-cabinet. On February 1, 1934 the Black committee informed him that it wanted to see him — and his files. That evening Colonel L. H. Britten, vice-president of Northwest Airways, and Gilbert Givvens, secretary to Harris Hanshue, the president of Western Air Express, appeared in MacCracken's office. MacCracken went over his files, took out papers reflecting on Western, and gave them to Givvens, who mailed them to Hanshue. Meanwhile Britten took the Northwest papers back to his office in the National Press Building and destroyed them.

On February 2, the next day, Black cross-examined Britten, who confessed to having obtained the papers from MacCracken. The two Republican Senators on the committee, Austin of Vermont, later American delegate to the United Nations, and White of Maine, later Senate majority leader, immediately joined Black in denouncing MacCracken and

Britten as guilty of contempt of the Senate. Black wrote out a resolution for the arrest of MacCracken, which the Senate, in an atmosphere of "intense excitement" as the press reported it, immediately adopted.

The next day MacCracken testified that the letters he had given to Givven were all "personal" and had nothing to do with air mail. He also contended he had a lawyer's right to protect his clients' confidence. But Givven was frightened and told the truth, confirmed by the eventual recovery of the letters; all had been letters dealing with air-mail contracts. Britten stuck to the story that the letters he received from MacCracken were personal. On February 5 Black asked the Senate to cite MacCracken, Britten, Hanshue, and Givven for contempt of the Senate, to be tried by the whole Senate. The Senate immediately did so. Meanwhile Black's investigators went through numerous sacks of rubbish in the basement of the National Press Building and pieced together a number of letters that had been torn up by Britten, which dealt with air-mail contract problems, and some of which had the phrase "MacCracken's copy" written at the top. Britten said these were not the letters he had brought back from MacCracken.

After a comic-opera interlude in which MacCracken at first defied the Senate and later submitted to arrest, the Senate, with Black as the moving spirit in examining the witnesses, found Givven and Hanshue not guilty in view of their defense that they had not understood that the Senate wanted the papers which they retrieved from MacCracken; but the Senate sentenced Britten and MacCracken for contempt to ten days each in the District of Columbia jail. Britten served his sentence at once. MacCracken litigated his case to the United States Supreme Court, which refused to interfere with the conviction, and then served his sentence.

On February 19, 1934, the date the army began to carry the mail, Black's investigation was an overwhelming success. A complete new system for government subsidies to air carriers was in the offing. The promoters and the financial adventurers who had been bleeding not only the government but the aviation industry were to be driven out. Political control was to end. A healthy competitive system was to take its place as the holding-company pyramid came down. The country was ready. As the *Des Moines Register-News* put it, if the carriers "are in an unpleasant mess, they may thank their own greed and the system that grew up in the Postoffice Department under Postmasters General who did not know an airplane from a toadstool."

Then came the collapse. The army was unable to carry the mail. The President had received the best of technical advice before he canceled the contracts. War Secretary Dern, after consultation with Chief of Staff Douglas MacArthur and his aeronautics officers, had assured the President that the army could do a prompt and efficient job. Former Brigadier General Billy Mitchell had said the same thing. But they were wrong. Twelve pilots died during army control. Only four of them were actually carrying mail, but the others were moving planes or supplies for auxiliary purposes.

The country was shocked and frightened. The explanations were two: first, that the army planes were not so well equipped as the commercial planes; and second, that the weather in February and March had been the worst in years. Both explanations were true, and the latter may have been controlling. Serious commercial crashes occurred in the same period, and airplane accidents have been known on more recent occasions to occur in clusters. But the tragedies gave Eddie Rickenbacker, for the air lines, an opportunity to shout "legalized murder" and to denounce the Presi-

dent's advisers as "traitorous." And then the air lines
wheeled their biggest gun into play.

In 1934 the only American who could rival Franklin D.
Roosevelt's popularity was Charles Lindbergh. Lindbergh,
who had received $250,000 worth of stock for signing up
with one of the air lines, and whose air-line salary was
$16,000 a year, testified that the air lines were without fault
and that the entire cancellation of contracts had been an
outrageous mistake. As Lindbergh testified and the deaths
went up, it became evident that President Roosevelt had a
political bear by the tail.

Black fought back for the administration on the floor of
the Senate and on the radio. He supported the cancellation
with the dramatic revelations of his investigation, and he
reiterated over and over again Farley's basic charge that
$28,000,000 in excessive, unnecessary, and illegal subsidies
was paid the carriers between the 1930 meetings and 1934.
He insisted that the cancellation had been a legal necessity,
since the government would have been bound by the fraud
of its agents if it had not canceled immediately upon its
discovery.

The upshot was compromise of the reforms originally
hoped for. Under the combination of new contracts and new
legislation, the holding-company system was largely overthrown. Rates to the government shot down on the new bids;
there was a forty-seven per cent saving in the first year, a
good share of which was due to elimination of previous excesses. On the other hand, the opportunity to achieve a
really competitive system was lost. The big four of the air
lines won back most of their original routes. Three lost
about twenty per cent of their mileage, and one gained
about the same proportion. The principal new concerns to
enter the field as the result of the new system were Braniff,
Delta, Northeastern, and Chicago & Southern. The last

company was dominated by the same Robertson whose troubles were recounted earlier. At last he secured a route without having to bribe anyone.

The air-mail investigation was a children's game compared to the public-utility holding-company investigation. There was a real fight, with a twelve-billion-dollar industry and almost the entire press massed solidly against the administration, and against Black.

The Wheeler-Rayburn bill of 1935, called the "death-sentence bill," was an administration measure, which Black enthusiastically supported, aimed at completely terminating utility holding companies. A public-utility holding-company system is, in classical design, a series of operating companies scattered about the country over which is layered a series of companies that hold stock in the operating companies and that in turn are dominated by others. At the top of the pyramid is the dominant holding company. For example, in the North American Company system there were at one time eighty corporations covering seventeen states. North American itself owned stock in ten corporations, several of which were themselves holding companies through which other companies were controlled.

This pyramidal device, manipulated by complicated systems of stock offerings in which insiders controlled the voting power, permitted promoters to exercise control far out of proportion to their investments. For example, one dollar's worth of stock in Corporation Securities Company gave its holder control of two thousand dollars' worth of money actually invested by others at the bottom of the pyramid. As the Supreme Court itself later put it, "Under such circumstances, a relatively small but strategic investment in common stock (with voting privileges) in the higher levels of a pyramided structure often resulted in absolute control of underlying operating companies with assets of hundreds of millions of dollars."

In the eyes of the New Dealers the system was a thoroughly bad one. The top concerns actually contributed substantially nothing. At the same time they drained off enormous sums which consumers of electricity eventually paid, and thereby kept the cost of electricity too high to make it completely available to all. There were many methods of making profits from a holding company. The holding company, for example, could charge their subsidiaries large sums for dubious "services." They could form other concerns to sell raw materials to the subsidiaries at high prices. They could themselves handle all security issues for the operating companies, keeping the profits for handling the securities. Sometimes, the New Dealers suspected, the holding companies caused operating companies to do unnecessary financing in order to have the profit of handling it. In short, in countless ways the holding-company system meant that the local power company was run for the benefit of men thousands of miles away rather than for the local community.

The "death-sentence" program passed the Senate by a majority of one vote. The propaganda campaign against the bill had been enormous. Thousands and thousands and thousands of letters and telegrams poured in on Senators and Representatives, seemingly from the people, assuring their Congressmen that they were opposed to the bill. There was a certain uniformity about the messages that indicated a surprising unanimity of adverse opinion. As the press screamed about the widows and orphans who would be deprived of their all by the destruction of their investments, the Congress was perceptibly yielding.

In the Senate Black remained an all-out supporter of the bill. He declared that he opposed the holding-company system not only in the utility field, but in every field, and that he had learned his opposition from the air-mail investigations in which it had taken his investigators months to find out how companies were organized. He said:

> I want it distinctly understood that I am not referring simply to holding companies in the power business; I am referring to an iniquitous system which has been built up in this country in other lines of business as well as in the power business, a blood-sucking business, a vampire, taking the lifeblood of commerce and trade and extracting money from those who have earned it by honest toil and putting it in the pockets of people whose only right to it is that by chicanery, by fraud, by manipulation within and without the law, they have been able to obtain that which they did not earn.

As the bill went to the House, the efforts of the holding companies were redoubled, and were successful. The entire holding-company system, within and without the power field, felt itself menaced. Automobiles and oil rallied to the support of power. Telegrams and messages apparently from the voters deluged the House, which on July 1, 1935 eliminated the death-sentence provision from the bill.

As a modified measure passed the House, it was sent to conference with the Senate. Then the administration hit upon its strategy. There would be a Black investigation of lobbying against the Wheeler-Rayburn bill; meanwhile the bill would be stalled in conference. On July 2, the day after the House defeat, Black introduced a resolution for investigation, and a committee was quickly authorized with Black as chairman, Minton of Indiana and Schwellenbach of Washington, two of Black's closest friends, as the other two Democratic members, and Frazier of North Dakota and Gibson of Vermont as Republican members. The whole committee was unanimous in every action it took.

Black began the investigation with a tip from Representative Driscoll, whose district included Warren, Pennsylvania. Driscoll had received over eight hundred telegrams against the bill signed by names of persons in Warren. He had become suspicious because so many of the telegrams were signed by persons whose names began with "B."

On July 16 J. A. Fisher, the manager of the Western Union office at Warren, testified before Black that R. B. Herron, a representative of Associated Gas & Electric Company (A.G.E.), one of the greatest of the holding companies, had dictated thirteen hundred telegrams, signing names picked by him from the city directory. He also testified that someone had got into Western Union files at Warren and had burned the files of original telegrams while the Senate was considering the lobby bill.

Once again there was a nation-wide burning of evidence in which the Senate might be interested. O. E. Wasser, comptroller of the A.G.E., had authorized a subordinate, Ursal E. Beach, to direct the destruction of all written evidence in A.G.E. files relating to lobbying. This, testified Beach, resulted in a complete destruction of records "From Maine to Florida, as far west as Illinois and as far southwest as Texas." E. W. O'Brien, the A.G.E. man at Erie, testified that, in March 1935, representatives from twenty-six states on the A.G.E. staff met at Ithaca and there planned their letter and telegram campaign, and other A.G.E. testimony admitted to $700,000 spent to oppose the Wheeler-Rayburn bill, much of it for false letters and telegrams. With so many records destroyed, Black found it hard, but not impossible, to check this figure.

As the Black committee pressed ahead, it discovered a nation-wide pattern of large sums, used for lobbying, charged to operating expenses, and thus passed on to consumers. The names of all the employees and their relatives were signed to letters or telegrams by one A.G.E. street railway company. At least one "signer" was dead. Scores of the same messages were sent over different signatures from another office. Of 14,782 messages against the bill sent from New York, Pennsylvania, Florida, and Texas, all but three were paid for by the utilities. For example, in early March 1936 the committee discovered that Stephen B. Severson, vice-president of the Republic Light, Heat & Power Company of Buffalo, had sent many telegrams opposing the Wheeler-Rayburn bill, all of which appeared to originate in Stoughton, Wisconsin. A sample instance involved a telegram purportedly signed by John Holton, a Stoughton tobacco-store owner. The following dialogue ensued:

> Senator Black: Did Holton authorize you to sign his name to this telegram to Representative Sauth-off?
> Severson: He did not.
> Q.: Did you ever discuss the Wheeler-Rayburn bill with him?
> A.: I do not remember.
> Senator Schwellenbach: And your purpose in sending these telegrams from Stoughton was to make this member of Congress, Mr. Sauthoff, think these constituents of his were opposed to the Wheeler-Rayburn bill?
> A.: I suppose so.

Black turned to Representative Patton of Texas and his package wrapped in newspaper. Patton had voted against the death sentence. He had called at the hotel of John W. Carpenter, president of a Texas subsidiary of Electric Bond & Share, another of the giant holding-company systems, and someone had seen him leave with the package. Unhappily for Carpenter and Patton, they were examined without an opportunity to refresh their recollections together. At the conclusion of their testimony it was not clear whether Patton had carried away a package of five-cent cigars or a package of Department of Agriculture pamphlets on livestock. Patton testified that Eugene B. Sellers was an intimate friend, and reliable. Sellers testified that a day or so after Patton carried away the cigars, or the pamphlets, or *something*, Patton's nephew said to Sellers: "Uncle has bought a bond and it's not payday." Patton testified that he had bought three thousand dollars' worth of bonds out of a few months' savings from his pay as Congressman. Two years later Patton vigorously denounced Black's appointment to the Supreme Court.

The committee also uncovered a man who had submitted to one of the holding companies a proposal to start a whispering campaign against Roosevelt's sanity in order to undermine confidence in the bill. There was no evidence, however, to show that the whispering campaign that did begin about that time actually originated with this particular suggestion.

As the Black committee disclosed the nature of the opposition, support came to the bill. The *Emporia Gazette*, for example, declared that though the Kansas Representatives had been fooled by the propaganda, "They should not stay fooled." At the same time the holding companies, seeing their victory slipping away, lashed out hard at Black and the committee. Black was charged with a "campaign of terrorism" by the chairman of the Committee of Public Utility Executives, and the press played up every attack made upon the investigation.

As Black found himself unable to get the story to the people through the press to his satisfaction, he took to the radio. He showed that a minimum of one and one-half million dollars had been paid for lobbying against the bill, and predicted that the total when all was known would be about $5,000,000. He showed that Patrick Hurley, Hoover's

Secretary of War, had been paid $25,000 for his efforts with Congress on the bill, and that Joseph Tumulty, Wilson's personal secretary, received $33,000. Total fees to three law firms for power lobby activities were $214,000.

It was probably the examination of Howard Hopson, president of A.G.E., that put the Wheeler-Rayburn bill across. Hopson ducked the committee's subpœna for weeks, hiding in various places along the east coast, but eventually he surrendered himself. On August 15, 1935 he faced Black.

Black kept Hopson on the witness stand for days. Oratorical defiance yielded to persistent pressure, and Black finally obtained Hopson's story: Hopson controlled A.G.E. His 350,000 investors in that top holding company had received no dividends for years, but he and his sisters were paid $3,187,000 between 1929 and 1933 because of his control of the network. He had managed the anti-Wheeler-Rayburn fight for his company and would admit that he had spent about $900,000 for that purpose. He had devised the emotional campaign, deciding that an appeal to reason would be insufficient, and he had invented the widows and orphans whose cries of anguish were supposed to stop the bill.

Hopson had himself not trifled with such propaganda devices as phony telegrams. His contribution had been contorical defiance yielded to persistent pressure, and Black advertising, which were increased or decreased in proportion to his satisfaction with the "news" and editorials published. He had not been able to control the *New York Times* to his satisfaction because, he believed, the *Times* was already under the control of the Morgan, Carlisle power interests, which were inimical to his; but he had been excellently satisfied with the service he received from the Gannett papers in upper New York and the Hearst chain. Payments to them had gone up accordingly. The testimony of August 16 showed that he dictated editorials in the form of direct communications to William Randolph Hearst which were printed almost verbatim. He also tried to influence the Scripps-Howard press, and he had no apologies for his advertising-bribery device, saying: "I felt it would be a good thing if other papers would take the same position as the Hearst and Gannett papers."

Hopson, on top of the faked messages, was more than the public would stand. With strong administration pressure and with Senator Barkley working hard to devise a compromise by which the House might save face, a bill only slightly modified passed the House and Senate.

When a bicameral legislature acts, it is not easy to say who is responsible. Many persons — Roosevelt, Barkley, Wheeler, Norris, Rayburn, among others — contributed to the passage of the Public Utility Holding Company Act. So did the five members of Black's committee. Ray Clapper, Washington columnist, wrote during the investigation: "If the death sentence finally goes into the utilities bill, it will be another notch in the gun of Senator Hugo Black."

The life of the Black committee on lobbying did not expire with the adoption of the Public Utilities Holding Company Act, and the committee continued to investigate political-pressure activities in 1936. This was the year of President Roosevelt's second election, but months in advance there was no assurance that his victory was to be the greatest landslide since 1820; and a whole group of organizations mushroomed for the double purpose of opposing New Deal legislation and of defeating Roosevelt. To the extent that such groups as the American Liberty League were influencing legislation, they were in the legitimate scope of the work of the Lobby Committee; and it may be assumed that Black was not distressed because any information acquired concerning lobbying would be equally useful in the 1936 campaign.

The principal object of the Black committee during the first months of 1936 was to let the general public know exactly who was behind the many beautifully named organizations that had spread through the country. The Liberty League was the principal such organization, and it was heavily sponsored by the du Ponts and by John J. Raskob, a former chairman of the Democratic National Committee. But there were many others.

For example, Black's investigations showed that there was the Farmers Independence Council of America, an organization that purported to speak for the farmers of the Middle West. At first glance it was an independent organization. Jouett Shouse, president of the Liberty League, issued a statement saying that there was no connection between his organization and the Farmers Council. The Black committee proceeded to lay before the country evidence that the principal organizer of the Council had been paid by the Liberty League, that its first office had been the Liberty League headquarters in the East, and that its Chicago office was the Liberty League office there. Black's evidence further showed that the funds for this organization had come from such well-known farmers as Lammot du Pont ($5,000); J. M. Pew, Jr., of the Sun Oil Company ($2,000); Arthur Beeter, attorney for Swift & Company ($3,500); Alfred P. Sloan, Jr., president of General Motors ($1,000); and many other "farmers" whose crops were cultivated within a few blocks of the corner of Broad and Wall Streets in New York City.

Another such organization was the Southern Committee to Defend the Constitution, which, under the leadership of John H. Kirby of Houston, had sponsored a "grass-roots" anti-Roosevelt convention in Georgia centering principally on Governor Talmadge of that state. This convention had purported to be representative of the South. The committee evidence showed that Raskob and Pierre du Pont had each contributed $5,000 for the "grass-roots convention" and that Sloan and other Northern industrialists and power-company officials had contributed the balance. Kirby and his associates had prepared pictures of Mrs. Roosevelt accompanied by two Negroes, which were given to each delegate to the Talmadge convention.

The next organization Black studied was the Sentinels of the Republic, which had raised $400,000 for an anti-administration movie. The picture had been endorsed by Al Smith and many others. The Black committee laid before the public an exchange of correspondence between Alexander Lincoln, Boston banker and president of the Sentinels, and W. Cleveland Runyon, a loyal supporter. Lincoln had declared that the real menace to America was "the Jewish threat" and had said: "I am doing what I can as an officer of the Sentinels" to stop that menace. His loyal admirer applauded, saying: "the old-line Americans of $1200 a year want a Hitler."

Throughout its investigations the Black committee was hampered by the fact that the concerns investigated burned their records as soon as they thought the committee was drawing near. The power to punish for contempt in these cases was inadequate in so far as it could not recover the records. To meet this situation, the Black committee subpœnaed the originals of telegrams in the offices of Western Union. For example, the information about the false telegrams of the Republic Light, Heat & Power Company of Buffalo quoted above was obtained from the originals, for seven thousand telegrams had disappeared from the files of the power company. The Black committee's choice was to get the originals or give up its job.

It had not been the practice of Western Union or Postal Telegraph to inform the senders before they delivered the copies to the Black committee. In March 1936 Western Union altered this policy, and a Chicago law firm secured a temporary injunction in the district court to enjoin the delivery of the telegrams. There followed a series of suits in which the Black committee retained Crampton Harris, Black's one-time partner, to represent it in the legal proceedings. The District of Columbia Court of Appeals, though it frowned on the practice, eventually held itself to be without jurisdiction.

As the fight over the subpœnas flared up in March 1937, Black took the worst beating from the press he ever received in his life except for the Court appointment. Just as Black had been investigating lobbying with an eye to aiding Roosevelt, so the entire press, which was almost unanimously supporting Landon, attempted to aid their candidate by attacking Black and his committee. This was no small fight. The Hearst and Gannett press, which had been unmasked by Black as direct recipients of holding-company bounties only a few months before, had every reason for frenzy; and the committee work was endangering the effectiveness of the Liberty League, which was the spearhead of the Landon campaign.

Black and the committee were denounced as dictators, Hitlers, tyrants, and violators of the sacred rights of man. A representative of the American Taxpayers League — an organization subsidized by Andrew Mellon, the Columbia Gas & Electric Company, and others — described the Black committee as a "Polecat Committee," and a Hearst cartoon showed Black as a skunk and a Peeping Tom.

Black's critics contended that the seizure of the telegram originals was unconstitutional. As vocal a critic as any was Senator Steiwer of Oregon, who denounced the committee as no better than the Russian secret police. Senator Steiwer's point was not that the committee could not properly seize telegrams, but rather that the committee could not use the so-called "dragnet subpœnas," which asked for "all telegrams sent" in a certain period by a certain concern. The issue was as narrow as this: must the committee ask for specific telegrams by name, or could it ask for a great number of telegrams and decide by looking at them whether it was interested?

Black made his principal address in support of the committee on March 20, 1936. He read into the record a statement by an attorney for Western Union saying: "From my personal knowledge, I can say that the company has been served with subpœnas in the general form — namely, all messages sent by A from or received by A at a point named during a period specified — for at least thirty-six years." Black laid before the Senate subpœnas used by Senate committees for years past which either were identical with those used by his committee or were even broader in their demands. He showed that committees of which Steiwer himself had been a member had called for "all correspondence by and between the aforesaid parties" and a great list of persons and corporations. He showed that Senator Walsh when investigating the Teapot Dome scandal had once subpœnaed all incoming or outgoing telegrams from an entire town in New Mexico for the better part of three years. He gave examples of telegrams in code that could not possibly have been identified in advance.

Ex-Senator James A. Reed of Missouri had described the Black committee subpœnas as "so Unamerican a thing as naturally to carry you back to the days of the Inquisition." Black read to the Senate a subpœna issued by a committee of which Reed had been chairman requiring a witness to bring "all letters by you received and copies of all

letters by you sent." At that earlier time Reed had said:
"It is utterly useless to hide behind the old dodge that
every lawyer has tried, saying 'put your finger on the paper you want and we will perhaps produce that paper.'
. . . Every man who has tried law suits knows that in cases
like this, that in all cases where fraud is charged, or where
there are any ramifications of corruption charged, you
have to start perhaps with a small fact, and trace that
fact through its various connections to develop other facts,
and finally you are able to expose the whole warp and woof
of an enormous fraud and a widespread conspiracy." Black
concluded his speech thus:

> Mr. President, the Senate may be assured that its
> committee intends to recognize every constitutional priv-
> ilege of every citizen. It is not going to be alarmed or
> frightened or intimidated by any manufactured senti-
> ment which some people think is free and voluntary, but
> behind which, in the main, we find someone pulling the
> strings because there is something he wants to conceal.
> I do not mean to make that statement about all who
> disagree as to the exact mechanics by which evidence
> should be secured. I would not leave that inference. But
> I say that in the main, now as in the Teapot Dome in-
> vestigation, now as in the Daugherty investigation, now
> as in the star-route investigation, now as in the crooked-
> elections investigation, now as in all the other investi-
> gations, the loudest noise comes from those who are
> afraid that something they have done will be exposed to
> the public view, and that they will be known for what
> they are instead of what they want the public to believe
> they are.

Black could not have been disappointed with the evidence he finally gave to the country. He showed that approximately a dozen organizations such as the Liberty
League, the Minute Men and Women of Today, the American Federation of Utility Investors, the Sentinels of the

Republic, and other euphoniously named groups purporting to represent mass sentiment had raised $1,084,000. Of that sum, $924,000 came from the following sources:

Du Pont family	$204,045.00
Du Pont associates	152,622.68
Pitcairn family	100,250.00
J. P. Morgan associates	68,226.00
Mellon associates	60,752.55
Rockefeller associates	49,852.56
Hutton (E. F.) associates	40,671.28
Sun Oil associates	37,260.00
Banks and brokers	184,224.83
Utility companies and associates	27,069.94
Total	$924,974.84

Black, with Tom Walsh, was one of the most effective Congressional investigators of this generation. Why? The answer is probably threefold. First was industrious preparation. Black worked all night, if need be, to be prepared to examine a witness. He himself prepared the advance questionnaires. He studied all the returns. He analyzed the correspondence. When a witness came to the stand, there were few questions that Black might ask him to which he would not already know or suspect the answer.

Second was his persistence. He kept after the point in which he was interested and did not allow himself to be diverted. If the witness began to wander or make speeches, he was sharply brought back to the point. If he hoped to divert the discussion by bringing in interesting but unrelated matters, he was unsuccessful. This was coupled with Black's skill as trial lawyer of asking the most penetrating possible question in the fewest possible words.

The third element was sufficient sternness to make a witness disinclined to ramble. When Hopson, for example, began to avoid answers by making speeches, he was reminded that refusal to answer meant imprisonment for contempt; and Black's record of convicting MacCracken and Britten showed that he meant business. Ray Clapper observed during the public-utilities investigation: "This slight, youngish-looking Alabama senator, who has the steel-trap flash of a county prosecutor, has utilities agents who are hauled up as witnesses before him so frightened that they instinctively address him as 'your Honor.' "

Black's critics charged that as an investigator he was unfair and over-harsh and that he obtained evidence illegally. The telegram episode is the only one suggested to support the latter point,[1] and the former is hard to analyze. This much is clear: Black was no respecter of persons. Men like MacCracken and Hopson and Severson were, socially, "the best people." Black treated them neither better nor worse than persons of less prominence he had examined in committee or in the courts.

The history of the regulation of the wages, hours, and conditions of labor in the United States is largely a history of a tight-rope walked between Supreme Court decisions. Today we know that the states and the federal government can regulate both wages and hours, but this is the new era. As of 1933, the decisions of the Supreme Court indicated that hours could in some circumstances be regulated by the states, but probably not by the federal government, and that wages could be regulated by neither. A federal statute prohibiting transportation of goods produced by child labor in interstate commerce had been held invalid by a five-to-four vote of the Court in 1918.

But depression and human misery make very little allowance for Supreme Court decisions. Black had been thinking about the problems of broader employment throughout his "reading period" during his first term as

---

[1] Occasional charges of wire-tapping against the committee are totally unsupported and seem not to have been seriously made. Black as chairman frequently declared that no wire-tapping would be used or tolerated.

Senator, and he finally determined to risk the judicial obstacles and offer a plan.

The plan he offered was based primarily on his own reading and thinking. When he introduced his thirty-hour bill, no union officials knew that it was forthcoming. But Black had read extensively about the control of hours and the minimum-wage laws of Europe. He had been particularly impressed with the English writer G. D. H. Cole, author among other works of *Economic Tracts for the Times* and *A Guide through World Chaos*. In addition there was an outpouring of American works on employment regulation during the depression, and Black read every available work on the subject, including, particularly, much writing by Stuart Chase.

Black finally reached his own decision that a limitation of hours would spread work, and that it was unlikely that wages would be reduced in correspondence with reduction of hours. He became convinced that except in war-time or in occasions of special crisis America can produce all it needs with a far shorter work week than has yet been achieved.

The result was the Black thirty-hour-week bill. It contained no minimum-wage provisions because the Supreme Court decisions seemed too hopeless an obstacle. Thirty hours were picked as what seemed to Black a sound figure, and at the same time one that would permit eventual compromise on forty hours, which was the best Black seriously expected to secure.

In February 1933 Black made his first formal speech to the Senate in behalf of his bill. He made no claim that the bill was a cure-all for the depression, stressing that many other plans, including that for federal unemployment insurance, were also necessary; but he reiterated repeatedly in the years that followed that shorter hours meant more jobs. They would not, he was to declare, mean lower wages, because the unions would hold wages where they were.

Black made this argument for his bill at the beginning: unemployment resulted from improved technology and long hours of work for those employed. The efficiency of machine production made it unnecessary to work as long as in earlier generations, and yet in many industries the average work week was from forty-nine to sixty hours. Were the work load cut to thirty hours, at least half the unemployed would be employed. As wages went down from 1926 to 1932, many profits went up; and industry could pay the difference required by the thirty-hour bill without cutting the weekly wage for labor.

At the last session of the Hoover Congress, there was no opportunity for such a bill; but in the first session of the Roosevelt Congress in 1933 Black's bill was reintroduced. It came up on the floor on April 3, 1933.

Black had prepared thoroughly for the discussion that followed. He had been on the Judiciary Committee for five years, and he had been studying constitutional law with the utmost intensity in order to meet the constitutional attack on his own bill. He was confident, he declared, that under the commerce clause Congress had power to enact such a statute. He for one would not admit that the child-labor decision was final. Instead, he said: "The Constitution is final," for six new members had come into the Court since 1918, and "no doctrine of *stare decisis* applies to opinions on constitutional interpretation." He expressed his basic conviction that constitutional interpretation was a product of the times in which men lived, and that "the tendency of today is to give a new and exalted emphasis to the more sacred right of human beings to enjoy health, happiness, and security justly theirs in proportion to their industry, frugality, energy, and honesty."

Meanwhile the administration had not yet made up its mind as to the kind of labor legislation it wanted. Senator Robinson, majority leader, offered an amendment to raise the hours from a six-hour maximum day and a thirty-hour week to an eight-hour maximum day and a thirty-six-hour week. The amendment lost by a vote of 41 to 48, and the Black thirty-hour bill passed the Senate on April 6, 1933 by a vote of 53 to 30.

But the path did not remain smooth. After consultation with the President, Senator Robinson announced that the administration would sidetrack the thirty-hour bill in the House in favor of the NRA, whose Blue Eagle was to crow over an improved, if voluntary, regulation of labor relations. For this, section 7(a) of the NRA was the base of labor's rights. While on vacation at the end of the session, the President wrote to Black:

My dear Hugo:
Before leaving I did not have an opportunity to thank you for your commendable and praiseworthy work during the Special Session in behalf of the limitation of hours for labor. You and Congressman David Lewis led the way in causing constructive public discussion. Largely as a result of this, public opinion was so moulded as to make it possible to include the projects in the Industrial Recovery Act. I want you to know my appreciation.

FRANKLIN D. ROOSEVELT

But appreciation was not the bill, and in 1935, when the NRA faltered and died, Black returned to the fight. The *Schecter* decision of the Supreme Court invalidating the NRA raised doubts in Senators' minds as to the validity of the thirty-hour proposal, and Black in May 1935 sought to convince the Senate that the vices of the NRA were not in his bill. This time Robinson as majority leader in control of the calendar was able to keep Black from getting the bill on the floor, and it stayed off for another two years.

The temporary end of discussion in the Senate did not mean the end of effort. In 1936 Black went to the Democratic convention as a member of the platform committee. At the sessions of that committee he first met the delegate from Michigan, Frank Murphy, who fought with Black for the principle of a wage-hour law in the committee and who was later to do much to protect it as a Justice of the Supreme Court. The alliance at Chicago was the beginning of a firm friendship. Black and Murphy may not have obtained as much as they might have desired, but they got a party commitment to do at least a vague something about "minimum wages, maximum hours, child labor, and working conditions."

Thus for the first time Black and his party abandoned the caution about the Supreme Court that had led to the earlier omission of child-labor and minimum-wage provisions from the bill. The New Deal had adopted so many laws that would be invalid if the child-labor case and certain other decisions were to stand that there was no longer point in caution.

In May 1937 Black in the Senate and Representative Connery in the House introduced the new wage-hour bill and called upon the party to perform. Five years of support for his bill had taught Black the necessity of compromise, and the new bill as he offered it had neither fixed hours nor fixed wages. There was to be a sliding scale of minimum wages, later fixed at from forty to eighty cents an hour, with a board to establish the precise level for particular industries. The number of hours was finally set at 40. Enforcement was to be by the Board.

For the next two months Black supported his bill on the

radio and in the Senate. He scented sure victory, and he spoke with exultation:

We have waited too long for it already — at what cost in dollars and cents as well as in flesh and blood no one will ever know.

Now we are through waiting. The Democratic Party has promised the country this kind of legislation. The President has pledged it. The mandate of the election has ordered it.

And at long last the American people are going to have it!

But there was still the Senate to face. On July 27, 1937 Black spoke to his colleagues of labor conditions in the South. He waved before the Senate Southern pay vouchers: "Here is one dated July 3, 1937, 4½ days, wages $3.57. Another, July 3, 1937, 4½ days, wages $4.48. Here is another voucher, 4 days, wages $2.68. That figures up, as I recall, to about 8 cents an hour."

But, said someone, some firms cannot stay in business without working employees at ten-cent-an-hour wages for ten hours a day. Said Black, such concerns must go out of business: "I think it is a practice which is indefensible. I do not believe our civilization requires any such sacrifice on the part of any large percentage of our people."

The bill had support in the North, both from unions and from part of industry. Most of the opposition came from the South, where wages were lowest and hours longest. Smith of South Carolina said: "Anti-lynching, two-thirds rule, and last of all, this unconscionable — I shall not attempt to use the proper adjective to designate, in my opinion, this bill! Any man on this floor who has sense enough to read the English language knows that the main object of this bill is, by human legislation, to overcome the splendid gifts of God to the South." Byrnes of South Carolina and Connally of Texas were among those who fought the bill, and Black finally declared that he was as good a Southerner as any Senator, and with as many ancestors in the Civil War; but that in this fight he spoke for "the little men and women of Alabama and the Nation."

The critical vote was 48 to 36 for the bill. It passed the Senate on July 31, 1937. It was a far different bill from the thirty-hour bill of five years before and was to be virtually completely rewritten in the House before it was enacted into law the next year, after Black was on the Court. Yet many of the essentials remained the same. The bill continued to forbid child labor, and it kept a forty-hour week and a forty-cent minimum wage. The proposed board disappeared, and the method of enforcement was radically changed.

The Fair Labor Standards Act of 1938 is one of the most important steps in the history of social legislation in America. War-time inflation soon drained the forty-cent minimum of much of its meaning, so that today comparatively few cases arise because of payments under the minimum, and there is now a strong movement to raise the minimum to sixty-five or eighty cents an hour. The most important effect was in the regulation of hours. The payment required for work over forty hours is so high that in peace-time there will be very little overtime work; while emergency overtime must now be paid for handsomely. Only twenty-five years ago the sixty-hour week had not yet become a general reality for industrial workers. Today the forty-hour week is virtually universal.

There is credit enough to go around. Madam Perkins is entitled to some of it for her support of wage-hour legislation in the administration; so is Representative Connery, whose name the bill also bore; so is Sidney Hillman, who marshaled labor support for the bill. So is Black.

Chapter V

THE APPOINTMENT

In the two years prior to the election of 1936 the Supreme Court had invalidated much of the New Deal program, and the decisions indicated the Wagner Act and the Social Security Act would be the next to go. Early in 1937 President Roosevelt struck back with a proposal, vigorously supported by Black, to add up to six new members to the Court. The President's Court plan split the country and the Democratic Party as have few issues in history. Many Americans thought that the plan was an assault on the very citadel of liberty, while a great many others felt that a majority of the holders of that citadel needed a sound public spanking. No few words here can even slightly recall the passions unloosed by the President's proposal.

The President's plan was defeated in Congress, in large part because the Court itself abandoned its previous path and upheld the Wagner Act and the Social Security Act, and because Justice Van Devanter, a member of the conservative majority, retired. In so doing he utilized the Retirement Act of 1937, which permitted him to retire on full salary.

President Roosevelt determined to fill the Van Devanter vacancy with the greatest of care, and he and Attorney

General Cummings assembled a long list of possible appointees. Slowly the list was whittled down. Finally on Sunday, August 8, 1937, Cummings telephoned Senator Sherman Minton of Indiana. Minton was working at his office, and after the usual commiserations about Sunday work Cummings invited Minton to have dinner with him that evening without giving any indication of the subject to be discussed.

In the course of dinner and the evening Cummings broached the subject of the Supreme Court appointment and asked Minton for his views. Cummings finally asked Minton for his opinion of Black as a possible appointee. Minton was emphatically enthusiastic, for Black was virtually his closest Senate friend.

Cummings's next question was whether Minton thought Black would accept. On this point Minton was uncertain, for he knew that Black loved the work of a senator; "but," said Minton shrewdly, "I think Mrs. Black would like her husband to accept, and she has great influence with him." The result of the discussion was the commission of Minton by Cummings to inquire whether Black would accept the appointment.

The next day Minton found Black in his office and broached the subject. As Minton had anticipated, Black was perplexed. He faced re-election the next year, and he told Minton: "I am facing the toughest primary fight of my life, for the conservatives in Alabama will do everything they can to get rid of me. But I have no serious doubt that I will win the primary handily next year."

The conversation drifted to the problem of confirmation. Both Senators realized that at least some of the Senators who had defeated the President's Court plan would oppose Black, but Minton was confident that a senatorial appointment would easily win confirmation. Black took the matter under consideration overnight so that he might talk to his wife.

The next day, August 10, Black told Minton that he would not ask for the appointment, but would accept it if offered. Minton immediately informed Cummings.

On the same day the President called Black and asked if he would visit the White House that evening. Black explained that this was the evening of a Democratic dinner for Senator Barkley and that he was anxious to be present as a token of his appreciation of Barkley's brilliant work in the Senate. It was agreed that he should call the next evening, August 11. On the evening of the 11th Mrs. Black went to the movie *The Good Earth* and wondered what the President would say, while Black went to the White House.

The President chatted about a number of things and finally reached into a drawer, pulled out what appeared to be a piece of paper, and said: "Hugo, this is a form for the nomination of a Supreme Court justice. May I fill in your name?" Black replied: "Mr. President, are you sure that I'll be more useful on the Court than in the Senate?" The President replied: "Hugo, I wish you were twins because Barkley says he needs you in the Senate; but I think you'll be more useful on the Court." The President then signed the appointment and asked Black not to mention it before the next noon.

The appointment was kept so close a secret for the next eighteen hours that few but the President, Cummings, the Blacks, and Senators Barkley, Minton, and Ashurst, chairman of the Judiciary Committee, knew of it. Steve Early, Roosevelt's press secretary, had just indicated to the reporters that there might be no Supreme Court appointment at the current session when the bell from the President's office rang for him late on the morning of August 12. He excused himself for a moment and then returned to the reporters almost bounding with excitement as he declared that a Supreme Court appointment had been sent to the Senate. "You'll have to get the rest of it from the Senate," he added.

Mrs. Black went to the Senate gallery alone since she had been admonished to tell no one. Shortly after 12 o'clock the messenger from the President came in, gave the appointments to the Clerk, and, instead of walking out as usual, stepped back to see what would happen. "A message from the President of the United States," was appropriately intoned, and the appointment was read: "Hugo L. Black to be Associate Justice of the Supreme Court of the United States."

The resultant silence was stupendous. The conservative Democrats and Republicans could not have been more horrified to learn that Satan himself had been appointed to the High Court. As Minton, LaFollette, and Schwellenbach rushed to congratulate Black, the stunned victors of the Court fight slowly realized that F. D. R. was having his revenge.

No record shows exactly why the President appointed Black. That he considered Black an able and ardent New Dealer is clear. How much he was influenced by two related considerations is not known: that the Senate could not possibly fail to confirm one of its own members, and that the appointment of one of the stoutest Roosevelt followers in the Senate was bound to leave the majority, which had just defeated Roosevelt, in a state of frustrated fury.

To the opponents of the Court plan, this was the ultimate defeat. There were those who had opposed the Court plan to protect what they regarded as the sanctity of the Court, and in that view the President could appoint whomever he desired so long as he did not create a Court of more than nine justices. But to many others the fight had not been against the plan as an abstraction, but against the New Deal as a reality. To Herbert Hoover, for example, the Black appointment meant, he said, that the Court was "one ninth packed" — that is, had a Roosevelt appointment. To what purpose the battle if the war should be lost?

Within a moment of the appointment Senator Ashurst invoked senatorial courtesy and asked immediate consideration of the nomination. But Senators Johnson of California and Burke of Nebraska had been fighting the New Deal too long to be open to appeal on the amenities, and they forced reference of the appointment to the Judiciary Committee. No witnesses were heard and the question of Black's Klan membership was not considered. In the committee the anti-Black argument, outlined by Republicans Austin and Borah, was that when Van Devanter left the Court at full pay under the 1937 act, he retired and did not resign. Therefore there was no vacancy on the Court. A second argument was that the boost in retirement pay was an increase of the emoluments of office during Black's term as a Senator, which would disqualify him. The related contention was that, on the theory that the Retirement Act kept Van Devanter on the Court though not in active service, Black was a tenth Justice and was therefore taking an office that had been created during his term in the Senate. Borah made very clear that had he not felt bound by these technical considerations, he would have been most pleased with the appointment.

The press, with the same near-unanimity with which it had opposed the re-election of Roosevelt and the Court plan, condemned the Black appointment. The *Chicago Tribune* said the President had "picked the one who would be generally regarded as the worst he could find." The *New York Herald Tribune* said the nomination was "as menacing as it is unfit." Columnist Hugh Johnson said:

"a petulant or a prejudiced appointment," and Columnist Dorothy Thompson said "cheap."

On the other hand, the *Louisville Courier-Journal* said: "Black will carry to the Supreme Court the liberalism for which the President has fought — all the liberalism which one man can carry." John L. Lewis said "admirable," and William Green said "pleasing and satisfactory to labor." Local unions the country over agreed. Sterling Black, twelve-year-old second son of the Blacks, when interviewed by the press, said: "I guess it's all right."

On August 17, 1937, Senator George W. Norris, of Nebraska, wrote the following letter to Senator Henry F. Ashurst, of Arizona:

> "I regret my illness prevents me from actively participating in the work of the Senate at this time, but I hope through your courtesy to communicate my views upon the confirmation of Senator Black's nomination to become an Associate Justice of the Supreme Court. My long and personal acquaintance with him and my intimate association with him in our official work have given me a true insight into his character. I feel greatly grieved at the bitter, unreasonable, and sometimes malicious attacks which are being made upon him. His work in the Senate must convince everyone that he possesses a superior ability and undaunted courage which are seldom equaled or surpassed. His nomination to that great tribunal expresses the wish and hope of the struggling citizen asking only for justice for all alike. The scales of justice in his hands will bring renewed hope to millions of our common people throughout the country, and his nomination meets with the hearty approval of a vast majority of our people. He is a worthy representative of the common people. He understands their hopes and ambitions, and their liberties in his hands will be safe."

Doubts based on Black's reputed former Klan connections were raised, but were not searched. The question was raised principally by Senator Copeland, who was a candidate for mayor of New York and who was badly in need of Harlem's votes. He had no facts, and his remarks were easily discounted as serving New York election purposes only.

Senator Borah, who would have opposed any nominee on the theory of lack of a vacancy and hence voted against Black, but who was otherwise sympathetic to the nomination, made the only statement in Black's behalf on the question of Klan membership:

> There has never been at any time one iota of evidence that Senator Black was a member of the Klan. No one has suggested any source from which such evidence could be gathered. . . . We know that Senator Black has said in private conversation, not since this matter came up but at other times, that he was not a member of the Klan, and there is no evidence to the effect that he is. . . . If I knew that a man was a member of a secret association organized to spread radical antipathies and religious intolerance, I should certainly vote against him for any position.

This is the passage which later gave rise to the charge that either Black had misled Borah or Borah had misled the Senate. On the day, six weeks after his confirmation, when Black made his speech admitting former membership in the Klan but disavowing its doctrines, Senator Borah stated publicly: "I understood he had been a member of the Klan but had not been a member since about eleven years."

Finally, after two days' debate and with a last plea from Senator Johnson of California that the vote be on the "merits," not on senatorial courtesy, the nomination was confirmed. The vote was 63 to 16, ten Republicans and six conservative Democrats voting against the nominee.

Raymond Clapper, columnist, disapproved of every aspect of the Black appointment, including the appointment itself. While he regretted the selection, he disapproved of Copeland's use of the incident for purposes of the New York mayoralty race, and he disliked Black's opposition. In describing the debate he wrote:

> And in the senators' private gallery sat an unusual number of men. Well-dressed men, leaning far over their seats, listening with hardset faces to the debate. They were the lobbyists, representing the numerous interests on whose toes Black had stepped in his investigations and who wanted to beat him because of his economic views. It was their fight that a number of Senators in the pit below were making. But of course during all the hypocritical debate, not a word was breathed about that.

The *Montgomery Advertiser* made a rare observation:

> What a joke it would be on Hugo's impassioned detractors if he should now turn out to be a very great Justice of the Supreme Court. Brandeis did it when every Substantial Citizen in the Republic felt that Wilson should have been impeached for appointing him. . . . We do not care to invite the scorn of posterity by denouncing a man whose worst sin was in being a 100 per cent Rooseveltian when this newspaper itself has been 80 per cent Rooseveltian.

A few days after the confirmation Black took his oath and sailed for Europe for a short vacation with his wife.

On September 13 the roof fell in. Ray Sprigle's articles began to appear in the *Pittsburgh Post Gazette*, and through it in the entire press of the country. Sprigle had gone to Birmingham and had apparently prevailed on one-time Grand Dragon James Esdale to turn over the records of the Klan. He presumably obtained everything there was to show Black's Klan connection. He discovered, essentially, three documents: Black's 1925 resignation from the Klan, a copy of his 1926 Grand Passport, and a copy of

stenographic notes of his speech given upon the award of
the Grand Passport. It was the Grand Passport that was
the most essential element of the Sprigle story, because
since it bore no termination date, it was possible to make a
theoretical argument that Black was still a member of the
Klan.

The Sprigle account was given in six stories which appeared on successive days, and the press fanned public
attention to the wildfire stage. The New York mayoralty
primary was nearing its close, and Copeland trumpeted
that Black was the issue. Virtually every figure in public
life was asked whether he thought Black should resign, and
those who were not asked issued statements. The President
declined comment until Black should return from Europe.
Ex-Wizard Hiram Evans said that Black was not a life
member, that he thought he would probably be a good
judge, but that he disapproved of his investigations and
his labor record. Evans also said that Copeland had been
a Klan candidate in the twenties. Norman Thomas said
Black should resign. Al Smith, who was campaigning for
Copeland, very carefully said nothing about Black. Senators Van Nuys of Indiana and Clark of Missouri said they
were sorry they had voted for confirmation. Senator Berry
of Tennessee said he was glad that he had voted for confirmation. So in effect did Senators Pepper and Andrews
of Florida and Schwartz of Wyoming. Senator Norris
stood solidly behind Black, saying: "Actually, Justice
Black is being subjected to all this criticism because he is a
liberal, because he wants to bring the Supreme Court closer
to the people — not because he is a Klansman."

In the press and among organizations the lines stayed
fairly generally as they were. Almost the entire press had
condemned the appointment, and they condemned all the
more. The *Philadelphia Record* was one of the few to shift

from strong pro-Black to strong anti-Black. Editor Bill Evjue of the Madison, Wisconsin, *Capitol Times* stuck with Black, as did columnist Heywood Broun.

The days that followed were the crisis of Black's life. Public opinion was being built up to the point of a demand for impeachment. In that crisis it was primarily labor solidarity that kept a substantial nucleus of public opinion on Black's side. The *Paper Makers' Journal* carried an editorial saying: "Workers and common people, for our own good and welfare, don't be played for suckers through these pleas to prejudice and bigotry." *Labor*, the organ of the Railroad Brotherhoods, which Black still reads regularly, said that the press handling of the Black case was a "national disgrace," and continued: "Whatever errors Mr. Justice Black may have made, the American people will forgive and forget — because of his splendid record in the Senate, but even more because of the character of his enemies."

In the midst of the uproar Edward Keating, editor of *Labor*, spoke to the international convention of the boiler-makers' union at Kansas City, Missouri. He described himself as Irish and a Catholic, obviously out of sympathy with the Klan. He then declared that Black was being attacked because he was a progressive, saying: "It was Senator Black who took his political life in his hands to introduce the first 30 hour week bill. It was Senator Black who again took his political life in his hands to expose the knavery of the great utility companies' lobby in his famous holding company investigation. It was Senator Black who took his political life in his hands in order to champion the hours and wages bill." "When the cheering delegates resumed their seats," said the press account, a resolution of confidence in Black was proposed. Before the vote the Canadian delegate rose: "We know something about the splendid record of Senator, now Justice, Black. . . . On behalf of a solid Canadian delegation, we want to join with the workers of the United States in expressing our faith and confidence in Justice Black."

Meanwhile Black in London was almost overwhelmed by the pressure of reporters asking for a statement. His spirits reached their lowest point when an over-enterprising reporter stepped out from a darkened hotel corridor to face him and his wife as they returned to their rooms one night and by his very unexpectedness badly frightened Mrs. Black. On September 30 the Blacks returned to Norfolk on a small ship that had taken ten days for the trip. Black declined to make any statement to the press, hinting that if he had anything to say, he would say it by radio. He made a radio address on the night of October 1.

Black's short speech was heard by what was estimated to have been the largest audience ever to hear a radio speech except for the abdication of Edward VIII. He said that in no ordinary situation should a justice of the Supreme Court discuss a political maneuver, but that this situation was extraordinary. He continued: "My words and acts are a matter of public record. I believe that my record as a Senator refutes every implication of racial or religious intolerance. It shows that I was of that group of liberal Senators who have consistently fought for the civil, economic and religious rights of all Americans, without regard to race or creed. . . . I did join the Klan. I later resigned. I never rejoined. I never have considered and I do not now consider the unsolicited card given to me shortly after my nomination to the Senate as a membership of any kind in the Ku Klux Klan. I never used it. I did not even keep it. Before becoming a Senator I dropped the Klan. I have had nothing whatever to do with it since that time."

He had never, at any meeting of any organization, said

anything denying complete religious liberty to all, the speaker continued; he was totally out of sympathy with any who would interfere in the slightest degree with religious freedom. He had supported candidates for public office without reference to their faith. Negroes, Catholics, and Jews had been his close friends, and Herman Beck, the Birmingham Jewish merchant, "stood so nearly in the place of a father to me that while in the Army in 1918 I designated this trusted Jewish friend as the sole executor of my will." A few words more, and Black said: "When this statement is ended my discussion of the question is closed."

In the preceding years Black had made countless radio speeches. Perhaps only Franklin D. Roosevelt was an abler radio speaker than he. The speech turned the tide. Before, a Gallup poll showed that 59 per cent of the people thought Black should resign. After, 56 per cent thought he should stay on the bench. As opinion changed, it became heavily partisan; two thirds of the Republicans thought he should resign, while two thirds of the Democrats thought he should not. Meanwhile Copeland had been roundly defeated in New York, and public attention turned back to the world series and to foreign policy as it was announced on Roosevelt's Western trip.

Sprigle, who received the Pulitzer prize for his story, discovered what thousands of Alabamans already knew. The front page of Alabama papers had carried the Grand Passport in 1932. Most of what he learned was unknown outside Alabama only because few outside of Alabama had cared to inquire. The one important exception was the September 2, 1926 speech. Sprigle's largest contribution was turning a local commonplace into a sensation by his dramatically effective writing, aided by the full force of the press.

The *Montgomery Advertiser* made a clear statement on the honest national distress and the manipulation which had caused it:

> American public opinion was profoundly disturbed by the revelations which to Alabamans is old stuff. But the hostility to the new Justice was honest hostility in the main. What is of special moment and significance is the fact that the engineers of the attack were not disturbed by the knowledge of his former Klan affiliations. They would have been as raw in their treatment of him — given the pretext — if he had been a Jew or a Roman Catholic or Negro. They hated him because of his record as a United States Senator.

On October 4, 1937, three days after the radio speech, Black for the first time sat as a member of the United States Supreme Court. The Court itself, without Black's participation, speedily disposed of two motions aimed at unseating him and he then settled down to the business of being a Justice.

Black meanwhile had only a few days in which to assemble a small office staff. Each Justice had a Negro messenger, and Black's was Spencer Campbell, whose mother was then, and whose sister became later, the Blacks' cook. Miss Anne Butt, a Catholic who had been on his staff in the Senate, he took with him to the Court as a secretary. For a law clerk he hastily phoned his former partner, federal district Judge Davis of Birmingham, and Davis sent him his own clerk, Jerome "Buddy" Cooper, a recent Harvard graduate whose father Black had known. Cooper was Jewish. The press thereupon asserted that Black was attempting to assuage minority feelings by appointing a Negro, a Catholic, and a Jew, and disparaged him accordingly.

Like any new appointee, Black had an enormous amount to learn, particularly about the technical aspects of the

Court's work; and because of his sensational entrance to the Court he was on trial as few Justices had been before him. He settled down to work with a vengeance. The *New York Times* soon reported that the new Justice was working hard and was frequently at his office from a little before ten in the morning until early evening. The reporter could not know that Black's day usually found him in his study at home for hours before coming to the office, and that he and his clerk frequently worked a fourteen- to sixteen-hour day.

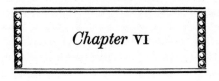

Chapter VI

THE OPINIONS

The latter portion of this book contains Black's own expressions on the issues of his first decade on the Court. Introductory comments to those opinions will assist in placing the particular opinions in their settings. But at the risk of some duplication in discussion of both the general and the particular, an outline summary of Black's general views is offered here.

1. *Control of the Economy*

Hugo Black has the usual doubts of a thoughtful man as to whether prosperity can be obtained by aid of legislation, but he has no doubt that it is a proper object of government to try. He conceives of the Constitution as a charter of power that permits the people of the United States to attempt most of what they think they must attempt to achieve a standard of living that meets the highest levels of which twentieth-century production is capable. Black's conceptions of the Constitution took their firm shape during the depression, and he reads the Constitution against a background of national needs that must be met.

In short, Black believes in dynamic government, and he thinks the Constitution gives abundant power for that kind of government to both the states and the federal system. In taking his position Black is completely outside the orbit of the old controversy between "states' rights" and "centralized power." With him the question is not which government shall prevail as between states and nation. For to him that classical question is meaningless. Instead the question is which government is actually prepared at this moment to do the actual job that some group in the community thinks ought to be done. For in the Black view the power to govern goes to the sovereign which would use it. The practical effect of this view is not only to broaden federal power, but also to give the states wider authority than they have ever had.

The constitutional power of state and federal government to control the economic affairs of the nation depends primarily on the interpretation of two clauses of the Constitution, the commerce clause and the due-process clause. Black's position is clear on both. He believes that the Constitution, by giving to Congress the power to regulate commerce, gives to Congress an absolutely comprehensive power to regulate the entire economic life of the country — every last bit of it if need be. His position is substantially what it was when he was advocating the Fair Labor Standards Act in the Senate, but the details have been filled in by the opinions that he has written or in which he has joined. The Court as a whole has since 1936 found no federal statute invalid because it was outside the power to regulate commerce.

The modern view is based on the conviction that commerce is a continuous activity that may be interrupted by blocking either the production of goods or their distribution. Hence both production and distribution fall within the commerce power. For example, a conspiracy to restrain trade in insurance is a restrain on "commerce," says Black in the *South-Eastern Underwriters* decision, and though some of his brethren quarrel with him about the form of words used by Congress in the particular case, none doubt that the power to regulate the whole insurance business exists if Congress cares clearly to use it. Even the production of grain on a farm to be fed to livestock on the farm is subject to the control of Congress under the commerce clause, a unanimous Court has held in an opinion in which Black joined. The commerce power has become the power by which Congress may undertake to solve any of the nation's economic problems. In this view the Wage Hour Act has been held clearly constitutional.

The power to regulate wages or prices or utility rates frequently involves a question of interpretation of the due-process clause. Black would reject utterly and completely the doctrine of the last forty-five years that the due-process clause gives to courts the power to determine the reasonableness of regulations. He says, in effect, that the decisions on this point immediately after the Civil War were correct and that the Court should never have departed from them. As far as he is concerned, the wisdom or the rightness and wrongness of regulatory legislation is entirely a question for the people to decide through their elected representatives.

This was substantially the view held by the majority of the Court as expressed by Chief Justice Waite in the 1870's. It is the diametrical opposite of the dominant 1900–36 view, which, behind much fancy legal language, meant substantially that a statute or administrative order was unconstitutional if the Court thought it was bad social policy. The intermediate position, held by Holmes, was that a statute is unconstitutional not if the Court merely disagrees with it, but only if it is so utterly unreasonable as to be capricious or arbitrary. Today a majority of the Court follows the Holmes view, as nearly as any view so unprecise may be said to have a following; while Black insists that the Waite position was correct and that the federal courts have no power at all under the due-process clause to review rate orders or any other form of regulatory legislation for reasonableness.

The principal practical difference is in the lower courts and in the future. The Holmes position leaves constitutionality of regulatory legislation largely subjective. Less tolerant justices in the future may subjectively move back toward the dominant 1900–36 position and yet scarcely seem to move at all. Further, the Supreme Court can review only a tiny number of the enormous mass of cases moving through the lower courts, and to a limited extent every local judge thus becomes something of a local oligarch. The Black position, which does not now seem likely to prevail, would cut out this judicial power of review wherever it exists, now and in the future. He is particularly concerned over the fact that in rate-regulation cases utilities have frequently frustrated the law by dilatory court tactics, which may not prevail in the long run but which afford swollen profits for many years. Black hit hard at such practices in a lone dissent case in his first term, and his position has strong adherents now.

One of the principal limitations on the power of the states either to regulate or to tax is, oddly enough, the commerce clause. This clause gives to Congress the power to regulate commerce, and hence it is argued that *only* Congress can regulate commerce. Therefore, runs the argument, the states may not regulate it by taxation or otherwise.

For the first sixty years of our national history the

Court struggled with this problem without reaching any definite conclusion. Chief Justice Taney, for one, thought that the commerce clause did not restrict the states at all until Congress had actually exercised its power; but this view did not prevail. The final but rather vague resolution of the problem in 1851 was that the states could regulate or tax businesses affecting commerce sometimes, but not other times; and the difference between the two situations had remained so vague and wavering that it is unnecessary for the purpose of this study to attempt to work it out.

Operating on this theory that at least sometimes the commerce clause invalidates state laws, the Court in recent years has held in the *Southern Pacific* case that Arizona did not have constitutional power to limit the length of trains running through it even though Arizona claimed that the restriction was necessary for safety. It has also invalidated many state taxes. For example, the Court recently held unconstitutional the Indiana gross income tax as applied to an Indiana resident who sold some stock on the New York stock exchange, on the ground that the tax improperly burdened the interstate transaction. This clause of the Constitution has become the foremost hobble today upon the regulatory and taxing power of the states.

In such cases Black has declared, in effect, that the original position of Chief Justice Taney seemed to him correct and that the commerce clause by itself should never be considered as ousting the states from the power to tax or regulate. If Congress wants some particular aspect of commerce free of state regulation, it has but to say so, asserts Black; and meanwhile the Court should keep out of the field altogether. The only case in which Black did not follow this position was one holding invalid a Virginia statute requiring segregation on interstate busses on the ground that the regulation improperly burdened commerce. Regarding it Black said that while he did not believe state statutes should ever be invalidated under the commerce clause, a majority of the Court disagreed with him; and he felt bound to acknowledge that if the majority general theory was right, this was a proper place for its application. Hence he would acquiesce.

Yet another restraint on state power is the contract clause, which forbids the states to impair the obligation of contracts. Interpretation before Black came to the Court read the limitation of reasonableness into this restraint, so that the clause is read as though it prohibited the states from interfering unreasonably or arbitrarily with contractual rights; and Black has been quick to find that state regulations concerning contracts were reasonable.

The composite effect of these views is a comprehensive charter to state and federal governments to do their jobs to the full. The federal government has wide power to act, and when it undertakes a particular regulatory program, the states may have to get out, with no tears on Black's part for state sovereignty. In the meantime, until the federal government acts, Black would leave the states fettered only by the requirement of respect for civil rights.

2. Regulatory Statutes

The contemporary approach to the Constitution is one that so largely removes the restraints on what Congress and legislatures may do that comparatively few big cases now deal with the naked question of power. Today's issues instead arise under the interpretation of particular statutes exercising legislative power.

TRADE REGULATION

Black's philosophy for the capitalist system can be summed up in the one word "competition." It is doubtful if any judge in history ever believed more wholeheartedly in the philosophy of the antitrust laws. The Sherman Act was passed to meet Populist pressures and was an important feature of Clay County political faiths. Black as a Senator had preached that only rigorously enforced competition could save the American enterprise system. As a Justice he displays the same convictions.

As a result Black has consistently supported enforcement of the antimonopoly laws and has been ingenious in finding full scope for them. He wrote the opinions condemning monopolistic practices by the insurance industry and by the Associated Press. He declared that the fashion industry could not cloak its designs from the use of competitors by private agreements.

But today we have passed beyond the stage in which competition can greatly be aided by terming large combinations "monopolies." It has become necessary to devise methods for putting a stop to those monopolies, and here the Court has shown a tendency to fall back without effective action. Black has been willing to support the devices that might actually break up the great monopolies.

This policy reaches into many aspects of the Court's work. Black supported the state of Georgia in the initial stage of its claim that the railroads of the country were making it difficult for the South and West to compete with the industrial North. He supported the Interstate Commerce Commission when it took some action toward solving the same problem. He supported a company which claimed that it should not have to pay certain charges for goods sold to it at allegedly illegal and discriminatory prices.

A special area that involves this same problem is the field of patents. Each patent is a monopoly, normally assigned to the corporation that hired the inventor, which gives to the corporaton many special privileges. As such each patent is an exception to our general antimonopoly policy. Pools or combinations of patents give large enterprises great power, which may be readily used in the violation of antimonopoly spirit. These patent privileges have fairly steadily been expanded by interpretation since the country's early years.

There are two basic ways of limiting abuse of patent monopolies. One is to be very strict in the definition of invention and not to allow patents for every insignificant contrivance. The other is to limit the uses to which the patent grant can be put. Black has done both. The first device, however, is very nearly useless because the Patent Office gives out patents by the thousand for every one the Supreme Court can invalidate. The second device is somewhat more effective, for through it certain general principles of law can be devised that can be readily applied by the lower courts. For example, Black recently wrote an opinion permitting assignees of patents to challenge the validity of the patent. This seemingly technical step should materially limit patent abuses.

LABOR RELATIONS

The three principal federal statutes of primary concern to labor that come regularly before the Supreme Court are the Wagner Act, the Wage-Hour Act, and the Federal Employees Liability Act. Black has supported to the hilt the broadest possible enforcement of all three.

The Wagner Act has raised countless problems, one of the most serious of which was ensuring that the lower federal courts would enforce the orders of the National Labor Relations Board. The Fifth Circuit Court of Appeals, covering the Southernmost states, including Alabama, early showed some tendency to set aside the orders of the Board very lightly. The Supreme Court cannot possibly review any great number of such cases, but in the *Waterman Steamship* case, included in this volume, Black tactfully but firmly utilized the supervisory power of the Court to ensure that the Fifth Circuit would give the fullest effect to the statute.

The Wage-Hour Act was Black's own, though as has been noted it was changed materially in the months between the time of his appointment to the Court and its passage. Lawyers have devised countless ingenious schemes for avoiding its apparently simple mandate that time-and-one-half must be paid for overtime. Justice Murphy had written most of the majority and dissenting opinions most favorable to the full and broad enforcement of the act, and Black has supported the Murphy position.

The Federal Employees Liability Act, or FELA, is one of the several federal statutes providing for compensation for injured workers who operate in fields particularly close to commerce. The FELA protects railroad workers, and other statutes apply to longshoremen, harbor workers, and seamen. This field is a favorite for Black. It is close to his own practice, and he is deeply interested in tort law. There are numerous ambiguities in these statutes, and Black's many opinions reflect a consistent attitude that the workman is entitled to the widest possible protection for injuries.

One other closely related subject is the Seventh Amendment, which provides for jury trial in civil cases. The past

hundred years have seen the invention of many legal devices
by which judges are able to substitute their opinions for
those of juries. Black has a deep and real faith, based on
hundreds of jury trials, in the wisdom, fairness, and substantial justice of the jury system. He was the first member of the Supreme Court in a hundred years to have a
really zealous desire to preserve that system. This particularly affects the injured worker or the disabled veteran,
for their cases go to juries in the federal courts, and juries
are far more likely to be generous to them than judges.
Justices Douglas, Murphy, Rutledge, and Burton have, as
they joined the Court, showed clear intention of joining to
re-establish an effective jury system in the federal courts,
and it now seems probable that, should the Court membership remain static, the jury will have returned to its strong
standing of a century ago within ten years. There is no
battle about which Black has felt more keenly.

Two Black positions to which at least portions of organized labor will take exception were his stand in the
Lewis injunction case, in which he agreed that the United
Mine Workers might be enjoined from striking, and his
opinion in the *Petrillo* case. In the latter opinion Black upheld the validity of the statute aimed at feather-bedding
practices by Petrillo's Musicians Union.

3. Civil Rights

Black's broad notions of the extent of the power to govern does not include sanction of a power to oppress, and
he is one of the strongest supporters of civil rights in the
history of the Supreme Court.

Perhaps the most dramatic general position held by
Black is that the entire Bill of Rights of the Constitution

is a limitation not only on the power of the federal government, but on the power of the states as well. The Bill of Rights, which guarantees such important liberties as freedom of speech, press, and religion, and which assures of a fair trial, was early held to limit the federal government only. As far as the Bill of Rights, taken by itself, is concerned, a state may oppress its citizens all it wants to.

The Fourteenth Amendment, adopted seventy-five years after the Bill of Rights, is commonly regarded as imposing at least some of the Bill of Rights as a limitation on the states. Here the contemporary battle begins, for Black's view is that the Fourteenth Amendment makes the entire Bill of Rights a limitation on the states as well as the federal government. Justice Douglas agrees with him fully, and Justices Rutledge and Murphy take a substantially similar position. The majority of the Court, however, holds that only the First Amendment, guaranteeing freedom of speech, press, and religion, is equally binding upon states and nation. This means, as a matter of practical consequence, that one is not guaranteed the same fair trial in state as in federal courts.

The principal point of difference involves the right to counsel. The Bill of Rights is interpreted to mean that no man who wants a lawyer can be tried in federal court without one. If he is too poor to pay for counsel, legal help must be furnished him. But the five-four majority holds that the same privilege does not extend to defendants in state courts. There a person may be tried and convicted without counsel in non-capital cases even though he plead for help because he has not sufficient funds to hire someone to assist him. *Betts* v. *Brady* is the most striking of these cases of deprivation of counsel, and Black's dissent in that case is included here.

The second serious aspect of criminal procedure arises when the state police use third-degree or torture methods to extract confessions. Black has been a vigorous fighter against third-degree methods since his prosecuting-attorney days, and he has written some of his most eloquent opinions in this field. Here he has usually prevailed, though occasionally over the sharp opposition of some of the Court.

Black has deviated from one hundred per cent defense of broadly claimed civil rights in only two important areas. He has not given a broad interpretation to the Fourth Amendment, protecting against search without warrant, and he yielded to some of the war-time trespasses by the military against civil rights. The most serious single large-scale invasion of civil rights in American history was the war-time military removal of the Japanese from the west coast to inland camps, which only the heroic efforts of a series of civilian administrators kept from being concentration camps of a Nazi variety. No one doubted that if any Japanese-Americans were disloyal, the government could deal with them; but here thousands of American citizens against whom there was no charge were wrenched out of their homes and scattered to desert camps.

The Supreme Court unanimously upheld the basic constitutional principles involved in the relocation, with the late Chief Justice Stone writing the majority opinion. Black stood with Stone, and later, in the case of *Korematsu*, Black applied those basic principles in an opinion for the Court, three justices dissenting, squarely upholding the evacuation.

This is not to say that Black approved every act of the army which came before him. A leading example to the contrary was the case of *Duncan*, in which he held invalid the army's system of martial law in Hawaii and in so doing presumably wrote an end to the use of martial law in labor disputes in the continental United States.

To Black the most important single passage in the Constitution is the First Amendment's guarantee of free speech. If he had to sacrifice all of the Constitution except one clause, that one would remain. No member of the Court has ever interpreted the First Amendment more broadly, though others may give it the same scope. As a Senator, Black defended freedom from the censor, and on the Court there has been scarcely a case in which he has found free expression to have been properly abridged. As one aspect of this attitude he has vigorously supported the right of the press and of individuals to criticize the courts.

Cases of claimed violation of freedom of religion have found him substantially as consistent. The two principal exceptions to this uniform attitude were the first Flag Salute case and the New Jersey School Bus case. In the Flag Salute case Mr. Justice Frankfurter for the Court held that a state or municipality could require school children to salute the Flag even though the salute violated the religious scruples of the children. Justices Black and Douglas joined in that opinion, but later reconsidered and in the second Flag Salute case voted to overrule the former decision.

In the School Bus case Black held for the Court, five to four, that a New Jersey town, if it cared to, could pay for the bus transportation of Catholic students to parochial schools. The dissent contended that this violated the principle of separation of church and state, but Black felt that this was closer to the category of poor relief than actual aid to one religious group. He did make clear the view of the whole Court that no substantial assistance could be given by the state to any form of religious education. A year later he wrote the opinion of the Court invali-

THE MAN

dating an Illinois system of utilizing the schools to aid in securing religious training. In the course of his opinion in the Illinois case Black said:

> The First Amendment rests upon the premise that both religion and government can best work to achieve their lofty aims if each is left free from the other within its respective sphere. . . . The First Amendment has erected a wall between Church and State which must be kept high and impregnable.

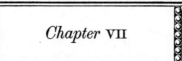

Chapter VII

THE CHIEF-JUSTICESHIP

Like the one-hoss shay the old Court fell apart all at once. When Van Devanter resigned, other resignations came quickly. Within four years of Black's appointment all the members of the old Court had been replaced except Stone and Roberts, and by now they too are gone. In the short period since 1937 Black has become the senior Justice.

The new personnel brought new alliances. The member of the new Court closest to Black, both intellectually and socially, is William O. Douglas. There have been terms in which no appreciable disagreement was recorded between them, and while there have been more frequent divergencies in recent terms, they are not as yet significant. The alliance has been of great mutual value, because each is more expert than the other in some fields of law. Douglas, for example, has had more experience than Black in matters of high finance, while Black has had more trial experience than Douglas. One came to the Court from the administrative branch of the government, and one from the legislative. Their frequent conversations are bound to be mutually useful.

Black's other two closest intellectual companions on the Court are Justices Murphy and Rutledge. The degree of his agreement with them is not quite so close as that with Douglas, but it is close enough to make the four a fairly cohesive bloc.

Of the remainder of the Court, Black is occasionally in important disputed cases in agreement with Justices Reed and Burton or Chief Justice Vinson, and he is very seldom in agreement with Justices Frankfurter or Jackson.

It is no secret that there have been sharp strains among the members of the new Court, for those strains have been reflected in the opinions. In recent years, however, the practice of using harsh words has been largely limited to Justices Frankfurter and Jackson, and particularly to the latter. Outward signs of the strains reached their high point at the time of the recent vacancy in the Chief-Justiceship.

When Chief Justice Stone died, the usual speculation over the vacancy began. There were two possibilities: one, that appointment would be made from within the Court, in which case someone would also have to be chosen as Associate Justice, the other that someone from outside the Court would be chosen as Chief Justice.

As the President poised undecided over the possibilities, the usual flood of rumors, mostly false, filled Washington and spilled out to the press. Justice Jackson was at that time in Nuremberg conducting the war trials and knew of the situation in Washington only what was in the press or in letters from friends. One of the rumors circulating in Washington was that Justice Black had told the President he would resign if Jackson were appointed.

The truth was that Black was doing nothing at all. For himself, he never thought for a moment that he might be appointed, feeling certain that, aside from numerous other circumstances, the time was not propitious for the appointment of so militant and open a supporter of the Roosevelt program. He also thought that for political or personal reasons there was no likelihood of the appointment of Murphy or Rutledge. His own preference was perfectly open to a few close friends; his first choice for the Chief-Justiceship — as for any other position he might desire — was Douglas, and if Douglas was not appointed, he hoped for Reed. (When toward the end of the period of waiting it became evident that Douglas was not going to be appointed, the supporters of both Black and Douglas swung to Reed, whose genial goodness made him an ideal moderator.) In short, from Black's standpoint, assuming that the appointment was to go to someone on the Court, the best practical possibility would be Douglas or Reed. If the choice was to go outside the Court, any of a dozen possibilities would have been excellent.

But Black was in no position to do anything active to support his preferences. He did not discuss the matter with the President, nor did he in any way tell the President that he would resign if Jackson were appointed. Columnists' accounts to the contrary were mistaken.

Then came the appointment of Treasury Secretary Vinson as Chief Justice. Though a surprise to Black, it was eminently satisfactory. He knew Vinson well enough to have high regard for him, and expressed his pleasure freely.

Between Vinson's appointment and confirmation came the Jackson letter from Nuremberg which the Judiciary Committees of both Houses of Congress received June 10, 1946. The background of this remarkable attack on Black is lost in intimate relations among the Justices of a sort which contemporary historians cannot penetrate. The superficial cause of the explosion had been a column by Miss Doris Fleeson, published in May 1946 in the *Washington Star* and many other papers. But for an understanding of the Fleeson column and the letter it is necessary to go back to the *Jewell Ridge* case.

The *Jewell Ridge* case was presented to the Supreme Court about a year before the vacancy in the Chief-Justiceship by Crampton Harris of Birmingham, attorney for the United Mine Workers and Black's partner of twenty years before. The legal issue was whether, under the Wage-Hour Act, miners were entitled to be paid for "time worked" for the protracted periods spent in uncomfortable and hazardous traveling from the mouth of the mine to the actual face of the coal and back. *Jewell Ridge* was the second portal-to-portal case to come to the Supreme Court, the first having arisen in Alabama and having also been presented to the Court by Harris a year before. The first case involved iron miners, and the Court, in a unanimous result though by divergent reasoning, had held for the miners.

Black participated in both cases. In neither the iron case nor the coal case had counsel suggested that Black should be disqualified by reason of his long-gone association with Harris or for any other reason. Nor had the point been raised in previous Harris cases, in at least one of which the Court had unanimously decided against Harris's client. In the five years preceding the *Jewell Ridge* case Black had seen Harris socially only once, and that for only a few minutes.

In the *Jewell Ridge* case Jackson dissented from the opinion of the Court, written by Justice Murphy, and joined in by Black, which gave judgment for the coal miners. Jackson saw a difference between the case of the iron miners and that of the coal miners and in his dissent went to great lengths to quote statements made by Black as Senator concerning the Wage-Hour Act, remarks which in Jackson's view were relevant to the *Jewell Ridge* issue.

Thereupon the coal companies' counsel moved for a re-hearing on the ground, among others, that Black was dis-qualified from hearing the case because of his previous association with Harris. The petition for rehearing was denied, with Justices Jackson and Frankfurter filing a short memorandum noting that they did not consider it within their province to express any view on the merits of the disqualification question. This was highly unusual, for motions relating to disqualification are normally decided by the whole Court without comment.

During the vacancy of the Chief-Justiceship reporter Fleeson came upon the unusual Jackson-Frankfurter state-ment, which had gone unnoticed a year before, and printed a column about it. According to Miss Fleeson, the special opinion on the point of disqualification had caused Black to react "with fiery scorn" to what he deemed a "slur upon his personal and judicial honor." Again according to Miss Fleeson, President Truman had been told of the dispute, and it was one of the reasons why Jackson was unlikely to be appointed.

The Fleeson story was only one more of the countless rumor-stories coming out of Washington. It was slightly more than a column long, and over half of it was direct quotation of Jackson's opinion. For some reason, Jackson regarded the story, according to his letter, as "the most direct specific attack on me." He remained silent until the appointment went to Vinson and then sent his letter.

Jackson began by saying that the "feud" among the Justices had been so well advertised that Congress "has a right to know the facts." He said too: "I also have personal reasons for wanting this situation made clear." According to the news that he was getting, "One of my colleagues made public threats to the President," and the upshot has been to give the appearance that "offensive behavior on my part is responsible for the feud."

Jackson then outlined the *Jewell Ridge* case as he saw it. He said that he had filed his special opinion on the ex-partner question because he had not wanted to "lend blind and unqualified approval." He then detailed the proposals of other members of the Court and the conference discussion. Said Jackson: "I told Justice Black in language that was sharp but no different than I would use again that I would not stand for any more of his bullying." He said that Black might deny that he had made "threats" to the President opposing Jackson, but that "it is equally sinister that a fabrication about a Justice should be so assiduously advertised without denial from any source."

Press reaction split several ways. David Lawrence expressed gratitude that Jackson had the courage to "expose the irregular situation." On the other hand, the Macon, Georgia, *News* took the position that "Justice Jackson is an ass." In an editorial thus headed, the *News* said that Black "has done no wrong and had been guilty of no impropriety in the particular case, except in the perverted imagination of a disappointed aspirant for the position of Chief Justice." Similarly the *Indianapolis Times* carried a front-page story headed: "Report Vinson Appointment Was Sharp Blow to Jackson." The extremely conservative press took the opportunity to say "a plague on both your houses." The *Richmond Times-Dispatch*, a moderate paper, was typical of those which felt that the essential issue was whether Black should have been disqualified, and that the paper would remain neutral until it knew more about the practice.

The Jackson letter was not altogether coherent. For example, at one point he declared that Black's participation in the *Jewell Ridge* case did not involve "lack of 'honor,'" and at another he said that if such an incident ever again occurred, "I will make my *Jewell Ridge* opinion look like a letter of recommendation in comparison." As nearly as it could be understood, the Jackson position appeared to reduce to three propositions: that Jackson thought he had been bullied; that Black had not taken steps to deny rumors about his preference for a Chief Justice other than Jackson; and that Black had wrongfully heard a case argued by a former partner.

The immediate problem was whether Black should respond to the charge, and the immediate answer was no. No statement could do anything but add to the damage already done to the Court. More important, it was an ethical absolute that a justice should never, under any circumstances, release to the public the events of the conference of the Supreme Court. The weekly Conference is so secret that the junior Justice of the Court is required to answer any knock at the door to receive any message that may be sent to any justice, for not even a messenger is allowed in the room. In the weekly conference, at which, according to Jackson's allegations, he had been "bullied," justices are supposed to speak their minds freely, safe in the knowledge that no word uttered there will ever be repeated. Their votes are recorded in locked volumes, and the opinions that emerge are set in type by several typesetters rather than one in order that no one shall know, either before or after an opinion, what the process of deliberation, argument, and concession may have been.

Not since a Justice was rumored to have told President Buchanan in advance how the Dred Scott case was to be decided in 1857 had, so far as historians know, a conference secret ever been deliberately breached. Black himself had for ten years been close-mouthed about the conference to the point of taciturnity; and no person not in association with the Court had ever heard him speak a word about the secret discussions of the brethren.

Black thus could not reply to Jackson. That Jackson had breached the confidence of the conference gave Black no leave to do so. Black maintained absolute silence.

Besides, there was nothing to say. Black had heard argument by a former partner. So, at one time or another, had Supreme Court Justices Field, Harlan, Blatchford, Butler, Holmes, Brandeis, Cardozo, and Stone. Diligent research fails to reveal that there was ever a case of a Supreme Court justice who had declined to sit for this reason. Jackson knew this as well as Black, for Jackson had once appeared as counsel before Justice Brandeis and was opposed by Brandeis's former partner.

The practice which Black followed was that not only of the Supreme Court but of the other federal courts and state supreme courts. Scrupulous judges do not hear former partners on matters that were in the office at the time of the termination of the partnership; but the Black-Harris partnership had terminated twenty years before these Harris cases arose. A poll covering thirty state supreme courts and nine of the intermediate federal appellate courts showed that thirty-one such courts had a consistent policy in respect to disqualification where ex-partners appear, and that in twenty-six of them the practice was that which Black had followed.

The real mystery remains: why did Jackson, a sophisticated and intelligent man, make a sensational charge against Black for doing exactly what almost every other judge in the country invariably does? Jackson may think the practice wrong, but could scarcely think it worth a congressional investigation. Indeed, the Judiciary Committees thought the charge so empty that they took no action at all.

Three answers circulated through the legal profession: first, that Jackson was a virtuous man, revealing an evil situation; second, that Jackson sought to wreak personal vengeance on the man he thought responsible for barring his path to the Chief-Justiceship; and third, that the enormous strain of the Nuremberg trial, a serious failure both in publicity and in results from a prosecutor's standpoint, caused an irresponsible act for which there is no rational explanation.

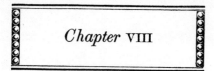

Chapter VIII

MAN AND JUDGE

The foregoing pages deal with what Black has done. A word may be added as to the manner of the man, the method of his work, and his status in the law.

Hugo Black today is a man of middling height, of slight build, and of almost incredible physical stamina. His principal physical recreation is tennis, which he plays incessantly during the summer and when work permits in spring and fall. At the age of sixty-two he still plays several sets on his own court on the hottest of days. When, a year or so ago, he pulled a muscle in his right arm which would have kept him off the court for the summer, he learned to play with his left arm and before long was giving his son Hugo, Jr., a good game.

Learning to play tennis with his left arm is typical of Black tenacity. He cannot give up, whether the task he has set for himself is playing a game, reading a book, or writing an opinion. This persistence aids him in mapping out long term activities and then finishing them. Recent summer reading programs of classical writing, or realistic jurisprudence, or economic history are examples.

A closely related quality is his inability to stop a job before it is finished. He has a completion mania, which accounts for his doing so large a volume of work on the

Court. When he starts on an opinion, he never stops. He works at it from early morning until late night, jealous of every interruption and occasionally even hurrying his meals. He will not hasten his work or cut corners, but he will not be happy until the opinion has gone to the printer. This compulsion is apparently growing stronger with the years, so that he is almost uneasy until his work is done. Jo-Jo, the Justice's young daughter, is one of the few persons who can easily interrupt him at work, for any problem of hers comes first. When she was much younger, many an evening at the office was interrupted with a tearful telephone inquiry about a difficult problem in fifth-grade arithmetic, and any such inquiry was carefully talked out.

Neither in the Senate nor on the Court have the Blacks participated extensively in the more elaborate types of Washington social life. Mrs. Black enjoys entertaining, but prefers to do it on the scale of small dinners, at which all the guests can enjoy each other in the course of the evening. As Sigrid Arne, A.P. feature writer, put it in 1941, in reference to the Black's entertaining, "It was Mrs. Black's delicate humor that kept the talkers relaxed. Typically, the dinner wasn't large. The Blacks never give come-one, come-all receptions. They invite people who can talk." Similarly, the Blacks prefer to attend small, rather than large, affairs. As the political complexion of Washington is changing, Black's personal friends are now less than formerly in political circles. His closest friend still in active politics is his successor in the Senate, Lister Hill, for whom he has the highest regard.

Neither of the Blacks has any taste for formality, an attitude shown in countless little ways. The Blacks live in one of the oldest and handsomest houses in Alexandria, where breakfast is virtually always served in the kitchen, the Justice making coffee, bacon, and eggs. The tennis court may be shared by any neighbors who will help keep it in good repair, and Black plays with everyone he can find, from his messenger to a recent vice-president of the United States. He frequently takes exercise in the morning by rolling on the floor of his study in various contortions assumed to be healthful. For years Black had his downtown meals at one restaurant because he enjoyed his conversations with one of the waiters.

At the same time Black has firm personal dignity and reserve. It is almost inconceivable that anyone would take advantage of his personal amiability to be unduly familiar. No one would slap Black on the back even if he were still running for office.

In deciding cases Black is frequently a sentimentalist about people. A vivid and dramatic imagination fills in details that may or may not exist. If a case involves an injured veteran, for example, Black sees the veteran, and his family, and his children. If it should be an injured railroad worker, the man becomes as real to Black on an abstract record as if Black himself were making the address to the jury. In these and in the farmer foreclosure cases, now less frequent than they were, Black's sympathies are so completely and automatically enlisted for the unfortunate that he is very nearly as much of a pleader as a judge.

Oddly enough for a man of firm opinions, Black is a good listener, and frequently changes his mind when convinced that he is wrong. He did so in the Senate and has done so on the Court.

At the same time Black is a very, very tough man. When he is convinced, he is cool steel hard. He knows clearly the kind of America he wants his children to grow up in, and he is absolutely impervious to blows that may fall upon him for trying to create that kind of America. His temper is usually in close control, but he fights, and his words may occasionally have a terrible edge. He can be a rough man in an argument.

Something as to Black's work-habits as a Justice has been said in the preceding paragraphs. His extreme diligence makes him, with Douglas, one of the two workhorses of the present Court. Black, Douglas, and Murphy among them last year wrote more than half the majority opinions of the Court.

If the case is of fair difficulty, Black usually begins by reviewing the entire subject of which the case is a part. He may spend a morning, or a day, or in rare cases of great importance as much as a week in reading everything he can find on the subject. He will read the texts, the law-review articles, and frequently the student notes. He may talk it through, perhaps with his clerk, perhaps with Justice Douglas, perhaps with one of the other members of the Court. His is the sort of mind that meets its difficulties most easily at the level of the spoken word, one of the reasons why the oral argument of cases carries so much more weight with him than with some other judges. Probably the greatest value to him of a law clerk is in giving him an audience with whom to think out loud.

From the general outline of the subject, he moves to the detailed decisions of the Court on the precise point at hand, and finally to a draft of the opinion. The draft is prepared occasionally from notes, but more often by collecting all useful references, including the briefs, on racks around his desk. The draft, like the earlier formulation of his thoughts, is done orally with the dictaphone.

The first draft then goes to the law clerk, who prepares his own suggestions. The Justice will then accept such of his clerk's suggestions as he thinks are helpful and will make his own revisions. This stage usually produces two more drafts.

If the opinion is of real importance, the Justice and his clerk may go over the opinion together, aloud, word for word. The objects will be threefold: first, to make the opinion as short as possible; second, to make it as clear as possible; and third, to put it in as simple language as possible. Citations that are merely cumulative, paragraphs that are repetitious, and words that can be deleted go out. A fourth draft is frequently shorter than any that preceded it, for Black prides himself on making his opinions as concise as possible. If the Justice hesitates as to which of two drafts of the same paragraph is more clear, both may go home to Mrs. Black for her opinion. Black seeks the simplest possible expression. As Heywood Broun once put it. "Black is certainly popular with newsmen, because he recently wrote a dissent in English as plain and simple and clear as a good running story on the first page. Naturally, reporters take to those who speak their own language. And it is a far finer tongue than that invented by Mr. Blackstone."

As a glance at the opinions in this volume will show, the Justice's style is usually clear and strong. He does not strive for artful phrases, and his prose does not skip or dance; it marches. It is not nearly so ponderous as the prose of the late Chief Justice Stone, an excellent legal writer; but it has only rare elements of the Holmes epigram or the Cardozo glowing phrase. Its strongest virtue is its simple clarity.

With probably at least half of his judicial career left before him, it would be aimless as well as ineffective to attempt a rounded estimate of Black's significance as a judge.

This is particularly true because rightly or wrongly we tend to measure the significance of a judge, like the significance of anyone else, in part by success. Peter V. Daniel, for example, or Morrison R. Waite, able Justices of the nineteenth century, are almost totally forgotten today because their views are so largely unaccepted. If the temper of the country and the Court continues to swing in conservative directions, Black's influence, no matter how ably he does his work, will diminish, in the short run at least. Yet even on a receding tide of the New Deal movement Black's power and color will make him a rallying-point, which will keep him in the forefront of legal attention; and like Holmes he will have disciples in dissent.

One oversimplification ought to be disposed of. Popular writers frequently refer to Black as a "leader" of one wing of the Court and Jackson or Frankfurter as the "leader" of another. This is a product of the fact that few newspaper writers follow the Court closely enough to keep track of nine individuals, and they are compelled, for their own convenience, to make a reduction to two or three personalities. Justices Black, Douglas, Murphy, and Rutledge are in agreement a very large share of the time, but Black's "leadership" consists largely in the fact that he is the senior member of the group on the Court, as well as the oldest in years, and has the opportunity to speak first in the conference. All four are strong and independent thinkers who were strong Roosevelt Democrats. There is no equivalent on the Supreme Court of either the party caucus or the floor-leader. Black is "leader" only to the extent that he can be persuasive in any individual case.

In the millions of words that have been spoken or written about Hugo Black in the past twenty years, he has been charged with almost every wrong that could possibly be scorned in the world of affairs. Yet one charge has never been made, and one seldom. No one has ever asserted that Black was not industrious, and few have asserted that he was not able. It is believed that in the last eight years one columnist is the only person to have publicly challenged Black's general competence. Some legal writers have of course occasionally doubted the skill of a particular opinion, but for the most part they have followed the early lead of Dean Harold Havighurst of Northwestern University in describing Black as an extraordinarily able jurist.

To the conservative press Black remains anathema. To those whose opinions he would value he is top-notch. On April 3, 1945 a testimonial dinner was given for Black upon the occasion of the presentation to him by the Southern Conference for Human Welfare of its Thomas Jefferson award. The late Senator Bilbo of Mississippi thought it an outrageous occasion and sent an agent to gather data, with which he denounced the affair in the Senate for its all-racial audience. But other persons present in person or by message took a different view.

Justices Reed, Douglas, Murphy, and Rutledge were present. So were Secretaries Ickes and Wallace, Senator Thomas of Utah, labor leaders Dan Tobin and Phil Murray. William Green sent a warm message. Senator Barkley was toastmaster, and Senator Pepper, Judge Sherman Minton, and President Frank Graham of the University of North Carolina spoke. Vice President Truman sent a message saying: "I think the country is to be congratulated on the fact that we have a man like Justice Black on the Supreme Court."

Charles Houston, a prominent member of the National Association for the Advancement of Colored People and an able Washington lawyer, referring to the Marian Anderson concert at the Lincoln Memorial in Washington, said:

"After the concert, Negroes sought Mr. Justice Black's autograph more than that of any other person except Marian Anderson herself. People have an uncanny instinct for recognizing their friends."

The then Federal Loan Administrator, Fred Vinson, said: "a lucid intellect and disciplined craftsmanship harnessed to the purposes of creative judicial democracy."

Mrs. Franklin D. Roosevelt said: "I know that all of us here are deeply conscious of the services which Justice Black has rendered to the liberal cause." President Roosevelt wrote: "Hugo L. Black deserves such honor. His own career has served to translate from history to public service the meaning of Jefferson's devotion to the rights of man."

A judge is not a legislator, and a court has no unrestrained freedom to translate its will into law. Particularly in the constitutional field the greatest good may lie in insisting, as Black so often does, that courts must be subordinate to the elected representatives of the people. But within those boundaries which are inherent in the nature of judging, there is wide range for judgment, policy, will.

Justice Black's fame as a jurist will ultimately be based on his sure instinct for the core of the case and his fertile legal imagination. He sees the social point of a case, its implication to the lives of people, in a flash; and he has the energy and the ability to devise ways — new ways if need be — of serving what in his conception is the largest good. He is a representative of that movement in American history which we have variously called the Grange, the Populists, the New Freedom, and the New Deal. He is one of the tiny handful of representatives of that movement ever to reach the Supreme Court of the United States. His significance as a Justice is that he knows what to do with the power thus given him.

THE OPINIONS

In the course of ten years Justice Black has written over three hundred majority and dissenting opinions. This selection of thirty-four means, then, the omission of ninety per cent of his written work for the decade. Hence the opinions have been selected on a basis of variety as well as general interest.

These opinions have been sharply edited. Most paragraphs of technical analysis either of jurisdiction or of previous decisions, and almost all footnotes and citations, have been omitted. The theory in cutting has been to avoid, as far as possible, much that an intelligent non-lawyer would find uninteresting. At the same time, in the interest of readability, ellipses (. . .) have been omitted wherever the text would make sense without them.

Because the intelligent non-lawyer may be curious as to exactly how an unedited opinion looks, one opinion, *Tiller* v. *Atlantic Coast Line,* is included in its entirety.

I.

CONTROL OF THE ECONOMY

EXTENT OF FEDERAL

POWER

United States v. *South-Eastern Underwriters' Association,* 322 U.S. 533 (1944)

[At the beginning of 1937, the year in which Justice Black was appointed to the Supreme Court, the interpretation of the commerce clause of the Constitution was the most serious constitutional issue for the New Deal. President Roosevelt's program had been one of expanded federal action, particularly in the control of labor relations and in the promotion of agricultural welfare. The rational constitutional basis for the President's program was the commerce clause of the Constitution: "Congress shall have power . . . to regulate commerce . . . among the several states." The then recent decisions of the Supreme Court indicated that the entire New Deal program was unconstitutional because Congress did not have the power under the commerce clause to regulate the production of crops or of goods.

This constitutional interpretation precipitated the Court fight. Even before the Black appointment the Court itself changed position on the commerce clause and upheld two of the most basic statutes of the program.

Thus when Black came to the Court, the general principle of wide federal power was clearly established. Black has since joined in all opinions giving wide scope to the federal power of regulation. His views on the Court remain what they were when he supported the Fair Labor Standards Act in the Senate. He adheres very closely to the general principles of Chief Justice Marshall in the first case on the commerce clause, that

Congress has the power to regulate that which is directly in commerce and that which, though not directly in commerce, affects the commerce of the country.

The *South-Eastern Underwriters'* case illustrates Black's basic philosophy. Here he held that the business of insurance was "commerce" and was subject to regulation under the Sherman Anti-Trust Act.

This is an action under the Sherman Act against the South-Eastern Underwriters' Association and its membership of approximately two hundred fire-insurance companies and twenty-seven persons. The government alleged that the defendants had monopolized the sale of fire insurance in six of the Southeastern states; that the defendants in conspiracy fixed prices for insurance in those states; and that by boycotts and coercion they forced all companies to comply with their standards, by various economic means forcing purchasers of insurance to buy only from those who participated in the plan.

The opinion of the Court, written by Justice Black and joined in by Justices Douglas, Murphy, and Rutledge, held that insurance was commerce and was covered by the act. In so doing the Court distinguished an 1869 decision, *Paul* v. *Virginia*. Chief Justice Stone and Justices Frankfurter and Jackson dissented on various grounds, their central position being that insurance could be regulated by Congress, but that it had not been by the statute at hand. Justices Reed and Roberts did not participate. Excerpts from so much of Justice Black's opinion as deals with the constitutional problem follow.]

Mr. Justice BLACK delivered the opinion of the Court.

For seventy-five years this Court has held, whenever the question has been presented, that the Commerce Clause of the Constitution does not deprive the individual states of power to regulate and tax specific activities of foreign insurance companies which sell policies within their territories. Each state has been held to have this power even though negotiation and execution of the companies' policy contracts involved communications of information and movements of persons, moneys, and papers across state lines. Not one of these cases, however, has involved an Act of Congress which required the Court to decide the issue of whether the Commerce Clause grants to Congress the power to regulate insurance transactions stretching across state lines. Today for the first time in the history of the Court that issue is squarely presented and must be decided. . . .

The record presents two questions and no others: (1) Was the Sherman Act intended to prohibit conduct of fire insurance companies which restrains or monopolizes the interstate fire insurance trade? (2) If so, do fire insurance transactions which stretch across state lines constitute "Commerce among the several States" so as to make them subject to regulation by Congress under the Commerce Clause? Since it is our conclusion that the Sherman Act was intended to apply to the fire insurance business we shall, for convenience of discussion, first consider the latter question.

I

Ordinarily courts do not construe words used in the Constitution so as to give them a meaning more narrow than one which they had in the common parlance of the times in which the Constitution was written. To hold that the word "commerce" as used in the Commerce Clause does not include a business such as insurance would do just that. Whatever other meanings "commerce" may have included in 1787, the dictionaries, encyclopedias, and other books of the period show that it included trade: business in which persons bought and sold, bargained and contracted. And this meaning has persisted to modern times. Surely, therefore, a heavy burden is on him who asserts that the plenary power which the Commerce Clause grants to Congress to regulate "Commerce among the several States" does not include the power to regulate trading in insurance to the same extent that it includes power to regulate other trades or businesses conducted across state lines.

The modern insurance business holds a commanding position in the trade and commerce of our Nation. Built upon the sale of contracts of indemnity, it has become one of the largest and most important branches of commerce. Its total assets exceed $37,000,000,000, or the approximate equivalent of the value of all farm lands and buildings in the United States. Its annual premium receipts exceed $6,000,000,000, more than the average annual revenue receipts of the United States Government during the last decade. Included in the labor force of insurance are 524,000 experienced workers, almost as many as seek their livings in coal mining or automobile manufacturing. Perhaps no modern commercial enterprise directly affects so many persons in all walks of life as does the insurance business. Insurance touches the home, the family, and the occupation or the business of almost every person in the United States.

This business is not separated into 48 distinct territorial compartments which function in isolation from each other. Interrelationship, interdependence, and integration of activities in all the states in which they operate are practical aspects of the insurance companies' methods of doing business. A large share of the insurance business is concentrated in a comparatively few companies located, for the most part, in the financial centers of the East. Premiums collected from policyholders in every part of the United States flow into these companies for investment. As policies become payable, checks and drafts flow back to the many states where the policyholders reside. The result is a continuous and indivisible stream of intercourse among the states composed of collections of premiums, payments of policy obligations, and the countless documents and communications which are essential to the negotiation and execution of policy contracts. Individual policyholders living in many different states who own policies in a single company have their separate interests blended in one assembled fund of assets upon which all are equally dependent for payment of their policies. The decisions which that company makes at its home office — the risks it insures, the premiums it charges, the investments it makes, the losses it pays — concern not just the people of the state where the home office happens to be located. They concern people living far beyond the boundaries of that state.

That the fire insurance transactions alleged to have been restrained and monopolized by appellees fit the above described pattern of the national insurance trade is shown by the indictment before us. Of the nearly 200 combining companies, chartered in various states and foreign countries, only 18 maintained their home offices in one of the six states in which the S. E. U. A. operated; and 127 had headquarters in either New York, Pennsylvania, or Connecticut. During the period 1931–1941 a total of $488,000,000 in premiums was collected by local agents in the six states, most of which was transmitted to home offices in other states; while during the same period $215,000,000 in losses was paid by checks or drafts sent from the home offices to the companies' local agents for delivery to the policyholders. Local agents solicited prospects, utilized policy forms sent from home offices, and made regular reports to their companies by mail, telephone or telegraph. Special travelling agents supervised local operations. The insurance sold by members of S. E. U. A. covered not only all kinds of fixed local properties, but also such properties as steamboats, tugs, ferries, shipyards, warehouses, terminals, trucks, busses, railroad equipment and rolling stock, and movable goods of all types carried in interstate and foreign commerce by every media of transportation.

Despite all of this, despite the fact that most persons, speaking from common knowledge, would instantly say that of course such a business is engaged in trade and commerce, the District Court felt compelled by decisions of this Court to conclude that the insurance business can never be trade or commerce within the meaning of the Commerce Clause. . . .

One reason advanced for the rule in the *Paul* case has been that insurance policies "are not commodities to be shipped or forwarded from one State to another." But both before and since *Paul* v. *Virginia* this Court has held that Congress can regulate traffic though it consists of intangibles. Another reason much stressed has been that insurance policies are mere personal contracts subject to the laws of the state where executed. But this reason rests upon a distinction between what has been called "local" and what "interstate," a type of mechanical criterion which this Court has not deemed controlling in the measurement of federal power. We may grant that a contract of insurance, considered as a thing apart from negotiation and execution, does not itself constitute interstate commerce. But it does not follow from this that the Court is powerless to examine the entire transaction, of which that contract is but a part, in order to determine whether there may be a chain of events which becomes interstate commerce. Only by treating the Congressional power over commerce among the states as a "technical legal conception" rather than as a "practical one, drawn from the course of business" could such a conclusion be reached. In short, a nationwide business is not deprived of its interstate character merely because it is built upon sales contracts which are local in nature. Were the rule otherwise, few businesses could be said to be engaged in interstate commerce.

Another reason advanced to support the result of the cases which follow *Paul* v. *Virginia* has been that, if any aspects of the business of insurance be treated as interstate commerce, "then all control over it is taken from the States and the legislative regulations which this Court has heretofore sustained must be declared invalid." Accepted without qualification, that broad statement is inconsistent with many decisions of this Court. It is settled that, for Constitutional purposes, certain activities of a business may be intrastate and therefore subject to state control, while other activities of the same business may be interstate and therefore subject to federal regulation. And there is a wide range of business and other activities which, though subject to federal regulation, are so intimately related to local welfare that, in the absence of Congressional action, they may be regulated or taxed by the states. In marking out these activities the primary test applied by the Court is not the mechanical one of whether the particular activity affected by the state regulation is part of interstate commerce, but rather whether, in each case, the competing demands of the state and national interests involved can be accommodated. And the fact that particular phases of an interstate business or activity have long been regulated or taxed by states has been recognized as a strong reason why, in the continued absence of conflicting Congressional action, the state regulatory and tax laws should be declared valid.

The real answer to the question before us is to be found in the Commerce Clause itself and in some of the great cases which interpret it. Many decisions make vivid the broad and true meaning of that clause. It is interstate commerce subject to regulation by Congress to carry lottery tickets from state to state. So also is it interstate commerce to transport a woman from Louisiana to Texas in a common carrier; to carry across a state line in a private automobile five quarts of whiskey intended for personal consumption; to drive a stolen automobile from Iowa to South Dakota. Diseased cattle ranging between Georgia and Florida are in commerce; and the transmission of an electrical impulse over a telegraph line between Alabama and Florida is intercourse and subject to paramount federal regulation. Not only, then, may transactions be commerce though non-commercial; they may be commerce though illegal and sporadic, and though they do not utilize common carriers or concern the flow of anything more tangible than electrons and information. These activities having already been held to constitute interstate commerce, and persons engaged in them therefore having been held subject to federal regulation, it would indeed be difficult now to hold that no activities of any insurance company can ever constitute interstate commerce so as to make it subject to such regulation; — activities which, as part of the conduct of a legitimate and useful commercial enterprise, may embrace integrated operations in many states and involve the transmission of great quantities of money, documents, and communications across dozens of state lines.

The precise boundary between national and state power over commerce has never yet been, and doubtless never can be, delineated by a single abstract definition. The most widely accepted general description of that part of commerce which is subject to the federal power is that given in 1824 by Chief Justice Marshall, "Commerce, undoubtedly, is traffic, but it is something more: it is intercourse. It describes the commercial intercourse between nations, and parts of nations, in all its branches. . . ." Commerce is interstate, he said, when it "concerns more States than one." No decision of this Court has ever questioned this as too comprehensive a description of the subject matter of the Commerce Clause. To accept a description less comprehensive, the Court has recognized, would deprive the Congress of that full power necessary to enable it to discharge its Constitutional duty to govern commerce among the states.

The power confided to Congress by the Commerce Clause is declared in the Federalist to be for the purpose of securing the "maintenance of harmony and proper intercourse among the States." But its purpose is not confined to empowering Congress with the negative authority to legislate against state regulations of commerce deemed inimical to the national interest. The power granted Congress is a positive power. It is the power to legislate concerning transactions which, reaching across state boundaries, affect the people of more states than one; — to govern affairs which the individual states, with their limited territorial jurisdictions, are not fully capable of governing. This federal power to determine the rules of intercourse across state lines was essential to weld a loose confederacy into a single, indivisible Nation; its continued existence is equally essential to the welfare of that Nation.

Our basic responsibility in interpreting the Commerce Clause is to make certain that the power to govern intercourse among the states remains where the Constitution placed it. That power, as held by this Court from the beginning, is vested in the Congress, available to be exercised for the national welfare as Congress shall deem necessary. No commercial enterprise of any kind which conducts its activities across state lines has been held to be wholly beyond the regulatory power of Congress under the Commerce Clause. We cannot make an exception of the business of insurance.

EXTENT OF

STATE POWER

Gwin, White & Prince, Inc., v. *Henneford,*
305 U.S. 434 (1939)

[Black is the strongest supporter of the power of the states of
the Union to regulate the economic affairs of men and concerns within their borders that the Court has had in more
than a hundred years. Indeed, fair argument can be made that
he is the most complete and consistent supporter of state
power of all the Justices in the history of the Court.

The power of the states to regulate business is limited
largely by three clauses of the Constitution, the commerce
clause, the contract clause, and the due process clause. Of
these the most important today is the commerce clause, and
the Supreme Court now invalidates or seriously challenges
more state regulatory statutes under this clause than under
the entire remainder of the Constitution.

For one hundred years most of the Justices of the Supreme
Court have believed that the commerce clause, which gives
Congress the power to regulate commerce among the several
states, to some extent at least precludes the states from exercising a concurrent power to regulate commerce. The Court
therefore frequently invalidates state tax or regulatory laws
that affect interstate business.

In these cases Black sets himself squarely against the majority. He returns to principles similar to those held a century ago by Chief Justice Taney, and says shortly that unless
the states directly discriminate against interstate commerce,
they have a complete right to regulate in the absence of con-

gressional direction to the contrary. The *Gwin, White* case illustrates this view in the field of state taxation.

In the *Gwin, White* case, the state of Washington imposed
a gross income tax of one half of one per cent on a local fruit-
marketing company. The company made many of its sales
across Washington state borders and was engaged in commerce. The Court held that the tax was a burden on commerce, and that it was invalid. Justice Stone wrote the majority opinion, joined by Justices Brandeis, Roberts, Reed,
and Chief Justice Hughes. Justices Butler and McReynolds
concurred specially. Justice Black dissented alone.]

Mr. Justice BLACK, dissenting:

In 1933, Washington's system of taxation failed to supply adequate revenue to support activities essential to the
welfare of its people. Mounting delinquencies due to burdensome taxes on property led the State legislature to
conclude that property taxes had to be reduced. This reduction was made. Then, forced to seek new sources of
revenue, the State turned — as did many other States
faced with similar needs — to a general, non-discriminatory excise tax upon business carried on in Washington,
measured by gross receipts. This general and non-discriminatory tax enabled "the common schools of the state . . .
to operate the full school term." While those engaged in
interstate businesses have enjoyed the property tax reduction in common with all Washington business, the exemp-
tion from taxation here granted appellant forces intrastate business to bear the entire burden of the excise that
replaced the repealed property taxes. Only intrastate business is required to contribute under this excise to the support of the State government that affords protection to
both interstate and local business.

Appellant, a Washington corporation, serves — under a

contract made in Washington — as sales agent for Washington apple growers. Its agents sell these Washington-grown apples in Washington and other States. The Washington excise tax is measured by appellant's gross income — received in Washington — and earned solely by selling apples grown in and shipped from that State.

No other State in which appellant's agents perform sales services has imposed a similar tax upon appellant measured by any part of its gross receipts. Such an eventuality — if it should occur — is given the title of "multiple taxation." And such conjectured "multiple taxation" would be — it is said — a violation of that Clause of the Constitution which gives Congress a power to regulate commerce among the States. Thus far, Congress has not deemed it necessary to prohibit the States from levying taxes measured by gross receipts from interstate commerce. While there are strong logical grounds upon which this Court has based its invalidation of State laws actually imposing unjust, unfair, and discriminatory burdens against interstate commerce as such, the same grounds do not support a judicial regulation designed to protect commerce from validly enacted non-discriminatory State taxes which do not — but may sometime — prove burdensome.

A business engaging in activities in two or more States should bear its part of the tax burdens of each. If valid, non-discriminatory taxes imposed in these States create "multiple" burdens, such "burdens" result from the political subdivisions created by our form of government. They are the price paid for governmental protection and maintenance in all States where the taxpayer does business. A State's taxes are not discriminatory if the State treats those engaged in interstate and intrastate business with equality and justice. If the combined valid and non-discriminatory taxes of many States raise a problem, only

Congress has power to consider that problem and to regulate with respect to it. Neither a State, nor a State with the approval of this Court, has the constitutional power to enact rules to adjust and govern conflicting State interests in interstate commerce.

Legislative inquiry might disclose to Congress that the speculative danger of injury to interstate commerce is more than offset by the certain injury to result from depriving States of a practical method of taxation. It might appear to Congress that the adoption of a rule against State taxes measured by interstate commerce gross receipts would deprive the States of a potent weapon useful in preventing evasion of State taxes.

This Court's rule would permit Washington to tax appellant's net income. But determination and collection of taxes on net incomes are often very difficult because corporate profits and income may be isolated or hidden by accounting methods, holding companies and intercorporate dealings. A substantial portion of the nation's commerce is carried on by corporations with far-flung business activities in many States. Intercorporate relations may assume "their rather cumbersome and involved nature for the purpose of evading [a state] . . . tax" on income and to "remove income from the state though still creating it within the state." Even "profits themselves are not susceptible of ascertainment with certainty and precision except as a result of inquiries too minute to be practicable."

Congress might conclude that the States should not be prohibited from utilizing non-discriminatory gross receipts taxes for State revenues, because there are "justifications for the gross Receipts tax . . . it has greater certitude and facility of administration than the net income tax, an important consideration to taxpayer and tax gatherer alike. And the volume of transactions indicated on the taxpayer's books may bear a closer relation to the cost of governmental supervision and protection than the annual profit and loss statement."

Only a comprehensive survey and investigation of the entire national economy — which Congress alone has power and facilities to make — can indicate the need for, as well as justify, restricting the taxing power of a State so as to provide against conjectured taxation by more than one State on identical income. A broad and deliberate legislative investigation — which no Court can make — may indicate to Congress that a wise policy for the national economy demands that each State in which an interstate business operates be permitted to apply a non-discriminatory tax to the gross receipts of that business either because of its size and volume or partially to offset the tendency toward centralization of the nation's business. Congress may find that to shelter interstate commerce in a tax exempt refuge — in the manner of the judgment here — is to grant that commerce a privileged status over intrastate business, contrary to the national welfare.

But Congress has both the facilities for acquiring the necessary data, and the constitutional power to act upon it. "The power over commerce . . . was one of the primary objects for which the people of America adopted their government, and must have been contemplated in forming it." The "disastrous experiences under the Confederation when the states vied in discriminatory measures against each other" united the Constitutional Convention in the conviction that some branch of the Federal government should have exclusive power to regulate commerce among the States and with foreign nations. Our Constitution adopted by that Convention divided the powers of government between three departments, Congress, the Executive and the Judiciary. It allotted to Congress alone the "Power . . .

to regulate Commerce with foreign Nations, and among the several states. . . ." Congress is the only department of our government — State or Federal — vested with authority to determine whether "multiple taxation" is injurious to the national economy; whether national regulations for division of taxes measured by interstate commerce gross receipts should or should not be adopted; and what regulations, if any, should protect interstate commerce from "multiple taxation." It "is the function of this Court to interpret and apply the law already enacted, but not under the guise of construction to provide a more comprehensive scheme of regulation than Congress has decided upon. Nor, in the absence of Federal action, may we deny effect to the laws of the State enacted within the field which it is entitled to occupy until its authority is limited through the exertion by Congress of its paramount constitutional power."

Until 1936, this Court had never stricken down — as violating the Commerce Clause — a uniform and non-discriminatory State privilege tax measured by gross receipts, and constituting an integral element of a comprehensive State tax program. In *Philadelphia Steamship Co. v. Pennsylvania*, decided half a century ago and relied upon to support the judgment here, this Court did not determine that such a general business tax — applied to all businesses within a State — could not be measured by interstate commerce gross receipts. On the contrary, the Court pointed out that the invalidated tax was "a tax on transportation only," and that even one engaged in transportation could "like any other citizen . . . be personally taxed for the amount of his property or estate, without regard to the source from which it was derived, whether from commerce, or banking, or any other employment." That, as the Court made clear, was "an entirely different thing from laying a special tax upon his receipts in a particular employment." Since the *Philadelphia Steamship Co.* case, this Court has sustained many State taxes measured by receipts both from interstate and intrastate commerce. It was not until the decisions in the cases of *Crew Levick Co.* v. *Pa.* and *United States Glue Co.* v. *Oak Creek,* decided 1917 and 1918, respectively, that this Court first tentatively announced, by way of dicta, a rule condemning State taxes based on gross receipts from interstate commerce. The full-blown rule under which the Federal courts strike down generally applied non-discriminatory State taxes measured by gross receipts from interstate commerce ripened into its present expanded form only eight months ago. This recent judicial restriction — still less than a year old — on the power of the States to levy general gross receipts taxes, cannot be justified or validated by claiming prestige from advanced age.

Since the Constitution grants sole and exclusive power to Congress to regulate commerce among the States, repeated assumption of this power by the courts — even over a long period of years — could not make this assumption of power constitutional. April 25, 1938, this Court overruled and renounced an unconstitutional assumption of power by the Federal courts based on a doctrine extending back through an unbroken line of authority to 1842. In overruling, it was said: "We merely declare that in applying the doctrine [declared unconstitutional] this Court and the lower courts have invaded rights which in our opinion are reserved by the Constitution to the several States." A century old rule had produced "injustice and confusion" and "the unconstitutionality of the course pursued . . . [had become] clear. . . ." That decision rested upon the sound principle that the rule of stare decisis cannot confer powers upon the courts which the inexorable command of the Constitution says they shall not have. State obedience to an unconstitutional assumption of power by the judicial branch of government, and inaction by the Congress, cannot amend the Constitution by creating and establishing a new "feature of our constitutional system." No provision of the Constitution authorizes its amendment in this manner.

It is as essential today, as at the time of the adoption of the Constitution, that commerce among the States and with foreign nations be left free from discriminatory and retaliatory burdens imposed by the States. It is of equal importance, however, that the judicial department of our government scrupulously observe its constitutional limitations and that Congress alone should adopt a broad national policy of regulation — if otherwise valid State laws combine to hamper the free flow of commerce. Doubtless, much confusion would be avoided if the courts would refrain from restricting the enforcement of valid, nondiscriminatory State tax laws. Any belief that Congress has failed to take cognizance of the problems of conjectured "multiple taxation" or "apportionment" by exerting its exclusive power over interstate commerce, is an inadequate reason for the judicial branch of the government — without constitutional power — to attempt to perform the duty constitutionally reposed in Congress. I would return to the rule that — except for State acts designed to impose discriminatory burdens on interstate commerce because it *is* interstate — Congress alone must "determine how far [interstate commerce] . . . shall be free and untrammelled, how far it shall be burdened by duties and imposts, and how far it shall be prohibited."

For these and other reasons set out elsewhere I believe the judgment of the Supreme Court of Washington should be affirmed.

Southern Pacific Company v. Arizona,
325 U.S. 761 (1945)

[Just as the commerce clause may be used to invalidate state taxes, as in the *Gwin, White* case, so it may be used to invalidate state regulations of business that affect commerce. Black has never stated his position on the subject more vigorously than in the *Southern Pacific* case, in which, as he conceived it, the majority let considerations of the financial welfare of the railroads outweigh the protection of the safety of the employees. In this case Chief Justice Stone, for a majority including Justices Roberts, Reed, Frankfurter, Murphy, and Jackson, held invalid a 1912 Arizona statute that made it unlawful to operate a railroad train of more than fourteen passenger cars or seventy freight cars. Justice Rutledge concurred in the result.

Chief Justice Stone declared that the statute violated the commerce clause by putting an "undue burden" on commerce, holding after analysis of the facts that the safety argument advanced by the state did not outweigh the adverse effect on transportation efficiency and economy. In the following opinion Justice Black protested that "undue burden" was a question of fact which the Arizona legislature had decided in favor of safety, and that the Court became a "super-legislature" by reviewing that factual question. Justice Douglas joined in the Black dissent and also dissented separately.]

Mr. Justice BLACK, dissenting:

For more than a quarter of a century, railroads and their employees have engaged in controversies over the relative virtues and dangers of long trains. Railroads have argued that they could carry goods and passengers cheaper in long trains than in short trains. They have also argued that while the danger of personal injury to their employees might in some respects be greater on account of the operation of long trains, this danger was more than offset by an increased number of accidents from other causes brought about by the operation of a much larger number of short trains. These arguments have been, and are now, vigorously denied. While there are others, the chief causes assigned for the belief that long trains unnecessarily jeopardize the lives and limbs of railroad employees relate to "slack action." Cars coupled together retain a certain free play of movement, ranging between 1½ inches and 1 foot, and this is called "slack action." Train brakes do not ordinarily apply or release simultaneously on all cars. This frequently results in a severe shock or jar to cars, particularly those in the rear of a train. It has always been the position of the employees that the dangers from "slack action" correspond to and are proportionate with the length of the train. The argument that "slack movements" are more dangerous in long trains than in short trains seems never to have been denied. The railroads have answered it by what is in effect a plea of confession and avoidance. They say that the added cost of running long trains places an unconstitutional burden on interstate commerce. Their second answer is that the operation of short trains requires the use of more separate train units; that a certain number of accidents resulting in injury are inherent in the operation of each unit, injuries which may be inflicted either on employees or on the public; consequently, they have asserted that it is not in the public interest to prohibit the operation of long trains.

In 1912, the year Arizona became a state, its legislature adopted and referred to the people several safety measures concerning the operation of railroads. One of these required railroads to install electric headlights, a power which the state had under this Court's opinion. Another Arizona safety statute submitted at the same time required certain tests and service before a person could act as an engineer or train conductor, and thereby exercised a state power similar to that which this Court upheld. The third safety statute which the Arizona legislature submitted to the electorate, and which was adopted by it, is the train limitation statute now under consideration. By its enactment the legislature and the people adopted the viewpoint that long trains were more dangerous than short trains, and limited the operation of train units to 14 cars for passengers and 70 cars for freight. This same question was considered in other states, and some of them, over the vigorous protests of railroads, adopted laws similar to the Arizona statute. . . .

Under those circumstances, the determination of whether it is in the interest of society for the length of trains to be governmentally regulated is a matter of public policy. Someone must fix that policy — either the Congress, or the state, or the courts. A century and a half of constitutional history and government admonishes this Court to leave that choice to the elected legislative representatives of the people themselves, where it properly belongs both on democratic principles and by the requirements of efficient government.

I think that legislatures, to the exclusion of courts, have the constitutional power to enact laws limiting train lengths, for the purpose of reducing injuries brought about by "slack movements." Their power is not less because a requirement of short trains might increase grade crossing accidents. This latter fact raises an entirely different element of danger which is itself subject to legislative regulation. For legislatures may, if necessary, require railroads to take appropriate steps to reduce the likelihood of injuries at grade crossings. And the fact that grade crossing improvements may be expensive is no sufficient reason to say that an unconstitutional "burden" is put upon a railroad even though it be an interstate road.

The Supreme Court of Arizona did not discuss the County Court's so-called findings of fact. It properly designated the Arizona statute as a safety measure, and finding that it bore a reasonable relation to its purpose declined to review the judgment of the legislature as to the necessity for the passage of the act. In so doing it was well fortified by a long line of decisions of this Court. Today's decision marks an abrupt departure from that line of cases.

There have been many sharp divisions of this Court concerning its authority, in the absence of congressional enactment, to invalidate state laws as violating the Commerce Clause. That discussion need not be renewed here, because even the broadest exponents of judicial power in this field have not heretofore expressed doubt as to a state's power, absent a paramount congressional declaration, to regulate interstate trains in the interest of safety. For as early as 1913, this Court, speaking through Mr. Justice Hughes, later Chief Justice, referred to "the settled principle that, in the absence of legislation by Congress, the States are not denied the exercise of their power to secure safety in the physical operation of railroad trains within their territory, even though such trains are used in interstate commerce. That has been the law since the beginning of railroad transportation." Until today, the oft-repeated principles of that case have never been repudiated in whole or in part.

When we finally get down to the gist of what the Court today actually decides, it is this: Even though more railroad employees will be injured by "slack action" movements on long trains than on short trains, there must be no regulation of this danger in the absence of "uniform regulations." That means that no one can legislate against this danger except the Congress; and even though the Congress is perfectly content to leave the matter to the different state legislatures, this Court, on the ground of "lack of uniformity," will require it to make an express avowal of that fact before it will permit a state to guard against that admitted danger.

We are not left in doubt as to why, as against the potential peril of injuries to employees, the Court tips the scales on the side of "uniformity." For the evil it finds in a lack of uniformity is that it (1) delays interstate commerce, (2) increases its cost and (3) impairs its efficiency. All three of these boil down to the same thing, and that is that running shorter trains would increase the cost of railroad operations. The "burden" on commerce reduces itself to mere cost because there was no finding, and no evidence to support a finding, that by the expenditure of sufficient sums of money, the railroads could not enable themselves to carry goods and passengers just as quickly and efficiently with short trains as with long trains. Thus the conclusion that a requirement for short trains will "burden interstate commerce" is a mere euphemism for the statement that a requirement for short trains will increase the cost of railroad operations.

In the report of the Senate Committee, supra, attention was called to the fact that in 1935, 6,351 railroad employees were injured while on duty, with a resulting loss of more than 200,000 working days, and that injuries to trainmen and enginemen increased more than 29% in 1936. Nevertheless, the Court's action in requiring that money costs outweigh human values is sought to be buttressed by a reference to the express policy of Congress to promote an "economical national railroad system." I cannot believe that if Congress had defined what it meant by "economical," it would have required money to be saved at the expense of the personal safety of railway employees. Its whole history for the past 25 years belies such an interpretation of its language. Judicial opinions rather than legislative enactments have tended to emphasize costs. A different congressional attitude has been shown by the passage of numerous safety appliance provisions, a federal employees' compensation act, abolition of the judicially created doctrine of assumption of risk and contributory negligence, and various other types of legislation. Unfortunately, the record shows, as pointed out in the *Tiller* case, that the courts have by narrow and restricted interpretation too frequently reduced the full scope of protection which Congress intended to provide.

This record in its entirety leaves me with no doubt whatever that many employees have been seriously injured and killed in the past, and that many more are likely to be so in the future, because of "slack movement" in trains. Everyday knowledge as well as direct evidence presented at the various hearings, substantiates the report of the Senate Committee that the danger from slack movement is greater in long trains than in short trains. It may be that off-setting dangers are possible in the operation of short trains. The balancing of these probabilities, however, is not in my judgment a matter for judicial determination, but one which calls for legislative consideration. Representatives elected by the people to make their laws, rather than judges appointed to interpret those laws, can best determine the policies which govern the people. That at least is the basic principle on which our democratic society rests. I would affirm the judgment of the Supreme Court of Arizona.

Wood v. *Lovett,* 313 U.S. 362 (1941)

[The Constitution declares that "No state shall . . . pass any law . . . impairing the obligation of contracts," and this passage, traditionally known as the contract clause, is one of the three basic clauses under which the Court has controlled state action. The Black position, which in general is also the accepted modern position on the contract clause, is that it prohibits not all interference with contractual relations, but only those which are "unreasonable." Some such modification is imperative if government is to function, for if the clause were interpreted rigidly, states could not, for example, grant divorces (impairment of the marriage contract); or tax profits from enterprise ("impairing" the profit portion of contracts); or vary the powers of its municipalities (a corporate charter is a "contract"); or provide for debt moratoria in financial crises.

The problem thus becomes one of determining the "reasonableness" of the modification of contractual relationships. Black has been in the forefront of those who would give the states wide latitude in this as in other respects. This is illustrated by his dissent in this case.

The case arose thus: In 1933 Arkansas acquired certain land for nonpayment of taxes. In 1935 the state legislature passed a statute providing that when the state sold such land acquired for taxes, the sales "shall not hereafter be set aside" for irregularities in the process by which the land was acquired. In 1936 Arkansas sold the land to Wood and an associate. In 1937 Arkansas repealed the 1935 statute. Meanwhile the interest of the original deliquent taxpayer had passed to Lovett. There had been irregularities in the original tax foreclosure by Arkansas.

The situation thus was that if the irregularities could be considered, then Arkansas had never properly acquired the land and therefore could not validly sell it to Wood. In that case Lovett would own the land. But if the 1935 act was applicable, as it had been when Wood bought the land, the irregularities could not be given legal effect, and the land would belong to Wood.

2. Extent of State Power

The Court held for Wood, believing that the 1935 statute was a part of his contract of purchase in 1936, and that the 1937 repeal was void as an impairment of the obligation of contract. Justice Roberts wrote the majority opinion for Chief Justice Hughes and Justices Stone, Reed, Frankfurter, and Jackson. Justices Douglas and Murphy joined in Justice Black's dissent. The dissent began with a discussion of the background of the tax-delinquency problem, presented next an argument that there was in fact no contract between Arkansas and Wood, and concluded with a proposed application of general principles of the contract clause to the case. Excerpts from the first and third of these divisions follow.]

Mr. Justice BLACK, dissenting:

There is far more involved here than a mere litigation between rival claimants to a few hundred acres of Arkansas land. In my view, the statute here stricken down is but one of many acts adopted both by Congress and by state legislatures in an effort to meet the baffling economic and sociological problems growing out of a nationwide depression. These problems — among them the owners' loss of homes and farms, chiefly through mortgage sales and tax forfeitures and the states' concomitant loss of tax revenues — challenged the wisdom and capacity of the nation's legislators.

Among the efforts of Arkansas' legislators to meet these problems was the legislation adopted by Act 142 of 1935 and repealed by Act 264 of 1937 — the repealing act being the statute here held invalid. It is quite apparent that considerations of public policy induced the Arkansas legislature to pass the 1935 act whereby Arkansas courts were prohibited from setting aside certain types of defective tax sales "by any proceedings at law or in equity." At the time that act was passed, more than 25% of the real property in

169

the state was tax delinquent. Loss of revenue from so substantial a portion of the state's total acreage was a serious matter. In the eyes of some people, the land could be sold and the lost revenues recouped if some of the formal grounds on which tax titles could be invalidated were rendered unavailing. It seems clear that the 1935 legislature was persuaded of the wisdom of such a step. But it also seems clear that the 1935 act was repealed in 1937 because the legislature became convinced that the law had worked directly contrary to the state's policy of obtaining the benefits believed to flow from continuity of possession by home owners and farmers, that it had accomplished inequitable results, that it had thereby "operated injuriously to the interests of the State, and that sound policy dictated its repeal." This is apparent from reading that part of section 2 of the repealing act of 1937 which declared that "said Act 142, Acts 1935, ignores jurisdictional prerequisites to effect valid sales of tax delinquent land, as prescribed by law, and has brought the laws of the State incident thereto into doubt and confusion. . . ."

Both the 1935 act and the 1937 act repealing it touch on Arkansas' policy as to taxation, tax forfeiture, and land ownership — matters of public policy which are of vital interest to the state and all its citizens. It was a matter of serious moment to Arkansas that 25% of the state's privately owned land — homes, farms, and other property — was in jeopardy of being taken from its owners because of inability to pay taxes. If only 50% of the forfeitures were homes and farms, simultaneous ouster of so many citizens could result in forced migrations and discontents disastrous in their consequences. The manifestations of financial distress revealed by the widespread delinquency spotlighted conditions which called for the best in legislative statesmanship. To seek a rational and fair solution to the problem was not only within the power of Arkansas' lawmakers, but was also their imperative duty. Without attempting to judge the wisdom or equities of either act, it is easy to see that both the 1935 and 1937 acts represented rational and understandable attempts to achieve such a solution. To hold that the contract clause of the federal Constitution is a barrier to the 1937 attempt to restore to the distressed landowners the remedy partly taken away by the 1935 act is, in my view, wholly inconsistent with the spirit and language of that Constitution. . . .

So nearly universal are contractual relationships that it is difficult if not impossible to conceive of laws which do not have either direct or indirect bearing upon contractual obligations. Therefore, it would go far towards paralyzing the legislative arm of state governments to say that no legislative body could ever pass a law which would impair in any manner any contractual obligation of any kind. Upon a recognition of this basic truth rests the decision in the *Blaisdell* case. Such recognition was made clear by the use of the following expressions, either quoted and implicitly approved, or used for the first time: "the prohibition is not an absolute one and is not to be read with literal exactness like a mathematical formula"; "No attempt has been made to fix definitely the line between alterations of the remedy, which are to be deemed legitimate, and those which under the form of modifying the remedy, impair substantial rights. Every case must be determined upon its own circumstances"; "In all such cases the question becomes therefore one of reasonableness, and of that the legislature is primarily the judge"; "The question is not whether the legislative action affects contracts incidentally, or directly or indirectly, but whether the legislation is addressed to a legitimate end and the measures taken are reasonable and appropriate to that end"; "If it be determined, as it must be, that the contract clause is not an absolute and utterly qualified restriction of the state's protective power, this legislation is clearly so responsible as to be within the legislative domain."

The *Blaisdell* decision represented a realistic appreciation of the fact that ours is an evolving society and that the general words of the contract clause were not intended to reduce the legislative branch of government to helpless impotency. Whether the contract clause had been given too broad a construction in judicial opinions prior to the *Blaisdell* decision is not now material. And whether I believe that the language quoted from the *Blaisdell* opinion constitutes the ultimate criteria upon which legislation should be measured I need not now discuss. For I am of the opinion that the Arkansas statute, passed in pursuance of a general public policy of that state, comes well within the permissible area of state legislation as that area is defined by the *Blaisdell* case and the decisions upon which that case rests. . . .

At the time of the forfeiture and sale to the state, Arkansas law protected the purchaser by providing that he should be reimbursed and made whole in case his tax purchase was set aside for irregularity. That protection is today afforded to the full extent that it was when appellants bought the land; the repealing act of which appellants complain did not take away any part of that right. From all of this it is manifest that the entire plan of the state in connection with tax sales, both before and after the repealing act of 1937, shows a scrupulous desire to provide compensation for the purchaser in order that he may not suffer pecuniary loss, whatever may be the consequences of a suit for the land. And the whole course of legislation in Arkansas shows a desire to be fair both to the purchaser of tax forfeited land and to the former owners whose land is about to be lost by reason of the drastic device of forfeiture. I cannot believe

that the true intent and interpretation of the contract
clause prohibits Arkansas from making such an effort to
preserve the rights of both the landowner and the one who
claims the landowner's forfeited property. Arkansas has
not here taken away respondent's "entire remedy" but has
done so "in part only." I am willing to concede that there
may be a "vast disproportion between the value of the land
and the sum for which it is usually bid off at such sales."
But assuming that the tax forfeited land here was obtained
at such a bargain, I am still of the opinion that these appellants — who have the right to their money, with interest
— have been denied no right guaranteed by the contract
clause. And in this connection it is not to be forgotten that
appellants could have obtained a perfect title by openly
and adversely holding possession of the land for two years
— a privilege which the state courts finally and authorita-
tively found had not been exercised.

Tax sold properties are undoubtedly bought with the
knowledge on the part of those who speculate in them that
states ordinarily adopt a liberal policy in order to protect
property owners from tax forfeiture. And even granting
that we could enter into questions of policy, I would be
unable to reach the conclusion that Arkansas, by repealing
its 1935 statute, acted "without . . . reason or in a spirit
of oppression." It would seem to me to be difficult to support an argument that Arkansas was acting either unreasonably, unjustly, oppressively, or counter to sound public
policy in adopting a law which, without depriving purchasers of the right to recover their money outlay, with
interest, sought to make the way easy for former home
owners and property owners of all types to reacquire possession and ownership of forfeited property. If under the
contract clause it is justifiable to seek to find "a rational
compromise between individual rights and public welfare,"

then it seems to me that this is a case for the application of
that principle. I do not believe that the Arkansas legislature is prohibited by the federal Constitution from adopting the public policy which the decision of the Arkansas
Supreme Court has upheld in this case. "Especial respect
should be had to such decisions when the dispute arises out
of general laws of a State, regulating its exercise of the
taxing power, or relating to the State's disposition of its
public lands."

Connecticut General Life Insurance Company v. *Johnson,* 303 U.S. 77 (1938)

[While in recent years the chief constitutional obstacle to
state commercial legislation has become the commerce clause,
ten years ago and for half a century before, the due process
clause of the Fourteenth Amendment was the principal judicial device for invalidating state statutes. Black's position
is that this judicial power should be obliterated altogether and
that, for example, Supreme Court review of state social legislation or state rate regulation is totally unwarranted by the
Constitution.

The language of the Fourteenth Amendment is: "No state
shall . . . deprive any person of life, liberty, or property,
without due process of law." When the Amendment was
adopted, after the Civil War, it was not generally supposed
that it applied to corporations at all, or that it gave the
Supreme Court power to do more than review the procedures
of government. But within thirty years after the close of the
Civil War the Court had interpreted the Amendment both as
applying to corporations and as giving the Court complete
power to consider whether any state statute was "reasonable"
in the opinion of the judges. This process of interpretation
was bitterly resisted because, as Justice Holmes once said, it
made the sky the limit for the substitution of judicial for
legislative will.

2. *Extent of State Power*

Justice Black has struck at this interpretation of the Fourteenth Amendment on many grounds. One is that the Amendment was not meant to cover corporations at all, that the word "person" as used in it means natural person only. In the *Connecticut General* case he expressed that view in dissent. He still stands alone on this position.

In this case the Court held invalid a California tax on a Connecticut insurance corporation doing business in California. The opinion of the Court was written by Justice Stone and was joined by Justices McReynolds, Brandeis, Butler, Roberts, and Chief Justice Hughes. A portion of Justice Black's dissent follows.]

Mr. Justice BLACK, dissenting:

It is contended that the due process clause of the Fourteenth Amendment prohibits California from determining what terms and conditions should be imposed upon this Connecticut corporation to promote the welfare of the people of California.

I do not believe the word "person" in the Fourteenth Amendment includes corporations. A constitutional interpretation that is wrong should not stand. I believe this Court should now overrule previous decisions which interpreted the Fourteenth Amendment to include corporations.

Certainly, when the Fourteenth Amendment was submitted for approval, the people were not told that the states of the South were to be denied their normal relationship with the Federal Government unless they ratified an amendment granting new and revolutionary rights to corporations. This Court, when the *Slaughter House* cases were decided in 1873, had apparently discovered no such purpose. The records of the time can be searched in vain for evidence that this Amendment was adopted for the benefit of corporations. It is true that in 1882, twelve years after its adoption, and ten years after the *Slaughter House* cases, an argument was made in this Court that a journal of the joint Congressional Committee which framed the Amendment, secret and undisclosed up to that date, indicated the Committee's desire to protect corporations by the use of the word "person." Four years later, in 1886, this Court in the case of *Santa Clara County* v. *Southern Pacific Railroad* decided for the first time that the word "person" in the Amendment did in some instances include corporations. A secret purpose on the part of the members of the Committee, even if such be the fact, however, would not be sufficient to justify such a construction. The history of the Amendment proves that the people were told that its purpose was to protect weak and helpless human beings and were not told that it was intended to remove corporations in any fashion from the control of state governments. The Fourteenth Amendment followed the freedom of a race from slavery. Justice Swayne said in the *Slaughter House* cases, that "by 'any person' was meant *all* persons within the jurisdiction of the State. No distinction is intimated on account of race or color." Corporations have neither race nor color. He knew the Amendment was intended to protect the life, liberty and property of *human* beings.

The language of the Amendment itself does not support the theory that it was passed for the benefit of corporations.

The first clause of Section 1 of the Amendment reads: "All persons born or naturalized in the United States and subject to the jurisdiction thereof are citizens of the United States and of the State wherein they reside." Certainly a corporation cannot be naturalized and "persons" here is not broad enough to include "corporations."

The first clause of the second sentence of Section 1 reads: "No State shall make or enforce any law which shall abridge the privileges or immunities of citizens of the United States." While efforts have been made to persuade this Court to allow corporations to claim the protection of this clause, these efforts have not been successful.

The next clause of the second sentence reads: "Nor shall any State deprive any *person* of life, liberty or property without due process of law. . . ." It has not been decided that this clause prohibits a state from depriving a corporation of "life." This Court has expressly held that "the liberty guaranteed by the Fourteenth Amendment against deprivation without due process of law is the liberty of natural, not artificial persons." Thus, the words "life" and "liberty" do not apply to corporations, and of course they could not have been so intended to apply. However, the decisions of this Court which the majority follow hold that corporations are included in this clause insofar as the word "property" is concerned. In other words, this clause is construed to mean as follows:

"Nor shall any State deprive any human being of life, liberty or property without due process of law; nor shall any State deprive any corporation of property without due process of law."

The last clause of this second sentence of Section 1 reads: "nor deny to any person within its jurisdiction the equal protection of the laws." As used here, "person" has been construed to include corporations.

Both Congress and the people were familiar with the meaning of the word "corporation" at the time the Fourteenth Amendment was submitted and adopted. The judicial inclusion of the word "corporation" in the Fourteenth Amendment has had a revolutionary effect on our form of government. The states did not adopt the Amendment with knowledge of its sweeping meaning under its present construction. No section of the Amendment gave notice to the people that, if adopted, it would subject every state law and municipal ordinance affecting corporations (and all administrative actions under them), to censorship of the United States courts. No word in all this Amendment gave any hint that its adoption would deprive the states of their long recognized power to regulate corporations.

This Amendment sought to prevent discrimination by the states against classes or races. We are aware of this from words spoken in this Court within five years after its adoption, when the people and the courts were personally familiar with the historical background of the Amendment. "We doubt very much whether any action of a State not directed by way of discrimination against the Negroes as a class, or on account of their race, will ever be held to come within the purview of this provision." Yet, of the cases in this Court in which the Fourteenth Amendment was applied during the first fifty years after its adoption, less than one-half of one percent invoked it in protection of the Negro race, and more than fifty percent asked that its benefits be extended to corporations.

If the people of this nation wish to deprive the States of their sovereign rights to determine what is a fair and just tax upon corporations doing a purely local business within their own State boundaries, there is a way provided by the Constitution to accomplish this purpose. That way does not lie along the course of judicial amendment to that fundamental charter. An Amendment having that purpose could be submitted by Congress as provided by the Constitution. I do not believe that the Fourteenth Amendment had that purpose, nor that the people believed it had that purpose, nor that it should be construed as having that purpose.

I believe the judgment of the Supreme Court of California should be sustained.

2. Extent of State Power

Polk Company v. *Glover*, 305 U.S. 5 (1938)

[Black would strip judges completely of the power they have taken in the past fifty years to pass on the "reasonableness" of state commercial legislation. He would interpret the due process clause of the Fourteenth Amendment as it was originally interpreted by Chief Justice Waite in 1877, leaving to the legislatures the determination of the reasonableness of legislation, and to the legislatures and state administration agencies the reasonableness of utility rate regulation. He began while in the Senate to attack the Supreme Court's interpretation of the due process clause as judicial usurpation, incompatible with democracy, and he has held to that line on the Court.

The Black position on due process is truly startling, essentially because it is a return to first principles. From 1890 to 1937 the Supreme Court repeatedly invalidated state legislation under the due process clause. That exercise of a judicial veto has in recent years been very rare, because a majority of Black's brethren, while not agreeing with him entirely, have by other doctrines largely dulled the due process knife. But a knife only dulled can be sharpened again in another generation, and Black would like to see it thrown away altogether. The *Polk Company* dissent shows his view.

In this case a Florida statute required that cans containing Florida orange juice should be embossed with the word "Florida." The plaintiff canners brought this action to enjoin the enforcement of the statute on the grounds principally that embossing would create defects in the cans which would affect the juice, and that they had substantial numbers of cans on hand at the time of the passage of the statute, which would result in their suffering loss were the statute enforced. The essential lament of the plaintiffs was denial of due process. The district court, without a trial but after looking at some cans and considering some affidavits, granted the state's motion to dismiss. The district court found that the canners would suffer no serious injury and that the statute was important to the welfare of Florida orange-growers.

The Supreme Court reversed, holding that the case could

not be decided on affidavits and observations of the district judge, but that he must grant a full hearing and take testimony before deciding the point. The opinion was "per curiam," which means that it was not attributed to any one justice, and was joined in by Chief Justice Hughes and Justices McReynolds, Brandeis, Butler, Stone, Roberts, and Reed. Justice Black dissented alone.]

Mr. Justice BLACK, dissenting:

The important consequences of this remand raise far more than mere questions of procedure. State laws are continually subjected to constitutional attacks by those who do not wish to obey them. Accordingly, it becomes increasingly important to protect State governments from needless expensive burdens and suspensions of their laws incident to Federal Court injunctions issued on allegations that show no right to relief. The operation of this Florida law has been suspended. Complaints seeking to invalidate and suspend the operation of State laws by invoking the "vague contours" of due process can irreparably injure State governments if we accept as a "salutary principle" the rule that all such complaints — though failing to state a cause of action — raise "grave constitutional questions" which require that "the essential facts shall be determined." Under this declared "salutary principle" specially applying to bills attacking the constitutionality of legislative acts, such bills must be defended against even though they fail to state a cause of action. This is contrary to the traditional general rule that fatally defective bills are dismissed on motion (formerly demurrer) in order to prevent needless litigation, delay and expense. The application of this special principle to bills attacking State legislation seriously undermines the historical presumption of the validity of

State acts. A refusal to determine whether or not the allegations of the bill are sufficient to strike down an act until evidence has been heard adds a special burden to the defense of State legislation, as though legislation were to be presumed invalid. I do not believe this principle leads to salutary results and I am of the opinion that we should now determine whether the allegations of the bill, if proven, would entitle petitioners to relief.

Even according to the presently prevailing interpretation of the Due Process Clause of the Fourteenth Amendment, I do not believe that the averments of petitioners' bill can sustain invalidation of this duly enacted Florida statute. The statute contains a legislative finding that "certain persons, firms and corporations in the State of Florida" had engaged "in the practice" of deceiving customers into the belief that non-Florida canned citrus products had been produced in Florida. The legislature further found that this practice operated to "the injury and detriment of the producers and canners of citrus fruit and citrus juices in the State of Florida . . ." and concluded that an effective method to prevent this fraudulent practice was to require the publication of the truth upon labels and containers. Averments of petitioners' bill, in their strongest light, go no further than to dent this legislative finding. They say to require publication of the truth in this manner on the cans and labels is burdensome and violates the Due Process Clause of the Fourteenth Amendment. They further charge here that this finding of the legislature is a "feigned" assumption and that "the facts alleged [in petitioners' bill] not only show the nonexistence of any basis for such assumption but demonstrates that the law will cause serious injury to the packer and marked curtailment of the sale of citrus products grown and canned in Florida." Petitioners' argument for reversal largely involves "this disputed question as to the existence of facts concerning the basis for the law, and . . . the preamble statement of the alleged evil which gave rise to its enactment. . . ."

Because, it is said, the embossing and labelling requirements raise grave constitutional issues, the State of Florida will be required to defend against two issues raised by petitioners' bill. The State must answer the charges: first, that — contrary to the legislative finding — there was no fraudulent practice under which the dealers in canned citrus products were led to believe that they were buying Florida products when in fact the canned goods were produced outside that State; second, that truthful labelling and embossing as required by the statute would financially injure citrus growers, producers, canners and the people of Florida rather than benefit them as found by the legislature.

In attacking the legislative finding that the act would bestow benefits on the State of Florida, petitioners allege that the law would require petitioners to spend extra money for labels; might cause them to lose some business; would afford the opportunity for spoiling and swelling of some cans on the theory that embossing without spoiling is difficult and could weaken the tin of containers thereby permitting acid to corrode the steel underneath the tin; that petitioners will suffer loss because they have on their hands cans that have not been embossed; and that Florida already has laws adequate to protect itself from fraudulent sales.

With reference to a State law regulating containers (for lard) this Court has already said:

"This may involve a change of packing by the company and the cost of that change, but this is a sacrifice the law can require to protect from the deception of the old method."

2. *Extent of State Power*

The real issue raised by petitioners' bill is not the cost incident to changing from the old method of labelling and embossing, but whether the Florida legislature — convinced that fraud existed — had the constitutional right to determine the policy which it believed would protect the people of Florida from that fraud. The cause is now sent back to a Federal District Court to review the facts underlying the policy enacted into law by the legislature.

Under our constitutional plan of government, the exclusive power of determining the wisdom of this policy rested with the legislature of Florida subject to the veto power of Florida's governor. This Court has taken judicial notice of the fact that citrus fruits support one of the great industries of the State of Florida and held that it "was competent for the legislature (of Florida) to find that it was essential for the success of that industry that its reputation be preserved in other States wherein such fruits find their most extensive market." The legislators of Florida are peculiarly qualified to determine the policies relating to one of their State's greatest industries. Legislatures, under our system, determine the necessity for regulatory laws, considering both the evil and the benefits that may result. Unless prohibited by constitutional limitations, their decisions as to policy are final. In weighing conflicting arguments on the wisdom of legislation they are not confined within the narrow boundaries of a particular controversy between litigants. Their inquiries are not subject to the strict rules of evidence which have been found essential in proceedings before courts. Legislators may personally survey the field and obtain data and a broad perspective which the necessary limitations of court litigation make impossible.

The legislative history of the Florida statute under review indicates that it was given the careful and cautious consideration which regulation of one of the State's major industries deserved. Companion measures were offered in the Florida House and Senate on the same day — April 28, 1937. In the House the measure was referred to the Committee on Citrus Fruits. The existence of such a standing committee is itself indicative of a legislative procedure designed to give careful consideration to the legislation concerning this important industry. May 4, 1937, the House Committee voted to report the bill, favorably, sixteen ayes, no nays, six members absent. June 1, the bill was made the special order of business and on June 2, the companion Senate bill previously passed by that body by a vote of twenty-four to one was substituted for the House measure and passed by a vote of seventy to nothing.

In the face of this history, petitioners insist that this statute duly passed by the legislature and signed by the Governor of Florida violates the Due Process Clause as an unreasonable, capricious, unjust, harsh and arbitrary measure. Therefore, if petitioners are to obtain relief on this theory it must be found that this statute was "fixed or arrived at through an exercise of will, or by caprice, without consideration or adjustment with reference to principles, circumstances or significance"; or that it was "despotic, autocratic (or) high-handed"; or that it is "irrational, senseless" or passed by those "not endowed with reasoning ability; non-conformable to reason"; or that it is capricious or freakish which "denotes an impulsive seemingly causeless change of mind, like that of a child or a lunatic."

The cause is remanded for the court below to determine whether the legislative requirement that cans and labels be truthfully marked is arbitrary, unreasonable, capricious, unjust or harsh. This makes it necessary for the court to weigh and pass upon the relative judgment, poise and rea-

2. *Extent of State Power*

soning ability of the one legislator who voted against the
law, as contrasted with the ninety-four legislators and the
governor who favored it. I do not believe that obedience to
this carefully considered legislative enactment would violate any of petitioners' property rights without due process of law or that — even under prevailing doctrine —
the averments of the complaint indicate that no known or
supposed facts could sustain it. The allegations of the complaint in this cause raise no more than questions of policy
for legislative determination, which the Florida legislature
has already considered and which can be presented to other
legislatures in the future.

The majority opinion apparently does not decide that
Florida has no power to require that the origin of citrus
products canned in Florida shall be truthfully shown. Petitioners' bill insists that Florida exercised its power so un-
wisely as to violate rights of property without due process,
because, as alleged, canning frauds did not exist, and could
be prevented by a wiser statute, less expensive and burdensome to petitioners. Thus they challenge the wisdom of the
Florida legislation. On remand of petitioners' bill which
fails to show that the Florida law is invalid, may the
Court, on evidence outside the bill, hold that the law violates due process because the court is convinced that the
legislature might have chosen a wiser, less expensive and
less burdensome regulation? If a court in this case and
under this bill has this power, the final determination of
the wisdom and choice of legislative policy has passed from
legislatures — elected by and responsible to the people —
to the courts. I believe in the language of the *Powell* case
that since all that has been "said of this legislation is that
it is unwise, or unnecessarily oppressive to those" canning
citrus products, that "petitioners' appeal must be to the legislature . . . not to the judiciary." I would affirm.

Federal Power Commission v. Natural Gas Pipeline Company, 315 U.S. 575 (1942)

[It would probably be impossible to estimate the number of billions of dollars paid by individual and industrial consumers to railroads, electric utilities, telephone companies, and similar concerns as a result of the Supreme Court's interpretation of the due process clause. For just as the Court has taken the power to pass on the "reasonableness" of general legislation as a matter of due process, so has it claimed the power to pass on the "reasonableness" of utility rates.

For fifty years the principal controversies in this field have turned on the methods that the Supreme Court would require the states (or the federal government) to apply in setting such rates. Of these methods, the so-called "fair value" device is most favored by the utilities. As Professor Bonbright, the leading American authority on rate regulation, said in his *Public Utilities and the National Power Policies,* "Partly, I suspect, because of its very tendency to cripple effective public control over rates, the 'fair value' doctrine has been strongly supported by utility officials and company attorneys. Indeed, the fear that it may be modified, if not renounced, by the present Supreme Court is one of the reasons why some of the newer members of this Court are not popular in the utility world."

If this is so, then Justice Black must stand high on the list of utility unpopulars. He would not quibble about the methods that the Court should require for evaluation. Rather he would renounce all judicial scrutiny of rate-making under the Constitution.

In the *Natural Gas Pipeline* case the Court, in an opinion by Chief Justice Stone and joined by Justices Roberts, Reed, Frankfurter, Byrnes, and Jackson, upheld the validity of a commission order fixing rates for the sale of natural gas. Justices Black, Douglas, and Murphy filed a joint concurrence, a portion of which is included here because it so clearly states their views that courts should keep out of rate-making and that if courts are to participate in rate-making, they should not require the "fair value" method. Justice Frankfurter concurred specially to note his disagreement with the Black, Douglas, Murphy opinion.]

Mr. Justice Black, Mr. Justice Douglas, and Mr. Justice Murphy, concurring:

I

We concur with the Court's judgment that the rate order of the Federal Power Commission, issued after a fair hearing upon findings of fact supported by substantial evidence, should have been sustained by the court below. But insofar as the Court assumes that, regardless of the terms of the statute, the due process clause of the Fifth Amendment grants it power to invalidate an order as unconstitutional because it finds the charges to be unreasonable, we are unable to join in the opinion just announced.

Rate making is a species of price fixing. In a recent series of cases, this Court has held that legislative price fixing is not prohibited by the due process clause. We believe that in so holding, it has returned, in part at least, to the constitutional principles which prevailed for the first hundred years of our history. The *Munn* and *Peik* cases, decided in 1877, Justices Field and Strong dissenting, emphatically declared price fixing to be a constitutional prerogative of the legislative branch, not subject to judicial review or revision.

In 1866, four of the Justices who had voted with him in the *Munn* and *Peik* cases no longer being on the Court, Chief Justice Waite expressed views in an opinion of the Court which indicated a yielding in part to the doctrines previously set forth in Mr. Justice Field's dissenting opinions, although the decision, upholding a state regulatory statute, did not require him to reach this issue. For an interesting discussion of the evolution of this change of position, see Swisher, Stephen J. Field, 372–392. By 1890, six Justices of the 1877 Court, including Chief Justice Waite, had been replaced by others. The new court then clearly repudiated the opinion expressed for the Court by Chief Justice Waite in the *Munn* and *Peik* cases, in a holding which accorded with the views of Mr. Justice Field. Under those views, first embodied in a holding of this Court in 1890, "due process" means no less than "reasonableness judicially determined." In accordance with this elastic meaning which, in the words of Mr. Justice Holmes, makes the sky the limit of judicial power to declare legislative acts unconstitutional, the conclusion of judges, substituted for those of legislatures, become a broad and varying standard of constitutionality. We shall not attempt now to set out at length the reasons for our belief that acceptance of such a meaning is historically unjustified and that it transfers to courts powers which, under the Constitution, belong to the legislative branch of government. But we feel that we must record our disagreement from an opinion which, although upholding the action of the Commission on these particular facts, nevertheless gives renewed vitality to a "constitutional" doctrine which we are convinced has no support in the Constitution.

The doctrine which makes of "due process" an unlimited grant to courts to approve or reject policies selected by legislatures in accordance with the judges' notion of reasonableness had its origin in connection with legislative attempts to fix the prices charged by public utilities. And in no field has it had more paralyzing effects.

II

We have here, to be sure, a statute which expressly provides for judicial review. Congress has provided in Section 5 of the Natural Gas Act that the rates fixed by the Commission shall be "just and reasonable." The provision for judicial review states that the "finding of the Commission as to the facts, if supported by substantial evidence, shall be conclusive." But we are not satisfied that the opinion of the Court properly delimits the scope of that review under this Act. Furthermore, since this case starts a new chapter in the regulation of utility rates, we think it important to indicate more explicitly than has been done the freedom which the Commission has both under the Constitution and under this new statute. While the opinion of the Court erases much which has been written in rate cases during the last half century, we think this is an appropriate occasion to lay the ghost of *Smyth* v. *Ames* which has haunted utility regulation since 1898. That is especially desirable lest the reference by the majority to "constitutional requirements" and to "the limits of due process" be deemed to perpetuate the fallacious "fair value" theory of rate making in the limited judicial review provided by the Act. . . .

As we read the opinion of the Court, the Commission is now freed from the compulsion of admitting evidence on the reproduction cost or of giving any weight to that element of "fair value." The Commission may now adopt, if it chooses, prudent investment as a rate base — the base long advocated by Mr. Justice Brandeis. And for the reasons stated by Mr. Justice Brandeis in the *Southwestern Bell Telephone* case there could be no constitutional objection if the Commission adhered to that formula and rejected all others.

Yet it is important to note, as we have indicated, that Congress has merely provided in Section 5 of the Natural Gas Act that the rates fixed by the Commission shall be "just and reasonable." It has provided no standard beyond that. Congress, to be sure, has provided for judicial review. But Section 19 (b) states that the "finding of the Commission as to the facts, if supported by substantial evidence, shall be conclusive." In view of these provisions we do not think it is permissible for the courts to concern themselves with any issues as to the economic merits of a rate base. The Commission has a broad area of discretion for selection of an appropriate rate base. The requirements of "just and reasonable" embrace among other factors two phases of the public interest: (1) the investor interest; (2) the consumer interest. The investor interest is adequately served if the utility is allowed the opportunity to earn the cost of the service. That cost has been defined by Mr. Justice Brandeis as follows: "Cost includes not only operating expenses, but also capital charges. Capital charges cover the allowance, by way of interest, for the use of the capital, whatever the nature of the security issued therefor; the allowance for risk incurred; and enough more to attract capital." Irrespective of what the return may be on "fair value," if the rate permits the company to operate successfully and to attract capital all questions as to "just and reasonable" are at an end so far as the investor interest is concerned. Various routes to that end may be worked out by the expert administrators charged with the duty of regulation. It is not the function of the courts to prescribe what formula should be used. The fact that one may be fair to investors does not mean that another would be unfair. The decision in each case must turn on considerations of justness and fairness which cannot be cast into a legalistic formula. The rate of return to be allowed in any given case calls for a highly expert judgment. That judgment has been entrusted to the Commission. There it should rest.

One *caveat* however should be entered. The consumer interest cannot be disregarded in determining what is a "just and reasonable" rate. Conceivably a return to the company of the cost of the service might not be "just and reasonable" to the public.

This problem carries into a field not necessary to develop here. It reemphasizes however that the investor interest is not the sole interest for protection. The investor and consumer interests may so collide as to warrant the rate-making body in concluding that a return on historical cost or prudent investment though fair to investors would be grossly unfair to the consumers. The possibility of that collision reinforces the view that the problem of rate-making is for the administrative experts, not the courts, and that the *ex post facto* function previously performed by the courts should be reduced to the barest minimum which is consistent with the statutory mandate for judicial review. That review should be as confined and restricted as the review, under similar statutes, of orders of other administrative agencies.

Section III

PROBLEMS OF

REGULATION

Krug v. *Santa Fe Pacific Railroad Company,*
329 U.S. 591 (1947)

[Most problems of business regulation involve interpretation of statutes. The question becomes that of the meaning of a word or a phrase as used by Congress against a background of past decisions, committee reports, and legislative debates. The judge must decide whether his task is done when he has studied the word, the dictionary, and past decisions about the word, or whether his researches will take him to a view of the entire problem with which Congress dealt.

The *Krug* case is included here, not because it is itself of great significance, but because it is a good example of Black's method. In this case the issue is the interpretation of the phrase "under any grant" in a statute.

In the nineteenth century Congress gave land grants to railroads to aid their construction. It required in return specially favorable rates over those roads for government transportation. Under a 1940 Act of Congress the special government rates were ended if the railroads would release all claims against the government for lands sought by the railroads "under any grant." The Sante Fe accepted the new rates and gave the release, but contended that it had not released its claim to lands described in the opinion. The Court, in this unanimous opinion by Justice Black, held that the statutory phrase covered these lands, and held against the railroad.]

192

3. Problems of Regulation

Mr. Justice BLACK delivered the opinion of the Court.

In the first half of the Nineteenth Century the United States acquired a vast new area of sparsely populated lands in the South and West. Settlement and absorption of this territory into the older part of the country became a national problem which demanded for its solution a more rapid and extensive means of transportation of goods and people than was provided by wagons, stagecoaches, and waterways. The building of railroads largely provided the answer. They made it possible for the frontier homesteads and communities to be established on the lands of the new territory and yet maintain live contact with the national economy and culture. To encourage a rapid railroad building program, Congress chose to make public grants of a large proportion of the new lands to underwrite and subsidize the participation of private individuals and privately owned companies in the program. In this congressional program of land grants "in aid of construction" were sown the seeds of the present lawsuit.

Enormous areas of public lands were granted railroads, almost equal to the acreage of the New England States, New York and Pennsylvania combined. Execution of the land-grant program was marked by innumerable complex and unforeseen difficulties; its course has been beset by claims and counterclaims asserted by and between settlers, railroads, and Government. Congress, the executive agencies, and the courts have been repeatedly called upon to help resolve these conflicting claims. The lapse of nearly a century since the program was instituted has not resolved all of them. This lawsuit requires consideration of old and recent congressional efforts to settle these persistently recurring controversies.

One substantial field of railroad-government controversy

has been the terms of the original land-grants acts which required the railroads to carry Government goods and personnel free of tolls. By reason of judicial interpretation of these terms, as supplemented by periodic legislation, land-grant railroads for more than half a century immediately prior to 1940 transported for the Government at one-half of the standard commercial rates. During the depression years beginning in the late 1920's and immediately following, railroad earnings declined considerably, and a movement began to relieve the roads of their land-grant rate obligations. Studies by some Government selected agencies recommended legislation for outright repeal of the provisions for rate concessions to the Government. Bills to accomplish this in the 75th and 76th Congresses failed to pass. But Section 321 of the Transportation Act of 1940 provided that land-grant roads could, by compliance with specified conditions, collect from the Government full commercial rates, except for the transportation of military and naval freight and personnel. In brief, it required that a railroad, to qualify for full rates, must execute within a year after passage of the Act, a release of any claim it might have "against the United States to lands, interest in lands, compensation, or reimbursement on account of lands or interests in lands, which have been granted, claimed to have been granted, or which it is claimed should have been granted to such carrier or any . . . predecessor in interest *under any grant* to such carrier or such predecessor in interest as aforesaid."

Shortly after passage of this Act respondent took advantage of it, and gave the Government a release framed substantially in the words of the Statute. Its predecessor in interest had obtained a grant to lands in Arizona and New Mexico, under an Act of 1866 containing the usual governmental rate concession terms. The 1866 Act had specifically recited that if the Government, because of prior settlement of part of the granted lands by homesteaders, could not give possession to some of the lands granted to the railroad, it could select, under the direction of the Secretary of the Interior, other public lands in lieu of them as an indemnity. Respondent had large outstanding claims against the Government for these "indemnity" lands when it signed the release and conceded that the release extinguished these claims.

But it had other so-called lieu land claims against the Government which it asserts were not extinguished. The railroad urges that these claims are not covered by the Act or the release. They, allegedly, are not claims "on account of" or "under any grant" of lands, but rest on contractual exchanges of congressional effort to settle conflicts among railroads, Government, and settlers which arose by reason of settlement by homesteaders on railroad-granted lands after the grants had been made. Both Acts provided that where settlers had so occupied railroad-granted lands, the railroad could, upon relinquishment of its title to them, select other lands in lieu of them. Before the 1940 Act, respondent had, under the 1874 and 1904 Acts, relinquished title to the Government to certain lands previously granted. In August 1940, and subsequently in March 1943, respondent filed applications with the Secretary of the Interior to select its lieu lands. After the respondent signed the release, and because of it, the Secretary rejected the applications. The railroad then filed this suit in a Federal District Court for relief by injunction or by way of mandamus to require the Secretary and other Interior Department officials to pass on its applications without regard to the release. The District Court dismissed the bill on the merits, holding that the statute and release barred the claims. It read the 1940 Act as defining a congressional purpose "to wipe the slate clean of such claims by any railroad which enjoyed the benefits of the rate concessions made by the Transportation Act. . . ." The Court of Appeals for the District of Columbia reversed, holding, as respondent urges in this Court, that the 1940 Act did not apply to the type of claims involved here. The importance of the question decided caused us to grant certiorari.

We agree with the District Court. We think, as it held, that the Secretary of the Interior's construction of the 1940 Act was clearly right. Therefore, we do not discuss the Government's contention that, since the Secretary's construction was a reasonable one, it was an allowable exercise of his discretion which should not be set aside by injunction or relief in the nature of mandamus.

The respondent argues the case here as though the 1940 Act only applied to claims for "lands under any grant." The language is not so narrow. It also required railroads to surrender claims for "*compensation, or reimbursement* on account of lands, or interests in lands which have been granted, claimed to have granted, or which it is claimed should have been granted . . . under any grant." This language in itself indicates a purpose of its draftsmen to utilize every term which could possibly be conceived to give the required release a scope so broad that it would put an end to future controversies, administrative difficulties, and claims growing out of land grants. Beyond a doubt the words "compensation" and "reimbursement" as ordinarily understood would describe a payment to railroads in money or in kind for the surrender of lands previously acquired by them "under a grant." If they do not have this meaning, their use in the Act would have been hardly more than surplusage. And when viewed in the context of the historical controversies and claims under the land grants, the conclusion that the 1940 Act covers claims such as respondent's seems inescapable.

The legislative history of the Act shows that Congress was familiar with these controversies. In 1929 it passed an Act intended to authorize and require judicial determination of land grant claims of the Northern Pacific Railroad in order — finally and completely — to set them at rest. The suit authorized by that Act was tried in a Federal District Court and was pending in this Court when the 1940 Act was passed. Our decision in it shows the complexity and ramifications of the numerous questions involved in land grant controversies. Reference to this case was made by Government officials in urging Congress to include in the predecessors of the 1940 Act a requirement that the railroad surrender all claims arising out of land grants as a prerequisite to any Government rate concessions. Here, as in the 1929 Act, which applied to the claims of only one railroad, we think Congress intended to bar any future claims by all accepting railroads which arose out of any or all of the land-grant acts, insofar as those claims arose from originally granted, indemnity or lieu lands. All the Acts here involved, the Acts of 1866, 1874, 1904, and 1940 relate to a continuous stream of interrelated transactions and controversies, all basically stemming from one thing — the land grants. We think Congress wrote finis to all these claims for all railroads which accepted the Act by executing releases.

National Labor Relations Board v. *Waterman Steamship Corporation*, 309 U.S. 206 (1940)

[Of all the New Deal statutes, the National Labor Relations Act has probably caused the greatest controversy. The statute has been repeatedly before the Court for interpretation and application, and Justice Black has been a consistent exponent of the view that the Board should be given full opportunity and responsibility for carrying out its duties.

The most difficult issue under the act has been the determination of the proper boundaries between Labor Board supremacy and judicial review. Early in its career the Board was blocked by federal court injunctions, and later it was almost as completely stopped by the refusal of the federal courts to enforce its orders. Black has contributed materially to the reversal of that policy by the courts. He has invariably insisted that the courts must not substitute their judgment for that of the Labor Board so long as Congress gives to the Board the primary responsibility for deciding whether particular labor practices are fair or unfair.

The *Waterman* case deals with this problem. The Board found that Waterman had drydocked two ships and discharged a number of employees working on those ships because the employees had affiliated with C.I.O. unions. The case first came before the Fifth Circuit Court of Appeals, which covers the states of the deep South, on a petition by the Board to compel the company to mend its ways. That Court refused to issue the order and in turn was reversed and was ordered to issue it in a unanimous opinion of the Supreme Court written by Justice Black. The quoted portions of the opinion include only one of the three factual issues discussed.]

Mr. Justice BLACK delivered the opinion of the Court.

The court below, upon petition of respondent to set aside an order of the Labor Board, decided that the Board's order was not supported by substantial evidence, said the order was based on mere suspicion, and declined to enforce it. Whether the court properly reached that conclusion is the single question here.

We do not ordinarily grant certiorari to review judgments based solely on questions of fact. In its petition, however, the Board earnestly contended that the record before the Court of Appeals had presented "clear and overwhelming proof" that the Waterman Steamship Company had been guilty of a most flagrant mass discrimination against its employees in violation of the National Labor Relations Act, and that the court had unwarrantedly interfered with the exclusive jurisdiction granted the Board by Congress. The Board's petition also charged that the present was one of a series of decisions in which the court below had failed "to give effect to the provisions of the Act that the findings of the Board as to facts, if supported by evidence, shall be conclusive."

In that Act, Congress provided, "The findings of the Board, as to the facts, if supported by evidence, shall . . . be conclusive." It is of paramount importance that courts not encroach upon this exclusive power of the Board if effect is to be given the intention of Congress to apply an orderly, informed and specialized procedure to the complex administrative problems arising in the solution of industrial disputes. As it did in setting up other administrative bodies, Congress has left questions of law which arise before the Board — but not more — ultimately to the traditional review of the judiciary. Not by accident, but in line with a general policy, Congress has deemed it wise to entrust the finding of facts to these specialized agencies. It is essential that courts regard this division of responsibility which Congress as a matter of policy has embodied in the very statute from which the Court of Appeals derived its jurisdiction to act. And therefore charges by public agencies constitutionally created — such as the Board — that their duly conferred jurisdiction has been invaded so that their statutory duties cannot be effectively fulfilled, raise questions of high importance. For this reason we granted certiorari. . . .

Respondent, the Waterman Company, has taken the position that when the crews of the "Bienville" and "Fairland" received their wages and signed off statutory articles in Mobile, all tenure of employment and employment relationship of these men were at an end. From this premise, the Company insists that vacancies were created as the men signed off and, under an outstanding contract with the I.S.U., preference in filling these vacancies had to be given to members of the I.S.U. unless contractual obligations were to be violated. However, the Board contends that the signing off of articles when the ship's voyage ended at Mobile served only to end employment "in respect of the past voyage or engagement" and, therefore, it proceeded to examine the evidence to determine whether there was, after completion of the voyages in question of the "Bienville" and "Fairland," a continuing relationship, tenure, term or condition of employment between the Company and its men. The Act provides that

"It shall be an unfair labor practice for an employer — To interfere with . . . (the employees' right of self-organization).

"By discrimination in regard to hire or tenure of employment or any term or condition of employment to encourage or discourage membership in any labor organization. . . ."

The protection to seamen embodied in the Federal statutes which have been referred to has existed in some form since the earliest days of the Nation. This statutory plan was never intended to forbid the parties from mutually undertaking to assure a crew the right to continue as employees and to re-sign if it desires after signing off articles at a voyage's end. The design was to protect seamen from being carried to sea against their will; to prevent mistreatment as to wages and to assure against harsh application of the iron law of the sea during voyages. The Board, therefore, properly heard evidence as to whether the crews of the "Bienville" and "Fairland" had, unless discharged for cause, a continuing tenure or relationship entitling them to re-sign when the temporary lay-ups of their ships ended. If, as the Board found, there were such continuing tenure and customary term or condition of employment, of course no vacancies occurred when the men of the "Bienville" and the "Fairland" signed off articles in Mobile. And respondent's contract with the I.S.U., which only provided preferential treatment of the I.S.U. (A.F. of L.) in filling vacancies, did not require the Company to discharge the N.M.U. (C.I.O.) men from these ships.

If, therefore, there was substantial support in the evidence for the findings that these crews had a continuing right to and customary tenure, term or condition of employment within the purview of the Act even though their ships were temporarily laid up, and that this relationship was terminated by the Company because of the crews' C.I.O. relationship, the court below was required to enforce the Board's order. . . .

Evidence of discrimination because of C.I.O. affiliation. About July 1, 1937, the entire crew of the "Bienville" and all but three of the "Fairland," previously I.S.U. (A.F. of L.), joined the N.M.U. (C.I.O.) in Tampa, Florida. Such action had been decided on in June by the crew of the "Bienville" while she was in Le Havre, France. After the crew of the "Bienville" changed to the C.I.O. at Tampa and before she reached Mobile, the A.F. of L. representative at Tampa informed the A.F. of L. representative at Mobile, by telephone, that the change had taken place. And the Mobile A.F. of L. representative "at that time" notified the Waterman Company of the change. Intervening scheduled stops of the "Bienville" were cancelled by a memorandum purporting to have been written on July 1 and ordering her to Mobile to "go on inactive status for a period of about twenty days." The port captain of the Waterman Company, who signed this memorandum, stated that it was written on July 1, "to the best of . . . [his] knowledge." He added that it had not been written until after the "Bienville" was on her return voyage from Le Havre. That was after the ship's crew had, in assembly, determined to turn C.I.O. No such cancellation was directed to the "Fairland." The "Fairland," he testified, was laid up because periodic repairs "were due." On the other hand, her master had no knowledge of any contemplated lay-up until she reached Mobile, and understood, according to advice given him, that she was laid up because "she was behind schedule . . . and they put her back to the next sailing." The Waterman port captain thought she was laid up because repairs "were due"; he had no knowledge that it was because she was behind schedule. Her master's testimony showed,

"Q. The laying-up plan, then, had been something that was contemplated in Tampa?"

"A. No, sir."

"Q. It was something that came into existence after you sailed from Tampa and before you came to Mobile, is that right?"

"A. Yes."

The "Fairland" is equipped with radio.

The ships were in Mobile by July 6. There was testimony that a member of the crew of the "Bienville," on the sixth, was asked by the executive vice-president of the Company why the change of unions was made and was told by that official "a man has to use his own head." This same witness testified that several of the discharged crew were given some work ashore and that "on a Saturday afternoon we collected three days pay, they held back two days in the

week, and about three o'clock in the afternoon the first
assistant came around there and I was working on some
safety valves on the boilers, and . . . [the assistant port
engineer of Waterman Company] said, 'Well, I got a
chance to fire you at last,' and I said, 'What is it?' And he
said, 'Well, you can get the rest of your money when you
are finished,' and I said, 'What's the matter, aren't we going to sail the ship?' And he said, 'No, not unless you go
back to the other place,' and I said, 'What other place?'
And he said, 'The I.S.U.' "

Pelletier, the steward on the "Bienville," worked for
Waterman from 1934 until discharged after joining the
N.M.U. (C.I.O.). When the "Bienville" arrived at Mobile,
Waterman's port steward went to the boat, and talked with
the mate, who informed him that some of the men had
joined the N.M.U. According to the port steward's testimony, he then asked the mate, "How is the Steward's Department?" and the mate replied, "Well, some of them
joined the N.M.U." ". . . and later on I [the port stew-
ard] found the steward in his room. . . . I asked Pelletier
did he join the N.M.U. and he said, 'Yes,' and I said 'What
about the rest of your crew?' and he said, 'Well, they all
did.' I asked him did they have any reason for it, and he
said, 'Yes, everybody did,' so I said, 'All right' and I left
the ship." He returned to the Company's office. Two hours
later, he came back to the ship, charged Pelletier with in-
competency and discharged him. Pelletier testified that the
port steward, when told that the crew and Pelletier had
turned N.M.U., said, "Well I have got orders to lay you
all off." Pelletier had been promoted just prior to the voyage in question. A new I.S.U. man was put on to finish up
his work and remained on as watchman practically the full
time the "Bienville" was laid up.

Although her captain had, prior to the coming aboard of

a Company official, expressed a desire to keep the "Fair-land's" crew, as one of her crew testified, the crew was informed by this official that they could not sail, "but if you take your books and give them to . . . the I.S.U. you can keep your jobs"; another Waterman official "told me I could not sail on any Waterman steamship as long as I was an N.M.U. man." According to this witness, he had left his clothes on the "Fairland" and slept aboard ship when she was in drydock with the understanding he would re-sign; he was, however, ordered off the ship.

An engineer on the Waterman vessel "Azalea City," eight years with the Company, O'Connor, a member of the M.E.B.A. (also affiliated with the C.I.O.), testified that he acted as spokesman for other engineers on his ship in complaining about working conditions, hours of employment, and rates of pay; when he discussed the complaint with the Company's representative, during July, he was told to take a vacation and left the ship on a promise of a more desirable job; neither the vacation, the promised job, nor re-employment of any kind was ever given him. . . .

One of the men who was given temporary repair work — subsequent to the Board's telegram of the seventh — testified:

"Q. While you were a member of the N.M.U., did you ever wear your N.M.U. badge or button?"

"A. Yes, Sir; I used to wear it on my cap, on the dock, while I was working down there."

"Q. Was there ever anything said to you at the Waterman Steamship about wearing it?"

"A. Mr. Ingram told me I would have to take that Maritime Union button off if I wanted to stay around there, and I took it off, and put it in my pocket." . . .

All of this is not to say that much of what has been related was uncontradicted and undenied by evidence offered

by the Company and by the testimony of its officers. We
have only delineated from this record of more than five
hundred pages the basis of our conclusion that all of the
Board's findings, far from resting on mere suspicion, are
supported by evidence which is substantial. The Court of
Appeals' failure to enforce the Board's order resulted from
the substitution of its judgment on disputed facts for the
Board's judgment — and power to do that has been denied
the courts by Congress. Whether the court would reach the
same conclusion as the Board from the conflicting evidence
is immaterial and the court's disagreement with the Board
could not warrant the disregard of the statutory division
of authority set up by Congress.

The cause is reversed and remanded to the Court of Appeals with directions to enforce the Board's order in its
entirety.

United States v. *Bethlehem Steel Corporation, et al.,* 315 U.S. 289 (1942)

[Control of war profits is one of the recurrent problems of
federal regulation, and Black feels that excessive profiteering
in war-time is nothing short of sinful. He feels that Congress
has abundant power to prevent war profits, whether by regulation, taxation, or government operation. At the same time
he believes that Congress must work out the program for
profit control, and he does not believe that the courts will help
solve the problem by hearing an occasional action for fraud.

In this most famous of his war-profits opinions Black held
at the very beginning of the recent war that the government
could not rely on fraud or duress actions for profit control
in the usual cases, and the opinion was so written as to come
close to inviting Congress to take comprehensive action to
control profits. Congress, in part as a response to that invitation, soon passed the Renegotiation Act, which provided

a comprehensive machinery for profit control, and under which, in conjunction with the tax laws, several billion dollars were cut off war profits.

This case arose because during the first World War the government entered into a contract for ships with a Bethlehem subsidiary. Under that contract Bethlehem claimed a profit of $24,000,000, or about twenty-two per cent, on ships the "actual cost" of which was $109,000,000. (In addition, among other benefits, Bethlehem Steel, the parent corporation, received such profits as there were on 43,000 tons of steel sold at maximum prices to its subsidiary shipbuilding corporation.) In this case the government sought to get back a portion of that profit and to avoid paying the remainder.

Justice Black delivered the opinion of the Court, upholding Bethlehem. He was joined by Justices Roberts, Reed, and Byrnes. Justice Murphy concurred specially, and Justice Douglas concurred in part and dissented in part. Justice Frankfurter dissented, and Chief Justice Stone and Justice Jackson did not participate. Excerpts from the opinion follow.]

Mr. Justice BLACK delivered the opinion of the Court.

III

. . . The Government further argues that if the half-savings clause must be taken as permitting Bethlehem to participate in savings however caused, the contracts are invalid because unconscionable. In invoking the asserted doctrine of unconscionability claimed to be applicable here, the government relies entirely upon the alleged existence of two elements: duress and profits grossly in excess of customary standards. And for reasons we shall set out, neither of these two elements exists here.

Duress. The word "duress" implies feebleness on one side, overpowering strength on the other. Here it is suggested that feebleness is on the side of the government of the

United States, overpowering strength on the side of a single private corporation. Although there are many cases in which an individual has claimed to be a victim of duress in dealings with the government, this, as far as we know, is the first instance in which the government has claimed to be a victim of duress in dealings with an individual.

The argument by which the petitioner seeks to establish that the contracts were made under duress is essentially this: Germany's submarine warfare made it imperative that the government secure the greatest possible number of ships in the shortest possible time; there was a scarcity of ships and shipbuilding facilities in the United States; Bethlehem, the largest shipbuilder in the world, not only had shipbuilding facilities available, but also a trained organization; at a time when Bethlehem's facilities and trained organization were vital to the prosecution of the war, it declined to accept terms proposed by the government, but insisted upon prices which some of the government's representatives thought too high; although Congress had authorized the Executive to commandeer shipbuilding facilities if necessary, Bethlehem's organization was also needed and the government was without power to compel performance by an unwilling organization; the government therefore had to accept contracts on whatever terms Bethlehem proposed or, doing without the ships which Bethlehem could produce, run the risk of military defeat.

Two basic propositions underlie this argument: (1) The government's representatives involuntarily accepted Bethlehem's terms, (2) The circumstances permitted the government no other alternative.

Upon reviewing the negotiations between the representatives of the government and the representatives of Bethlehem, we cannot find support for the first proposition. The Master found, and the courts below agreed, that "the contracts resulted from negotiations in which both parties were represented by intelligent, well informed and experienced officers whose sole object was to make the best trade possible, under conditions which included the uncertainties of war time contingencies, the results from which were not and could not have been known at the time the contracts were made." Two of the three principal negotiators for the Fleet Corporation have testified in the proceedings before the Master. It is abundantly clear from their testimony that, during the course of the negotiations, they did not consider themselves compelled to accept whatever terms the other side proposed. In the disposition of the two main differences between the negotiators there is no evidence of that state of overcome will which is the major premise of the petitioner's argument of duress. . . .

The other major difference between the negotiators was on the matter of price. There is evidence that some of the Fleet Corporation's representatives considered Bethlehem's demands high, but we cannot conclude that the figure finally accepted by the Fleet Corporation was accepted because its representatives felt themselves powerless to refuse. On the contrary, Bethlehem by letter voluntarily offered to accept contracts on terms to be fixed by the Fleet Corporation's general manager. This offer was rejected, one of the Fleet Corporation's negotiators testifying that it preferred to make contracts rather than assume the attitude of dictating terms. Moreover, the general manager of the Fleet Corporation, in whom final authority was vested and who approved these contracts, was of the opinion that high estimated cost figures would be advantageous to the government because "care must be exercised that they be not placed at too low a figure, for if they are, the probabilities are that the contractor will lose interest in keeping the cost down." And one of the negotiators for the Fleet Corporation has given

testimony that he was not so much concerned with the cost
as with speed of production since "legislation was already
in the offing in the form of war profit taxes . . . to take
care of extreme cases." We must therefore conclude that
the negotiations do not show that Bethlehem forced the
government's representatives to accept contracts against
their will.

If the negotiations do not establish duress, the government finds it in the circumstances themselves. The petitioner concedes that the government could have commandeered Bethlehem's plants, but it contends that if the plants
had been commandeered, Bethlehem's organization would
have been unwilling to serve the government in them. Heavy
reliance is placed on an observation in the Master's report
that "the Government did not have power to compel performance by an unwilling organization." We shall later
consider the alleged lack of power. We now point out that
the alleged unwillingness is an assumption unsupported by
findings or evidence. Since the possibility of commandeer-
ing appears not even to have been suggested to Bethlehem,
we have no basis for knowing what its reaction would have
been. We cannot assume that if the negotiations failed to
produce contracts acceptable to both sides, Bethlehem would
have refused to contribute to the war effort except under
legal compulsion. We cannot lightly impute to Bethlehem's
whole organization, composed as it was of hundreds of
people, such an attitude of unpatriotic recalcitrance in the
face of national peril.

But even if we were to assume, as we do not, an initial
attitude of unwillingness, we do not think that the government was entirely without means of overcoming it. For the
representatives of the Fleet Corporation, an agent of the
United States, came to Bethlehem armed with bargaining
powers to which those of no ordinary private corporation

can be compared. If it chose to, the Fleet Corporation could have foregone all negotiation over price, compelling Bethlehem to undertake the work at a price set by the President with the burden of going to court if it considered the compensation unreasonably low. And the power to commandeer Bethlehem's entire plant and facilities, in accordance with authority specifically delegated by the President, provided the Fleet Corporation with an alternative bargaining weapon difficult for any company to resist.

Profits. The general common law rule of unconscionability on which the petitioner relies is said to deny enforcement to contracts when the profits provided for are grossly in excess of a standard established by common practice. Whether there is such a rule, what is its scope, and whether it is part of the body of law governing these contracts, we need not decide. For high as Bethlehem's 22% profit seems to us, we are compelled to admit that so far as the record or any other source of which we can take notice discloses, it is not grossly in excess of the standard established by common practice in the field in which Congress authorized the making of these contracts. And in particular, it may be added, the Master found that the ships built by Bethlehem cost the government less than comparable ships built by other shipbuilders. The government made no attempt to establish, nor is there any indication in the record, that the profits realized by other shipbuilders were any less than Bethlehem's.

If the profits earned under government contracts in general are taken as the standard of comparison the 22% claimed here is overshadowed in too many instances for it to be regarded as extraordinary. The Hughes report referred to above, for example, points out that most of the airplane production during the last war was under contracts providing for much higher profits. To take an example of profits made on food products, the Federal Trade Commission determined that in 1917, profits on the sales of salmon canneries, a major portion of whose output was purchased by the government, ranged from 15 to 68% of cost, averaging 52%. In the shipbuilding industry itself, even in peace times, profits were found by a special committee of the Senate which investigated the munitions industry to have been from 25% to 37% on the cruisers built in 1927, about 22% in 1929, and of like range for other years.

If the comparison is made with industrial profits, not limited to profits on government contracts alone, the 22% asked for here likewise loses all claim to distinction. An exhibit, the accuracy of which the government has not challenged, incorporated into the record of this case, indicates that in terms of profit on gross sales, the largest American steel company made 49, 58, and 46% during the years 1916, 1917, and 1918. As computed by the Federal Trade Commission, net earnings in 1917 of the same company on all its business were 25% of total investment, and the Commission cites instances of other steel companies whose earnings thus measured ranged from 30 to 320%. Profits of lumber producers, again in terms of return on investment, ranged as high as 121%; and of producers of petroleum products, as high as 122%, over half of the industry earning more than 20%. During the first six months of 1917, one of the two major sulphur producers in the country sold its product at an average price of $18.11 per ton, more than 200% above cost which was $5.73 per ton; the other major producer earned 236% on its investment during the first eleven months of the same year. The Federal Trade Commission's collection of data for various other industries, a collection which the Commission stated was "by no means a complete catalog," affords many additional examples of the same kind. But further confirmation should be unnecessary for a conclusion no businessman would question: that the profits claimed here, seen in their commercial environment, cannot be considered exceptional.

The profits claimed here arise under contracts deliberately let by the Fleet Corporation under authority delegated by the President in accordance with an Act of Congress. Neither Congress nor the President restricted the freedom of the Fleet Corporation to grant measures of profits common at the time. And the Fleet Corporation's chosen policy was to operate in a field where profits for services are demanded and expected. The futility of subjecting this choice of policy to judicial review is demonstrated by this case, coming to this Court as it does more than twenty years after the ships were completed. In any event, we believe the question of whether or not this policy was wise is outside our province to decide. Under our form of government we do not have the power to nullify it, as we believe we should necessarily be doing, were we to declare these contracts unenforceable on the ground that profits granted under Congressional authority were too high. The profits made in these and other contracts entered into under the same system may justly arouse indignation. But indignation based on the notions of morality of this or any other court cannot be judicially transmuted into a principle of law of greater force than the expressed will of Congress.

IV

The problem of war profits is not new. In this country, every war we have engaged in has provided opportunities for profiteering and they have been too often scandalously seized. To meet this recurrent evil, Congress has at times

3. Problems of Regulation

taken various measures. It has authorized price fixing. It has placed a fixed limit on profits, or has recaptured high profits through taxation. It has expressly reserved for the government the right to cancel contracts after they have been made. Pursuant to Congressional authority, the government has requisitioned existing production facilities or itself built and operated new ones to provide needed war materials. It may be that one or some or all of these measures should be utilized more comprehensively, or that still other measures must be devised. But if the Executive is in need of additional laws by which to protect the nation against war profiteering, the Constitution has given to Congress, not to this Court, the power to make them.

Associated Press v. *United States,* 326 U.S. 1 (1945)

[As a citizen and as a Senator, Black believed that the Sherman Antitrust Act should be enforced rigorously against every form of monopoly. As a Supreme Court Justice he interprets the Sherman Act so as to enforce it against every form of monopoly. As he declared as a Senator, he very strongly believes that the successful maintenance of the capitalist system requires the maintenance of free competitive enterprise, and he conceives of the laws against restraints of trade as the statutory expression of the policy for free competitive enterprise.

The *Associated Press* case shows Black's willingness to apply the act to a combination of publishers. The case was an antitrust action brought by the United States against the Associated Press, charging that, under all the circumstances, certain bylaws of the Associated Press violated the Sherman Act. The A.P. is a co-operative association of more than twelve hundred members which collects news and disseminates it to the members. Under the bylaws, members could not sell news to non-members, and any member could easily block a non-member from membership. This meant, for example, that

213

the *Chicago Sun*, a morning competitor of the *Chicago Tribune*, could not get the Associated Press news without the *Tribune's* consent, which was not forthcoming.

The majority opinion, written by Justice Black and joined by Justices Douglas and Rutledge, held that the A.P. was restraining trade by its monopoly of the dissemination of the news. Justices Frankfurter and Douglas filed concurring opinions and Justices Roberts and Murphy and Chief Justice Stone dissented. Justice Jackson did not participate.]

Mr. Justice BLACK delivered the opinion of the Court.

The By-Laws provide a very simple and non-burdensome road for admission of a non-competing applicant. The Board of Directors in such case can elect the applicant without payment of money or the imposition of any other onerous terms. In striking contrast are the By-Laws which govern admission of new members who do compete. Historically, as well as presently, applicants who would offer competition to old members have a hard road to travel. . . .

In 1931, the By-Laws were amended so as to extend the right of protest to all who had been members for more than 5 years and upon whom no right of protest had been conferred by the 1900 By-Laws. In 1942, after complaints to the Department of Justice had brought about an investigation, the By-Laws were again amended. These By-Laws, presently involved, leave the Board of Directors free to elect new members unless the applicants would compete with old members, and in that event the Board cannot act at all in the absence of consent by the applicant's member competitor. Should the old member object to admission of his competitor, the application must be referred to a regular or special meeting of the Association. As a prerequisite to election, he must (a) pay to the Association 10% of the

3. *Problems of Regulation*

total amount of the regular assessments received by it from old members in the same competitive field during the entire period from October 1, 1900 to the first day of the month preceding the date of the election of the applicant, (b) relinquish any exclusive rights the applicant may have to any news or news picture services and when requested to do so by his member competitor in that field, must "require the said news or news picture services, or any of them, to be furnished to such member or members, upon the same terms as they are made available to the applicant," and (c) receive a majority vote of the regular members who vote in person or by proxy. These obstacles to membership, and to the purchase of A.P. news, only existed where there was a competing old member in the same field.

The court below found, and we think correctly, that the By-Laws on their face, and without regard to their past effect, constitute restraints of trade. Combinations are no less unlawful because they have not as yet resulted in restraint. An agreement or combination to follow a course of conduct which will necessarily restrain or monopolize a part of trade or commerce may violate the Sherman Act, whether it be "wholly nascent or abortive on the one hand, or successful on the other." For these reasons the argument, repeated here in various forms, that A.P. had not yet achieved a complete monopoly is wholly irrelevant. Undisputed evidence did show, however, that its By-Laws had tied the hands of all of its numerous publishers, to the extent that they could not and did not sell any part of their news so that it could reach any of their non-member competitors. In this respect the Court did find, and that finding cannot possibly be challenged, that A.P.'s By-Laws restrained the sale of interstate news to non-members who competed with members.

Inability to buy news from the largest news agency, or

any one of its multitude of members, can have most serious effects on the publication of competitive newspapers, both those presently published and those which, but for these restrictions, might be published in the future. This is illustrated by the District Court's finding that in 26 cities of the United States, existing newspapers already have contracts for A.P. news and the same newspapers have contracts with United Press and International News Service under which new newspapers would be required to pay the contract holders large sums to enter the field. The net effect is seriously to limit the opportunity of any new paper to enter these cities. Trade restraints of this character, aimed at the destruction of competition, tend to block the initiative which brings newcomers into a field of business and to frustrate the free enterprise system which it was the purpose of the Sherman Act to protect.

It has been argued that the restrictive By-Laws should be treated as beyond the prohibitions of the Sherman Act, since the owner of the property can choose his associates and can, as to that which he has produced by his own enterprise and sagacity, efforts or ingenuity, decide for himself whether and to whom to sell or not to sell. While it is true in a very general sense that one can dispose of his property as he pleases, he cannot "go beyond the exercise of this right, and by contracts or combinations, express or implied, unduly hinder or obstruct the free and natural flow of commerce in the channels of interstate trade." The Sherman Act was specifically intended to prohibit independent businesses from becoming "associates" in a common plan which is bound to reduce their competitor's opportunity to buy or sell the things in which the groups compete. Victory of a member of such a combination over its business rivals achieved by such collective means cannot consistently with the Sherman Act or with practical, everyday knowledge be attributed to *individual* "enterprise and sagacity"; such hampering of business rivals can only be attributed to that which really makes it possible — the collective power of an unlawful combination. That the object of sale is the creation or product of a man's ingenuity does not alter this principle. It is obviously fallacious to view the By-Laws here in issue as instituting a program to encourage and permit full freedom of sale and disposal of property by its owners. Rather, these publishers have, by concerted arrangements, pooled their power to acquire, to purchase, and to dispose of news reports through the channels of commerce. They have also pooled their economic and news control power and, in exerting that power, have entered into agreements which the District Court found to be "plainly designed in the interest of preventing competition."

It is further contended that since there are other news agencies which sell news, it is not a violation of the Act for an overwhelming majority of American publishers to combine to decline to sell their news to the minority. But the fact that an agreement to restrain trade does not inhibit competition in all of the objects of that trade cannot save it from the condemnation of the Sherman Act. It is apparent that the exclusive right to publish news in a given field, furnished by A.P. and all of its members, gives many newspapers a competitive advantage over their rivals. Conversely, a newspaper without A.P. service is more than likely to be at a competitive disadvantage. The District Court stated that it was to secure this advantage over rivals that the By-Laws existed. It is true that the record shows that some competing papers have gotten along without A.P. news, but morning newspapers, which control 96% of the total circulation in the United States, have A.P. news service. And the District Court's unchallenged finding was that "A.P. is a vast, intricately reticulated organization, the largest of its kind, gathering news from all over the world, the chief single source of news for the American press, universally agreed to be of great consequence."

Nevertheless, we are asked to reverse these judgments on the ground that the evidence failed to show that A.P. reports, which might be attributable to their own "enterprise and sagacity," are clothed "in the robes of indispensability." The absence of "indispensability" is said to have been established under the following chain of reasoning: A.P. has made its news generally available to the people by supplying it to a limited and select group of publishers in the various cities; therefore, it is said, A.P. and its member publishers have not deprived the reading public of A.P. news; all local readers have an "adequate access" to A.P. news, since all they need do in any city to get it is to buy, on whatever terms they can in a protected market, the particular newspaper selected for the public by A.P. and its members. We reject these contentions. The proposed "indispensability" test would fly in the face of the language of the Sherman Act and all of our previous interpretations of it. Moreover, it would make that law a dead letter in all fields of business, a law which Congress has consistently maintained to be an essential safeguard to the kind of private competitive business economy this country has sought to maintain.

Finally, the argument is made that to apply the Sherman Act to this association of publishers constitutes an abridgement of the freedom of the press guaranteed by the First Amendment. Perhaps it would be a sufficient answer to this contention to refer to the decisions of this Court. It would be strange indeed, however, if the grave concern for freedom of the press which prompted adoption of the First Amendment should be read as a command that the government was without power to protect that freedom. The First

Amendment, far from providing an argument against application of the Sherman Act, here provides powerful reasons to the contrary. That Amendment rests on the assumption that the widest possible dissemination of information from diverse and antagonistic sources is essential to the welfare of the public, that a free press is a condition of a free society. Surely a command that the government itself shall not impede the free flow of ideas does not afford nongovernmental combinations a refuge if they impose restraints upon that constitutionally guaranteed freedom. Freedom to publish means freedom for all and not for some. Freedom to publish is guaranteed by the Constitution, but freedom to combine to keep others from publishing is not. Freedom of the press from governmental interference under the First Amendment does not sanction repression of that freedom by private interests. The First Amendment affords not the slightest support for the contention that a combination to restrain trade in news and views has any constitutional immunity.

Hartford-Empire Company v. *United States,*
323 U.S. 386 (1945)

[Modern antitrust litigation divides into two quite distinct parts. The first is the determination of whether the defendant has operated in restraint of trade. The second is determining what to do about it. Today the antitrust laws are weakly enforced because the courts, although they frequently find the defendants in violation, are tender in their application of penalties.

The Black position is that violation of the antitrust law is a serious business, and that the remedy should be sufficient to stop it. This issue sometimes takes the form of a controversy over whether a monopoly that is based on abuses of patents should thereafter be allowed to keep the patents and charge others for them, or whether such a monopoly should be required to make the patents available without charge. In the *Hartford-Empire* case defendants were charged with monopolizing the production of glassmaking machinery, the restricting of the making of glass products, and controlling glass prices. Four members of the Court, in an opinion by Justice Roberts, joined by Justices Reed and Frankfurter and Chief Justice Stone, found that the defendants were violating the law. The Roberts opinion eliminated, however, a provision in the order of the trial court which required that the defendants should thereafter license others without royalty to use the patents upon which the defendants' illegal monopoly had been constructed. Justices Black and Rutledge dissented on this point. Justices Douglas, Murphy, and Jackson did not participate.]

Mr. Justice BLACK, dissenting in part:

I agree with the Court's judgment insofar as it sustains the decree of the District Judge.

I cannot, however, agree to many of the modifications of that decree. These appellants have violated the antitrust laws. The District Court's decree, taken as a whole, is an effective remedy, admirably suited to neutralize the consequences of such violations, to guard against repetition of similar illegal activities, and to dissipate the unlawful aggregate of economic power which arose out of, and fed upon, monopolization and restraints. Many of this Court's modifications seriously impair the decree and frustrate its purposes.

It would probably serve no useful purpose to state at length the reasons which justify the District Court's decree, since they are set forth clearly and well in its opinion. In particular, however, it is my belief that any reasonable assurance that these appellants will not continue to violate the antitrust law requires that we leave intact the District Court's decree.

The District Court found that these defendants started out in 1916 to acquire a monopoly on a large segment of the glass industry. Their efforts were rewarded by complete success. They have become absolute masters of that domain of our public economy. They achieved this result largely through the manipulation of patents and licensing agreements. They obtained patents so as to retain their dominance in that industry. The history of this country has perhaps never witnessed a more completely successful economic tyranny over any field of industry than that accomplished by these appellants. They planned their monopolistic program on the basis of getting and keeping and using patents, which they dedicated to the destruction of free competition in the glass container industry. Their declared object was "To block the development of machines which might be constructed by others . . ." and "To secure patents on possible improvements of competing machines, so as to 'fence in' those and prevent their reaching an improved state." These patents were the major weapons in the campaign to subjugate the industry; they were also the fruits of appellants' victory. The restoration of competition in the glass container industry demands that appellants be deprived of these weapons. The most effective way to accomplish this end is to require, as the District Court did, that these patents be licensed royalty free.

The decree of the court below was well-fashioned to prevent a continuation of appellants' monopolistic practices. The decree as modified leaves them free, in a large measure, to continue to follow the competition-destroying methods by which they achieved control of the industry. In fact, they have received much milder treatment from this Court than they anticipated. This is shown by a memorandum of one of

Hartford's officers made in 1925. That memorandum, which discussed plans for suppression of a number of competitors, with particular reference to possible prosecutions under the Sherman Act, read in part as follows:

"Of course, the court might order that we transfer the entire Federal licensing business to some other party and turn over to that party the Federal patents. This, of course, would simply restore to a certain extent the existing situation and establish a competitor. . . . I . . . do not see much danger of having any of these deals upset. . . . If they are upset, I still believe that by that time, we will be in a better position even with such dissolution than we would be otherwise; and I see no danger whatsoever of any criminal liability because the cases are necessarily so doubtful in the matter of law that they could never get any jury to convict and I doubt if any prosecuting officer would ever attempt any criminal action. Criminal action in cases of this sort, so far, has practically been non-existent."

I would sustain the decree of the District Court, for the reasons it gave, in all of the paragraphs mentioned.

Goodyear Company v. *Ray-O-Vac Company,* 321 U.S. 275 (1944)

[A patent is for all practical purposes a monopoly granted to the inventor, or to the corporation that hires an inventor, to exploit the results of the invention for a certain period of time. As such, every patent is a legal exception to the general policy of our laws against monopoly. Black would confine the patent system strictly, so as not to encroach upon the normal principles of competition except where the Constitution and laws clearly authorize that encroachment. Hence he is very strict in his standard of invention, for the Court is not supposed to approve of a patent unless a genuine invention is involved.

3. Problems of Regulation

In this case the issue was the validity of a patent for a leakproof dry cell for a flashlight battery. The Court, in an opinion by Justice Roberts, joined by Chief Justice Stone and Justices Reed, Frankfurter, and Rutledge, upheld the invention. Justice Black dissented, joined by Justices Douglas and Murphy. Justice Jackson dissented separately.]

Mr. Justice BLACK dissenting:

Those who strive to produce and distribute goods in a system of free competitive enterprise should not be handicapped by patents based on a "shadow of a shade of an idea." The practice of granting patents for microscopic structural or mechanical improvements inevitably must reduce the United States Patent Office to a mass production factory for unearned special privileges which serve no purpose except unfairly to harass the honest pursuit of business. If the patentee here has "discovered" anything, it is that the creamy substance in a dry cell will not leak through a steel jacket which covers and is securely fastened to the ends of the cell. For that alleged discovery this patent is today upheld. I do not deny that someone, somewhere, sometime, made the discovery that liquids would not leak through leakproof solids. My trouble is that, despite findings to the contrary, I cannot agree that this patentee is that discoverer. My disagreement is not based solely on the narrow ground that the record shows previous patents have been issued to others who put jackets of metal and other substances around dry cells. Antiquarians tell us that the use of solid containers to hold liquids predated the dawn of written history. That the problem of the quality and strength of the walls of such containers was one to which ancient people turned their attention appears from the widespread currency at an early age of the maxim that "new wine should not be put in old bottles." It is impossible for me to believe that Congress intended to grant monopoly privileges to persons who do no more than apply knowledge which has for centuries been the universal possession of all the earth's people — even those of the most primitive civilizations.

Interstate Commerce Commission v. *Inland Waterways,* 319 U.S. 671 (1943)

[The regulatory activities of Congress affect every group in society, and the next four opinions are selected because they show typical problems for three such groups. The *Inland Waterways* opinion is of interest because it indicates the general attitude with which Black approaches problems concerning farmers as a group. This case raises the traditional conflict between farmers and their transportation companies, and finds Black indignant at a momentary triumph for the railroads which he considers wholly unauthorized by statute.

In this case certain of the Eastern railroads filed proposed rates with the Interstate Commerce Commission requiring that grain brought to Chicago by water be shipped from Chicago to the East at a higher rate than grain brought to Chicago by train. The practical effect of this section would be to deprive farmers of the benefit of the low-cost barge system leading from the inland waterways to Chicago and would instead force them to use railroad transportation at greater expense.

For various reasons of procedure and substance the Court left the proposed Eastern railroad rates in effect. Justice Jackson wrote the majority opinion, joined by Chief Justice Stone and Justices Roberts, Reed, and Frankfurter. Justice Black filed a dissent from which these exceptions are taken, in which Justices Douglas and Murphy joined. Justice Rutledge did not participate.

This is one of the hardest-hitting dissents Black has ever written. The same problem returned to the Court in 1947 in

somewhat different procedural posture and Black then wrote
the opinion of the Court, in effect sustaining the views expressed here in dissent.]

Mr. Justice BLACK, dissenting:

The issue in this case is whether the farmers and shippers
of the middle west can be compelled by the Interstate Commerce Commission and the railroads to use high priced rail
instead of low priced barge transportation for the shipment
of grain to the east. I agree that, in the words of Division 2
of the Commission, "this record is replete with complexities
and technicalities" which have almost, but I think not quite,
successfully obscured that simple issue. The District Court,
which held that the Interstate Commerce Commission's order
"discriminates against water competition by the users of
barges" understood the issue. The railroads, which proposed the increase in the cost to barge shippers, also understood the issue as is shown by the frank statement of their
representatives at the Commission hearing: "We made this
proposal, as I have stated several times, and filed these tar-
iffs with the hope that we could drive this business off of the
water and back on the rails where it belongs. . . . We are
not in love with water transportation . . . and we believe
that we are entitled to that grain business." From behind
a verbal camouflage of "complexities and technicalities"
there emerges one single easily understandable question:
Railroads pick up grain in Chicago which may be brought
there by rail, lake transport, or inland waterway barge. Is
it lawful for a railroad to deprive midwestern grain farmers and shippers of the benefits of cheap barge transportation by charging a higher tariff for re-shipment of grain
originally transported to Chicago by barge than the same
railroad charges for re-shipment of the same grain from

Chicago to the same places when the grain is brought to the re-shipping point by rail or by lake?

I think that approval of this tariff is a defiance of the Transportation Act of 1940. This Act declared it to be "the national transportation policy of the Congress to provide for fair and impartial regulation of all modes of transportation subject to the provisions of this Act, so administered as to recognize and preserve the inherent advantages of each." The Act commands the Interstate Commerce Commission that "all of the provisions of this Act shall be administered and enforced with a view to carrying out the above declaration of policy." Congress, fearful, in the words of several members, that the Commission was "essentially a railroad minded body," took every precaution to prevent discrimination against water carriers.

Senators, particularly those from the midwestern states where the barge lines involved here were operating, were especially fearful that the Commission would do substantially what it has done in this case. They required repeated assurance by the Chairman of the Interstate Commerce Committee of the Senate that the bill was written in such manner that the Commission could not if it desired permit discrimination against water carriers. At great length the Chairman of that Committee explained to the apprehensive Senators that the bill contained provisions in three different places which imposed upon the Commission the imperative duty of standing in constant opposition to discrimination against shippers by water.

House Members shared the same fears. The first conference report was defeated in the House because it was believed that the bill did not offer adequate protection for water carriers against hostile Interstate Commerce Commission action. A proponent of the bill told the House that "It is not fair to suggest, in my opinion, that the Commission and the courts will not look to this declaration of policy whenever they are called upon to make such construction of the statute and application of it. . . . The specific provisions of the bill carry out the declaration of policy. The courts and commissions will recognize that. . . ." Defending the policy provisions as a complete protection against Commission action antagonistic to barge transportation, another sponsor of the bill, opposing a safeguarding amendment, declared that to consider it necessary "You will have to further assume that the Interstate Commerce Commission will not enforce it. You will have to assume that if a case goes to the courts, the courts will neither construe nor enforce the provisions of this policy." As I see it, the Commission in this case has declined to enforce Congress's policy and the Court has failed to construe and enforce the Act as Congress clearly intended it should.

This is not all. The first conference report having been defeated, the second conference report brought in changes intended to offer more protection to water carriers. The conferees reported that: "This measure will place upon the Interstate Commerce Commission, not only the power, but the duty, to protect and foster water transportation and preserve its inherent advantages." As a closing, clinching argument intended to persuade the House that the Commission would be fair to water carriers, the statement of Commissioner Eastman (who dissented from the order of the Commission here) was quoted. Eastman assured the Congressmen interested in water transportation that certain provisions of the bill "coupled with the admonition in the declaration of policy in section 1 that the provisions of the act be so administered as to recognize and preserve the inherent advantages of each mode of transportation, will afford adequate protection in this respect. If experience should show that further protection is needed, contrary to our expectation, Congress can amend the act, but such a restriction as is now proposed is, we believe, both unnecessary and undesirable."

Although these proceedings were not initiated under the 1940 Act, the Commission should have felt itself bound by that congressional expression of policy. Yet the legislative history just recited makes it clear that the Commission has flagrantly flouted the express mandate of Congress. It is said, however, that the Commission reserves the right to take further action in a "proper proceedings" in which it "*might* prescribe proportional rates (on the ex-barge traffic) or joint barge-rail rates lower than the combinations." At some future day the Commission may correct this discrimination. But the day for Commission action was the day this case was decided, and the day for action by this Court is now. The Commission is not bound by the technical procedures of the common law, and it should not strain to avoid the enforcement of congressional will because of the formal fashion in which questions are presented to it.

Congressman Bland, who opposed the 1940 Act on the ground that it lacked sufficient safeguards to prevent action by the Commission hostile to water transportation, called attention to the procedural delays in rate cases before that body, delays which he declared would be used to strangle financially weak water carriers, forcing them to "yield or transfer their operation to other streams." He pointed out this "would mean the death of water carriers"; that the railroads knew how to obtain delay and knew the disastrous consequences that would follow to their competitors; that railroads "seek to profit" by procedural delay; and that the diversity of their interests and extent of their revenues was so great that they could survive delays which would be unendurable for their competitors. The Congressman was a good observer and a sound prophet.

United States v. *Jackson,* 302 U.S. 628 (1938)

[Even in our formalized legal system a judge cannot completely separate his notions about law from his notions about justice. To Black it is a basic principle of justice that veterans who have served their country should not be precluded by legal higgling or technicality from receiving any awards that their country has promised them. Where the law is reasonably open to a construction favoring the veteran, Black gives it that construction.

The *Jackson* case illustrates this attitude. During the first World War it was the practice of the Government to allow soldiers one hundred and twenty days after enlistment in which to take out insurance, and they were credited with having applied for the insurance if they were killed or totally and permanently disabled within that time even though they had not made formal application. This was called "automatic insurance." The Economy Act of 1933 cut off certain previously existing veterans' benefits. Justice Black for a unanimous Court found that the Economy Act did not affect "automatic insurance" and hence that a soldier's son could recover. The conclusion of the opinion follows.]

Mr. Justice BLACK delivered the opinion of the Court.

It is to be remembered that automatic insurance applied to that particular group of American soldiers who either were killed, died, or became wholly or permanently incapacitated before they had a reasonable opportunity to obtain insurance of any kind. It may be that Congress did not believe it proper to economize at the expense of those veterans who came out of the army with health completely destroyed or to the detriment of the beneficiaries of soldiers who lost their lives in service without a reasonable opportunity to apply for insurance.

Certainly the reason which prompted the passage of the express provisions of Section 401 is such that, in the absence of subsequent legislation equally express, they are not overthrown by mere inference or implication. Only clear and unequivocal language would justify a conclusion that benefits, provided by a grateful government because of death and permanent incapacity of its soldiers, are to be wholly withdrawn for reasons of economy. Special provisions benefiting either soldiers who became incurably helpless in the Army or the dependents of soldiers who died or were killed in the service of their country cannot justifiably be repealed by implication. There is no irreconcilable conflict between Section 401 and the Economy Act and effect can reasonably be given to both. The judgment of the Court of Appeals is therefore

Affirmed.

Tiller v. Atlantic Coast Line Railroad, 318 U.S. 54 (1943)

[This opinion is chosen for two reasons: First, because it illustrates one of Black's deepest convictions, the conviction that injuries to workmen are as much a part of the cost of industry as raw materials or building construction, and that industry should pay all its costs. Second, because as a matter of the technique of opinion-writing, the case illustrates particularly well Black's efforts to understand and interpret the law by getting at the factors that underlie the law. This opinion is unedited and is printed with citations and footnotes in order that the lay reader may see one opinion in

3. Problems of Regulation

the form in which it is actually recorded in the United States Reports.

In this case the plaintiff's husband, a railroad policeman, was killed by a train while making an inspection. His widow brought this action for damages under the Federal Employers' Liability Act, and lost in the lower courts because of a belief by those courts that the husband had "assumed the risk." The Supreme Court in this opinion by Justice Black held that this was no defense. Justice Frankfurter concurred specially.]

Mr. Justice BLACK delivered the opinion of the Court.

The petitioner's husband and intestate, John Lewis Tiller, was a policeman for the respondent railroad. Among his duties was that of inspecting the seals on cars in railroad yards to make sure that no one had tampered with them. He had held this position for some years, was familiar with the yard, and was aware, in the words of the court below, that respondent's employees "are instructed that they must watch out for the movement of the trains as no employee watches out for them and no lights are used at night on the head end of back-up movements except when an employee is placed at the back end with a lantern to protect a road crossing." The Circuit Court of Appeals found that there was evidence sufficient to sustain the following account of the tragedy:

On the night of March 20, 1940, Tiller was standing between two tracks in the respondent's switch yards, tracks which allowed him three feet, seven and one-half inches of standing space when trains were moving on both sides. The night was dark [1] and the yard was unlighted. Tiller, using

[1] It was so dark that when the engineer after the accident asked the fireman to pick up an object near the tracks, the fireman replied, "No, I am afraid to go down in the dark by myself; you come with me."

a flashlight for the purpose, was inspecting the seals of the train moving slowly on one track when suddenly he was hit and killed by the rear car of a train backing in the opposite direction on the other track. The rear of the train which killed Tiller was unlighted although a brakeman with a lantern was riding on the back step on the side away from Tiller. The bell was ringing on the engine but both trains were moving and the Circuit Court found that it was "probable that Tiller did not hear cars approaching" from behind him. No special signal of warning was given.

Petitioner brought this suit to recover damages under the Federal Employers' Liability Act, 45 U.S.C. Section 51 *et seq.* The complaint alleged negligent operation of the car which struck defendant and failure to provide a reasonably safe place to work. Respondent denied negligence, pleaded contributory negligence on the part of the defendant, and set up as a separate defense that the deceased had assumed all the risks "normally and necessarily incident to his employment." After the plaintiff's evidence had been heard the defendant moved for a directed verdict on the grounds (a) that the evidence disclosed no actionable negligence and (b) that the cause of the death was speculative and conjectural. The motion was granted, judgment was accordingly entered for the defendant and the Circuit Court of Appeals, interpreting the decision of the district court as resting on a conclusion that the evidence showed no negligence, affirmed. 128 F. 2d 420. This result was based on a holding that the deceased had assumed the risk of his position and that therefore there was no duty owing to him by respondent. We granted certiorari because of the important question involved in the Circuit Court of Appeals' interpretation of the scope and effect of the 1939 amendment to the Federal Employers' Liability Act, 53 Stat. 1404, 45 U.S.C. 54. The amendment provides that an "employee shall not be held to have assumed the risks of his employment in any case where such injury or death resulted in whole or in part from the negligence of any of the officers, agents, or employees of such carrier."

The Circuit Court distinguished between assumption of risk as a defense by employers against the consequence of their own negligence, and assumption of risk as negating any conclusion that negligence existed at all. The court reasoned that if, for example, the respondent had negligently failed to provide a workman with a sound tool, and he was thereby injured, it could not under the amendment claim that he had assumed the risk of using the defective implement; but that if a workman were injured in the ordinary course of his work, as in such a switching operation as this, the assumption of risk might still be relied upon to prove that the respondent had no duty to protect him from accustomed danger. The court rejected petitioner's argument that since the doctrine of assumption of risk had been abolished "the carrier can no longer interpose it as a shield against the consequences of its neglect and hence is liable for injuries to its employees in its railroad yards or elsewhere, unless it takes precautions for their safety commensurate with the danger that they are likely to encounter." In rejecting this argument the court below put the core of its decision in these words: "The conclusion is inescapable that Congress did not intend to enlarge the obligation of carriers to look out for the safety of their men when exposed to the ordinary risks of the business, and that in circumstances other than those provided for in the amended section of the statute, *the doctrine of the assumption of the risk must be given its accustomed weight.*"

We find it unnecessary to consider whether there is any merit in such a conceptual distinction between aspects of assumption of risk which seem functionally so identical, and hence we need not pause over the cases cited by the court below, all decided before the 1939 amendment, which treat assumption of risk sometimes as a defense to negligence, sometimes as the equivalent to non-negligence.[2] We hold that every vestige of the doctrine of assumption of risk was obliterated from the law by the 1939 amendment, and that Congress, by abolishing the defense of assumption of risk in that statute, did not mean to leave open the identical defense for the master by changing its name to "non-negligence." As this Court said in facing the hazy margin between negligence and assumption of risk as involved in the Safety Appliance Act of 1893, "Unless great care be taken, the servant's rights will be sacrificed by simply charging him with assumption of the risk under another name"; [3] and no such result can be permitted here.

Perhaps the nature of the present problem can best be seen against the background of one hundred years of master-servant tort doctrine. Assumption of risk is a judicially created rule which was developed in response to the general impulse of common law courts at the beginning of this period to insulate the employer as much as possible from bearing the "human overhead" which is an inevitable part of the cost — to someone — of the doing of industrialized business.[4] The general purpose behind this devel-

---

[2] See, e.g., Toledo, St. L. R. v. Allen, 276 U.S. 165, 171, 172; Mo. Pac. Co. v. Aeby, 275 U.S. 426, 430. It is sometimes said that courts have held the master blameless in actions by employees who have entered and remained in hazardous occupations on the premises that the employee assumed the risk; but the theory has not always appeared under the name "assumption of risk" since the same result is reached by assigning a given case to one of three practically interchangeable categories: (a) the employee assumed the risk; (b) he was guilty of contributory negligence; (c) the master was not negligent. See 35 Am. Jur. 719 and 8 Labatt, Master and Servant, 2d ed. par. 1164–1172, 1205, 1210. The court below thought the Amendment eliminated defense (a) but in effect retained defense (c).

[3] Schlemmer v. Buffalo, Rochester, etc. Ry., 205 U.S. 1, 12, 13.

[4] The following table drawn from the 51st through the 55th Reports

opment in the common law seems to have been to give maximum freedom to expanding industry.[5] The assumption of risk doctrine for example was attributed by this Court to "a rule of public policy, inasmuch as an opposite doctrine would not only subject employers to considerable and often ruinous responsibilities, thereby embarrassing all branches of business," but would also encourage carelessness on the part of the employee.[6] In the pursuit of its general objective the common law took many forms and developed many doctrines. One of the first was the fellow servant-assumption of risk rule which originated in *Priestly* v. *Fowler.*[7] In *Priestly* v. *Fowler,* the Court said, "The servant is not bound to risk his safety in the service of his master, and may, if he thinks fit, decline any service in which he reasonably apprehends injury to himself; and in

---

of the Interstate Commerce Commission, indicates that a substantial number of railroad employees are killed and injured each year:

Employees Killed and Injured on Steam Railways

	Killed	*Injured*
1936	593	9,021
1937	557	9,294
1938	386	6,481
1939	400	6,988
1940	475	7,956

[5] See 35 Am. Jur. 717; and for discussion of this view see Pound, Economic Interpretation of Torts, 53 Harv. L. Rev. 365, 373.

[6] Tuttle *v.* Detroit, G. H. & M. R., 122 U.S. 189, 196. Representative Claiborne, advocating a bill to abolish assumption of risk as a defense under the Federal Employers' Liability Act at a Committee Hearing in the 75th Congress, expressed a contrary view as to the usefulness of the doctrine as an accident preventive: "The Courts went along and commenced to weave into the decisions this assumption of risk doctrine. . . . They said for one thing that it is good public policy to hold the employee liable when he knew of certain conditions and did not protect himself against them; that by doing that, you made the man better regard his two legs, or better regard his two hands, or better regard his stomach. Why, no employee of a railroad company is going out there and lose an arm or an eye or a leg and rely on a jury to make him whole." Hearings before Sub-committee Number 4 of the Committee on the Judiciary, House of Representatives, 75th Cong., 1st Session, on H.R. 5755, H.R. 7336, and H.R. 7621, p. 62.

[7] 3 M. & W. 1, 6 (Ex. 1837); on the question of which was the first case creating this doctrine, cf. Chicago M. & St. P. R. Co. *v.* Ross, 112 U.S. 377, 386.

most of the cases in which danger may be incurred, if not in all, he is just as likely to be acquainted with the probability and extent of it as the master."

As English courts lived with the assumption of risk doctrine they discovered that the theory they had created had become morally unacceptable but of such legal force that it could not be repudiated.[8] The English sought to eliminate the fellow servant rule, which placed the burden of an employee's negligence as it affected another employee on the injured person rather than on the business enterprise, by the Employers' Liability Act of 1880[9] and found that the assumption of risk doctrine still left the employee in a hopelessly unprotected position. In the leading case of *Thomas* v. *Quartermaine*, 18 Q.B.D. 685 (1887), the court held that an employee standing on a three foot runway between two unfenced vats who was attempting to dislodge a piece of wood from one of the vats and who by accident fell into the other and was scalded was barred from recovery. Since he had long known of the possible dangers of the narrow passage he was held to have assumed the risk of his position. In 1897 the English finally abandoned the common law remedy altogether as a protection for injured employees and adopted a workmen's compensation law. 60 & 61 Vict. c. 37.

[8] "Morally speaking, those who employ men on dangerous work without doing all in their power to obviate the danger are highly reprehensible, as I think the company were in the present instance. The workman who depends on his employment for the bread of himself and his family is thus tempted to incur risks to which, as a matter of humanity, he ought not to be exposed. But looking at the matter in a legal point of view, if a man, for the sake of employment, takes it or continues in it with a knowledge of its risks, he must trust himself to keep clear of injury." Woodley v. Metropolitan Dist. Ry. Co., L.R. 2 Ex. Div. 384 (1877).

[9] For brief discussion of the English experience see Packer, Workmen's Compensation, Sen. Doc. 618, 62nd Cong., p. 5; Cohen, Workmen's Compensation in Great Britain, chap. 5. For an account covering the history of English and American Workmen's Compensation laws see Dodd, Administration of Workmen's Compensation, chaps. 1 & 2.

3. Problems of Regulation

This Court accepted the assumption of risk doctrine as applied to railroad employees, at least in part, in 1879.[10] That decision placed the employee's assumption of risk upon the theory that an agreement to assume the risk was implied from the terms of the employment contract.

Prior to the passage of the Federal Employers' Liability Act of 1906 the assumption of risk doctrine, except for a considerable vagueness as to its relation with contributory negligence, was fairly well known.[11] It had already been applied generally at the time of the adoption of the Act because of acceptance of the theory that the employee's compensation was based upon the added risk to his position and that he could quit when he pleased. *Tuttle* v. *Milwaukee Railway, supra;* and compare for a restatement of this view after the passage of the Employers' Liability Act, *Seaboard Air Line* v. *Horton,* 233 U.S. 492, 504.[12] Federal and state courts, with some notable exceptions, accepted and applied the rule with all of its implications and consequences except when expressly prohibited from doing so by statute.[13]

[10] Hough *v.* Texas & Pac. Railroad Co., 100 U.S. 213, 217. See also Narramore *v.* Cleveland, etc. Ry. Co., 96 F. 298 (C. C. A. 6, 1899).

[11] See Warren, Volenti Non Fit Injuria, etc., 8 Harv. L. Rev. 457 (1895); Bohlen, Voluntary Assumption of Risk, 20 Harv. L. Rev. 14, 91 (1906).

[12] Senator Neely, sponsor of the 1939 amendment, explicitly rejected the economic theory which was the basis of the early opinions: "The contention that you have advanced apparently implies the theory that the employee . . . voluntarily assumed the risk in spite of the fact that the employer said, in effect, 'You take the risk or you get no job.' In these days when millions of unemployed must find work in order to save themselves and their families from distress, the situation is so desperate that men will sign any sort of waiver or agreement in order to obtain employment." Hearings, Subcommittee of the Senate Judiciary Committee, 76th Cong., 1st Session, on S. 1708, p. 33.

[13] For collections of early state cases, see 49 L.R.A. 33 and 97 Amer. State Rep. 877. Early state and foreign statutes are summarized in the Report of the House Judiciary Committee on the 1906 Act, Rept. No. 2335, p. 2, and decisions on state statutes are collected in the Am. State Rep. note, 891. The Seaboard Air Line case, *supra,* held these statutes inapplicable to actions under the federal act.

Congress took a major step toward modification of the common law barrier against employee recovery in accident suits in the Federal Employers' Liability Act of 1906, 34 Stat. 232, repassed with alterations not material in 1908, 35 Stat. 65. This Act, in its principal features, abolished the fellow servant rule, substituted comparative negligence for the strict rule of contributory negligence, and allowed survivors' actions for tort liability. Section 4 of that Act, as interpreted by this Court in *Seaboard Air Line Railway* v. *Horton, supra,* perpetuated the defense of assumption of risk.[14] Unfortunately, from the standpoint of legal clarity, the Act as interpreted required careful distinction between assumption of risk and contributory negligence, since assumption of risk was an absolute bar to recovery while contributory negligence merely reduced the amount of recovery. The great uncertainty existing prior to the Act as to what the margin between these doctrines was [15] thus became of real significance. The language of the statute itself seemed to impel the courts to practice "the niceties if not casuistries of distinguishing between assumption of risk and contributory negligence, conceptions which never originated in clearly distinguishable categories but were loosely interchangeable until the statute attached such vital differences to them." *Pacheco* v. *N.Y., N.H. & H. R. Co.,* 15 F. 2d 467 (C. C. A. 2, 1926). For an attempt to distinguish between the doctrines, see *Schlemmer* v. *Buffalo Rail-*

[14] For a vigorous attack on this decision, see Buford, Assumption of Risk Under the Federal Employers' Liability Act, 28 Harv. L. Rev. 163; and see Peterson, The Joker in the Federal Employers' Liability Act, 80 Cent. L. J. 5. The House Judiciary Committee in reporting a bill aimed at making some minor modification in the assumption of risk rule stated that the 1908 Congress never "dreamed, when it passed this former law, that this defense (assumption of risk) would ever be raised by the use of" Section 4 of the Act. Report of the House of Representatives Committee on Judiciary, 76th Cong., 1st Sess., Rept. No. 1222, on H.R. 4988, p. 4.

[15] See 49 L.R.A. 33, 49 (Relation Between Defenses of Assumption of Risk and Contributory Negligence), and 35 Am. Jur. 719 (Pragmatic Distinctions Shown to be Lacking).

way, supra, 205 U.S. 12, and the same case at 220 U.S. 590, 596.

The assumption of risk clause in the statute became the subject of endless litigation. The Federal Code Annotated, and the United States Code Annotated, devote over 30 pages of fine type merely to the citation and brief summary of the reported decisions and the number of unreported and settled cases in which the defense was involved must run into the thousands.[16] Aside from the difficulty of distinguishing between contributory negligence and assumption of risk many other problems arose. One of these was the application of the "primary duty rule" in which contributory negligence through violation of a company rule became assumption of risk. *Unadilla Valley Ry.* v. *Caldine,* 278 U.S. 139; *Davis* v. *Kennedy,* 266 U.S. 147. Other complications arose from the introduction of "promise to repair," "simple tool," and "peremptory order" concepts into the assumption doctrine.[17] In the disposition of cases the question of a plaintiff's assumption of risk has frequently been treated simply as another way of appraising defendant's negligence,[18] as was done by the court below in the instant case.

It was this maze of law which Congress swept into discard

---

[16] For some analysis of the cases, see Note, 32 Col. L. Rev. 1384, 53 Harv. L. Rev. 341, 71 A.L.R. 451, 89 A.L.R. 693. For an estimate of their quantity see Schoene and Watson, Workmen's Compensation on Interstate Railways, 47 Harv. L. Rev. 389, 394.

[17] "In thousands of cases the doctrine is complicated by 'promise to repair,' 'peremptory order,' and other special incidents. The 'simple tool' doctrine also arose as an exception. The 'promise to repair' aspect of the question is further confused by two superimposed theories; that the employee may rely upon such promise for a reasonable time and, next, that if the danger was so manifest that no reasonable person would act upon such promise, then assumption of risk is reestablished." House Committee Report, *supra,* Note 14, p. 4. For a collection of citations on all of the assumption of risk problems, see 2 Roberts, Federal Liability of Carriers, 2nd ed., Chapter 39. For a discussion of the "simple tool" doctrine see Jacob *v.* New York, 315 U.S. 752, 756.

[18] Harper, The Law of Tort, 292.

with the adoption of the 1939 amendment to the Employers' Liability Act, releasing the employee from the burden of assumption of risk by whatever name it was called. The result is an Act which requires cases tried under the Federal Act to be handled as though no doctrine of assumption of risk had ever existed.

If this were not sufficiently clear from the language of the amendment, any doubt would be dissipated by its legislative history. The 1939 bill [19] was introduced by Senator Neely and was supported at the hearings by the railway labor unions. It was accepted both by the unions and the railroads that the bill would utterly and completely abolish the defense of assumption of risk.[20] The report of the Senate Judiciary Committee struck at the basic reasons advanced by common law courts for the existence of the doctrine, declared it unsuited to present day activities, and described them as out of harmony with the equitable principles which should govern determinations of employer-employee responsibilities.[21] The bill, as described in the

[19] S. 1708, 76th Cong., 1st Session.

[20] Substantially the same proposal as that finally adopted in 1939 was before the 75th Congress in H.R. 7336. The chief labor exponent of that bill said: The "bill in its nature is intended to relieve the servant from the assumption-of-risk doctrine as interpreted and applied by our United States Supreme Court." Hearings, *supra*, Note 6, p. 69. Or, as it was put by the principal railroad representative at the 1939 Senate hearings, "Here . . . the proposal is to abolish the defense of assumed risk, to abolish it in toto." Hearings, Note 12, *supra*, p. 37, 38.

[21] "But such simple doctrines do not apply equitably under the complexities of modern industrial practices when one's fellow servants may be numbered by hundreds or even thousands, and unlimited output and maximum speed are watchwords on every hand. The common-law doctrine of assumption of risk, as applied to the worker in a small factory, cannot be fairly applied to the railroad man, whose services are performed over 150 miles of railroad track, or in a large and congested railroad yard.

"The present rule apparently ignores the fact that the master, and not the servant, has control over the conditions which affect the safety of employees. . . . The existing rule not only permits the employer to be careless about the condition of his premises, but, in effect, places a premium upon his carelessness. . . .

"Under present economic conditions, employees must, of necessity, report, was clearly aimed at making the principles of comparative negligence the guiding rules of decision in accident cases: "The adoption of this proposed amendment will, in cases in which no recovery is now allowed, establish the principle of comparative negligence which permits the jury to weigh the fault of the injured employee and compare it with the negligence of the employer, and, in the light of the comparison, do justice to all concerned." [22]

The purpose of the Act is made clearer upon analysis of the House bill which was rejected by the conference committee in favor of the Senate bill which is now the law. The House bill [23] was intended to preserve some part of the doctrine of assumption of risk, preserving that defense except "where said employee had not had actual notice of any negligently maintained condition or practice." The bill, unlike the Senate bill as the Representative reporting it explained, left untouched the rule of *Toledo, St. L. & W. R. Co.* v. *Allen*, 276 U.S. 165, "namely, that in the absence of special custom or unusual circumstances, a man who is run over by a switching movement cannot recover." [24] It was the Allen opinion on which the court below in the instant case particularly relied. But the House bill, which the chief railroad counsel appearing before the Senate Com-

---

continue to work under unsafe conditions or frequently sacrifice the fruits of many years of accumulated seniority, go on relief, or beg their bread."

Report of the Senate Committee on Judiciary, 76th Cong., 1st Sess., Rept. No. 661, p. 4.

22 One statement by the bill's chief supporter at the Senate Hearings comes very close to covering the instant case: "It gets back to our original argument that the courts have so enlarged upon this doctrine that we are confronted with such a situation as this: A poor fellow working in a yard, intent upon his work, and somebody kicks a car on top of him, and the courts, notwithstanding he has no knowledge of it, if he is struck, hold that he has no right to recover. It may be that he was negligent, but again I say the comparative negligence doctrine should be applied." Hearings, Note 12, *supra*, p. 78.

23 H. R. 4988, 76th Cong., 1st Sess.

24 House Report, Note 14, *supra*, p. 6.

mittee conceded would make no change in the existing law,[25] was rejected in conference. The *Allen* case was specifically and caustically discussed at the Senate hearings, and the Senate bill was clearly aimed at ending its rule.[26]

The doctrine of assumption of risk can not be "abolished in toto" [27] and still remain in partial existence as the court below suggests. The theory that a servant is completely barred from recovery for injury resulting from his master's negligence, which legislatures have sought to eliminate in all its various forms of contributory negligence, the fellow servant rule, and the assumption of risk, must not, contrary to the will of Congress, be allowed recrudescence under any other label in the common law lexicon. The Act of 1908 and the amendment of 1939 abolish the post-*Priestly* v. *Fowler* defenses and authorize comparison of negligence instead of barring the employee from all recovery because of contributory negligence. They leave for practical purposes only the question of whether the carrier was negligent and whether that negligence was the proximate cause of the injury.

In this situation the employer's liability is to be determined under the general rule which defines negligence as the lack of due care under the circumstances; or the failure to do what a reasonable and prudent man would ordinarily have done under the circumstances of the situation; or doing what such a person under the existing circumstances would not have done.[28] A fair generalization of the rule is given in the Senate Committee report on the 1939 amendment: "In justice, the master ought to be held liable for

[25] Senate Hearings, Note 12, *supra*, p. 61.
[26] Senate Hearings, Note 12, *supra*, p. 14, 17, 76, 81.
[27] *Supra*, Note 20.
[28] Baltimore P. R. Co. *v.* Jones, 95 U.S. 439, 442; Texas & Pacific Railway *v.* William K. Barrett, 166 U.S. 617, 619; Grand Trunk Railroad Co. *v.* Ives, 144 U.S. 408.

injuries attributable to conditions under his control when they are not such as a reasonable man ought to maintain in the circumstances." [29] Of course in any case the standard of care must be commensurate to the dangers of the business. *Hough* v. *Texas & P. Railway Co.*, 100 U.S. 213, 218; cf. *Northern Pacific Railroad Co.* v. *Herbert*, 116 U.S. 642, 652.

No case is to be withheld from a jury on any theory of assumption of risk and questions of negligence should under proper charge from the court be submitted to the jury for their determination. Many years ago this court said of the problems of negligence, "We see no reason, so long as the jury system is the law of the land, and the jury is made the tribunal to decide disputed questions of fact, why it should not decide such questions as these as well as others." *Jones* v. *E. Tennessee etc. Railroad Co.*, 128 U.S. 443, 445. Or as we have put it on another occasion, "Where the facts are in dispute, and the evidence in relation to them is that from which fair-minded men may draw different inferences," the case should go to the jury.[30]

We think that the question of negligence on the part of the railroad and on the part of the employee should have been submitted to the jury. The decision below is reversed

[29] Sen. Report, *supra,* Note 21, p. 4.

[30] Washington etc. Railroad Co. *v.* McDade, 135 U.S. 554, 572. See also Kane *v.* North Central Railway, 128 U.S. 91, 95, 96; Hough *v.* Texas & Pacific Co., *supra,* 225; Jacob *v.* City of New York, 315 U.S. 752, 757. It appears to be the clear Congressional intent that, to the maximum extent proper, questions in actions arising under the Act should be left to the jury: "At the beginning this defense (assumption of risk) was deemed to be at most a jury question. But repeated holdings have encroached more and more upon the right of the employee and various new doctrines or amplifications of previous principles have tended constantly to treat this defense as one to be determined by the courts as 'matter of law' — taking it away from the jury; and the courts have decided now it is a question of law." House Report, *supra,* Note 14, p. 1. Cf. Delaware etc. R. Co. *v.* Koske, 279 U.S. 7, 11; Toledo, St. Louis, and W. R. Co. *v.* Allen, 276 U.S. 165, 170.

and the case is remanded for further proceedings in conformity with this opinion.

It is so ordered.

Mr. Justice FRANKFURTER concurred specially.

Galloway v. *United States,* 319 U.S. 372 (1943)

[Justice Black has probably done as much to restore the civil jury to a place of effectiveness in American law as any judge of the twentieth century. The Seventh Amendment of the Constitution requires that there shall be juries in civil suits in the federal courts. For a hundred years this Amendment had been interpreted in such fashion as to whittle down the power of that jury. Perhaps it is because Black long ago discovered that in the American legal system the best friend of the injured veteran and the injured workman is the average juror that he has been so enthusiastic for the jury system. For whatever reason, he is enthusiastic, and the result, which transfers power in lawsuits from the judge to the jury, is to give considerable benefit to the injured veteran and the injured workman. Today in the federal courts the jury is more important and has more power than it has had for at least seventy-five years. To a considerable extent this is Black's doing.

In this case the plaintiff, a veteran, sued for total and permanent disability benefits. The essential issue was whether, as a matter of fact, he was insane on May 31, 1919, the date his government insurance lapsed. If he was insane then, he was entitled to recover in this suit. The trial court held that there was not sufficient evidence on this point to go to the jury, and decided the case against the veteran. The question as it came to the Supreme Court was whether the case should had gone to the jury.

Justice Rutledge wrote the opinion of the Court, holding that the veteran had not presented enough evidence to take the case to the jury. Justices Stone, Roberts, Reed, Frankfurter, and Jackson agreed with him. Justice Black in this dissent, in which Justices Douglas and Murphy concurred, argued that the case should have gone to the jury. In the portion of the dissent set forth here, Black discussed the history of the civil jury and his attitude toward its proper role.]

Mr. Justice BLACK, dissenting:

The Seventh Amendment to the Constitution provides:

"In suits at common law, where the value in controversy shall exceed twenty dollars, the right of trial by jury shall be preserved, and no fact tried by a jury shall be otherwise re-examined in any Court of the United States, than according to the rules of the common law."

The Court here re-examines testimony offered in a common law suit, weighs conflicting evidence, and holds that the litigant may never take this case to a jury. The founders of our government thought that trial of fact by juries rather than by judges was an essential bulwark of civil liberty. For this reason, among others, they adopted Article III, § 2 of the Constitution, and the Sixth and Seventh Amendments. Today's decision marks a continuation of the gradual process of judicial erosion which in one hundred fifty years has slowly worn away a major portion of the essential guarantee of the Seventh Amendment.

I

Alexander Hamilton in The Federalist emphasized his loyalty to the jury system in civil cases and declared that jury verdicts should be re-examined, if at all, only "by a second jury, either by remanding the cause to the court below for a second trial of the fact, or by directing an issue immediately out of the Supreme Court." He divided the citizens of his time between those who thought that jury trial was a "valuable safeguard to liberty" and those who thought it was "the very palladium of free government." However, he felt it unnecessary to include in the Constitution a specific provision placing jury trial in civil cases in the same high position as jury trial in criminal cases.

Hamilton's view, that constitutional protection of jury trial in civil cases was undesirable, did not prevail. On the contrary, in response to widespread demands from the various State Constitutional Conventions, the first Congress adopted the Bill of Rights containing the Sixth and Seventh Amendments, intended to save trial in both criminal and common law cases from legislative or judicial abridgement. The first Congress expected the Seventh Amendment to meet the objections of men like Patrick Henry to the Constitution itself. Henry, speaking in the Virginia Constitutional Convention, had expressed the general conviction of the people of the Thirteen States when he said, "Trial by jury is the best appendage of freedom. . . . We are told that we are to part with that trial by jury with which our ancestors secured their lives and property. . . . I hope we shall never be induced, by such arguments, to part with that excellent mode of trial. No appeal can now be made as to fact in common law suits. *The unanimous verdict of impartial men cannot be reversed.*" The first Congress, therefore, provided for trial of common law cases by a jury, even when such trials were in the Supreme Court itself.

In 1789, juries occupied the principal place in the administration of justice. They were frequently in both criminal and civil cases the arbiters not only of fact but of law. Less than three years after the ratification of the Seventh Amendment, this Court called a jury in a civil case brought under our original jurisdiction. There was no disagreement as to the facts of the case. Chief Justice Jay, charging the jury for a unanimous Court, three of whose members had sat in the Constitutional Convention, said: "For, as on the one hand, it is presumed that juries are the best judges of fact; it is on the other hand presumable that the courts are the best judges of law. But still, both objects are lawfully within your power of decision." Similar views were held by state courts in Connecticut, Massachusetts, Illinois, Louisiana and presumably elsewhere.

A long step toward the determination of fact by judges instead of by juries was the invention of the directed verdict. In 1850, what seems to have been the first directed verdict case considered by this Court was presented for decision. The Court held that the directed verdict serves the same purpose as the demurrer to the evidence, and that since there was "no evidence whatever" on the critical issue in the case, the directed verdict was approved. The decision was an innovation, a departure from the traditional rule restated only fifteen years before in *Greenleaf* v. *Birch*, in which this Court had said: "Where there is no evidence tending to prove a particular fact, the courts are bound so to instruct the jury, when requested; but they cannot legally give any instruction which shall take from the jury the right of weighing the evidence and determining what effect it shall have."

The substantial evidence rule did not spring into existence immediately upon the adoption of the directed verdict device. For a few more years federal judges held to the traditional rule that juries might pass finally on facts if there was "any evidence" to support a party's contention. The rule that a case must go to the jury unless there was "no evidence" was completely repudiated in *Improvement Co.* v. *Munson*, upon which the Court today relies in part. There the Court declared that "some" evidence was not enough — there must be evidence sufficiently persuasive to the judge so that he thinks "a jury can properly proceed." The traditional rule was given an ugly name, "the scintilla rule," to hasten its demise. For a time traces of the old formula remained, but the new spirit prevailed. The same transition from jury supremacy to jury subordination through judicial decisions took place in State courts.

Later cases permitted the development of added judicial control. New and totally unwarranted formulas, which should surely be eradicated from the law at the first opportunity, were added as recently as 1929 in *Gunning* v. *Cooley*, which, by sheerest dictum, made new encroachments on the jury's constitutional functions. There it was announced that a judge might weigh the evidence to determine whether he, and not the jury, thought it was "overwhelming" for either party, and then direct a verdict. *Gunning* v. *Cooley* also suggests quite unnecessarily for its decision, that "When a plaintiff produces evidence that is consistent with an hypothesis that the defendant is not negligent, and also with one that he is, his proof tends to establish neither." This dictum, which assumes that a judge can weigh conflicting evidence with mathematical precision and which wholly deprives the jury of the right to resolve that conflict, was applied in *Pennsylvania Railroad Co.* v. *Chamberlain*. With it, and other tools, jury verdicts on disputed facts have been set aside or directed verdicts authorized so regularly as to make the practice commonplace while the motion for directed verdict itself has become routine.

The story thus briefly told depicts the constriction of a constitutional civil right and should not be continued. Speaking of an aspect of this problem, a contemporary writer saw the heart of the issue: "Such a reversal of opinion [as that of a particular state court concerning the jury function], if it were isolated, might have little significance, but when many other courts throughout the country are found to be making the same shift and to be doing so despite the provisions of statutes and constitutions there is revealed one aspect of that basic conflict in the legal history of America — the conflict between the people's aspiration for democratic government, and the judiciary's desire for the orderly supervision of public affairs by judges."

The language of the Seventh Amendment cannot easily be improved by formulas. The statement of a district judge in *Tarter* v. *United States* represents, in my opinion, the minimum meaning of the Seventh Amendment:

"The Seventh Amendment to the Constitution guarantees a jury trial in law cases, where there is substantial evidence to support the claim of a plaintiff in an action. If a single witness testifies to a fact sustaining the issue between the parties, or if reasonable minds might reach different conclusions from the testimony of a single witness, one of which would substantially support the issue of the contending party, the issue must be left to the jury. Trial by jury is a fundamental guaranty of the rights of the people, and judges should not search the evidence with meticulous care to deprive litigants of jury trials."

The call for the true application of the Seventh Amendment is not to words, but to the spirit of honest desire to see that Constitutional right preserved. Either the judge or the jury must decide facts and to the extent that we take this responsibility, we lessen the jury function. Our duty to preserve this one of the Bill of Rights may be peculiarly difficult, for here it is our own power which we must restrain. We should not fail to meet the expectation of James Madison, who, in advocating the adoption of the Bill of Rights, said: "Independent tribunals of justice will consider themselves in a peculiar manner the guardians of those rights; . . . they will be naturally led to resist every encroachment upon rights expressly stipulated for in the Constitution by the declaration of right." So few of these cases come to this Court that, as a matter of fact, the judges of the District Courts and the Circuit Courts of Appeal are the primary custodians of the Amendment. As for myself, I believe that a verdict should be directed, if at all, only when, without weighing the credibility of the witnesses, there is in the evidence no room whatever for honest difference of opinion over the factual issue in controversy. I shall continue to believe that in all other cases a judge should, in obedience to the command of the Seventh Amendment, not interfere with the jury's function. Since this is a matter of high constitutional importance, appellate courts should be alert to insure the preservation of this constitutional right even though each case necessarily turns on its peculiar circumstances.

II.

CIVIL RIGHTS

BASIC THEORY

Adamson v. *California,* 332 U.S. 46 (1947)

[The largest single innovation in Justice Black's thinking about civil rights is his belief that the Bill of Rights of the federal Constitution is a protection of the people not only against the federal government, but also against the states of the Union. The Bill of Rights, which includes the rights to freedom of speech, press, and religion, the guarantee of a fair trial, and immunity from cruel and unusual punishments, was placed in the Constitution almost simultaneously with the adoption of the Constitution itself. These provisions were so worded as to be construed as protections to the people against the federal government only. But after the Civil War the argument was made that the fourteenth amendment, added as a result of that war, extended the protection of the Bill of Rights against state action as well as against federal action.

This has never been the majority view. It is the Black view, and is now held substantially by Justices Black, Douglas, Murphy, and Rutledge — four of the five Justices necessary to make it an effective portion of the Constitution. In the Black view, the citizen is protected by the Fourteenth Amendment and the Bill of Rights against denials of free speech, unfair trials, or cruel and unusual punishments or against any other violation of the Bill of Rights by either the federal government or the state governments.

This point of view is most fully developed in the Black dissent in the Adamson case. Adamson was convicted of murder in a California state court. Certain provisions of California procedure had the practical effect of either forcing Adamson to testify against himself or else leaving him in a very embarrassing position if he did not. Under the Bill of Rights "no person shall be . . . compelled in any criminal case to be a witness against himself."

The majority of the Court, in an opinion by Justice Reed, joined by Justices Frankfurter, Jackson, Burton, and Chief Justice Vinson, held that the provision of the Bill of Rights was not binding upon the state and that California was free to follow its practice. Justice Frankfurter also concurred specially.

Justice Black dissented, including with his dissent an extensive historical appendix containing materials showing that the framers of the Fourteenth Amendment had meant to make the Bill of Rights applicable to the states. Justice Douglas concurred completely with Justice Black and Justices Rutledge and Murphy noted their substantial agreement. Excerpts from the dissent follow.]

Mr. Justice BLACK, dissenting:

The argument is that (1) permitting comment upon his failure to testify has the effect of compelling him to testify so as to violate that provision of the Bill of Rights contained in the Fifth Amendment that "No person . . . shall be compelled in any criminal case to be a witness against himself"; and (2) although this provision of the Fifth Amendment originally applied only as a restraint upon federal courts, the Fourteenth Amendment was intended to, and did, make the prohibition against compelled testimony applicable to trials in state courts.

This decision reasserts a constitutional theory spelled out in *Twining* v. *New Jersey*, that this Court is endowed by the Constitution with boundless power under "natural law" periodically to expand and contract constitutional standards to conform to the Court's conception of what at a particular time constitutes "civilized decency" and "fundamental liberty and justice." Invoking this *Twining* rule, the

Court concludes that although comment upon testimony in a federal court would violate the Fifth Amendment, identical comment in a state court does not violate today's fashion in civilized decency and fundamentals and is therefore not prohibited by the Federal Constitution as amended.

The *Twining* case was the first, as it is the only decision of this Court, which has squarely held that states were free, notwithstanding the Fifth and Fourteenth Amendments, to extort evidence from one accused of crime. I agree that if *Twining* be reaffirmed, the result reached might appropriately follow. But I would not reaffirm the *Twining* decision. I think that decision and the "natural law" theory of the Constitution upon which it relies, degrade the constitutional safeguards of the Bill of Rights and simultaneously appropriate for this Court a broad power which we are not authorized by the Constitution to exercise.

The first ten Amendments were proposed and adopted largely because of fear that Government might unduly interfere with prized individual liberties. The people wanted and demanded a Bill of Rights written into their Constitution. The Amendments embodying the Bill of Rights were intended to curb all branches of the Federal Government in the fields touched by the Amendments — Legislative, Executive, and Judicial. The Fifth, Sixth, and Eighth Amendments were pointedly aimed at confining exercise of power by courts and judges within precise boundaries, particularly in the procedure used for the trial of criminal cases. Past history provided strong reasons for the apprehensions which brought these procedural amendments into being and attest the wisdom of their adoption. For the fears of arbitrary court action sprang largely from the past use of courts in the imposition of criminal punishments to suppress speech, press, and religion. Hence the constitutional limitations of courts' powers were, in the view of the Founders, essential supplements to the First Amendment, which was itself designed to protect the widest scope for all people to believe and to express the most divergent political, religious, and other views.

But these limitations were not expressly imposed upon state court action. In 1833, *Barron v. Baltimore* was decided by this Court. It specifically held inapplicable to the states that provision of the Fifth Amendment which declares: "nor shall private property be taken for public use, without just compensation." In deciding the particular point raised, the Court there said that it could not hold that the first eight Amendments applied to the states. This was the controlling constitutional rule when the Fourteenth Amendment was proposed in 1866.

My study of the historical events that culminated in the Fourteenth Amendment, and the expressions of those who sponsored and favored, as well as those who opposed its submission and passage, persuades me that one of the chief objects that the provisions of the Amendment's first section, separately, and as a whole, were intended to accomplish was to make the Bill of Rights applicable to the states. With full knowledge of the import of the *Barron* decision, the framers and backers of the Fourteenth Amendment proclaimed its purpose to be to overturn the constitutional rule that case had announced. This historical purpose has never received full consideration or exposition in any opinion of this Court interpreting the Amendment.

In the *Twining* case itself, the Court was cited to a then recent book, Guthrie, Fourteenth Amendment to the Constitution (1898). A few pages of that work recited some of the legislative background of the Amendment, emphasizing the speech of Senator Howard. But Guthrie did not emphasize the speeches of Congressman Bingham, nor the part he played in the framing and adoption of the first section of the Fourteenth Amendment. Yet Congressman Bingham may, without extravagance, be called the Madison of the first section of the Fourteenth Amendment. In the *Twining* opinion the Court explicitly declined to give weight to the historical demonstration that the first section of the Amendment was intended to apply to the states the several protections of the Bill of Rights. It held that that question was "no longer open" because of previous decisions of this Court which, however, had not appraised the historical evidence on that subject. The Court admitted that its action had resulted in giving "much less effect to the Fourteenth Amendment than some of the public men active in framing it" had intended it to have. With particular reference to the guarantee against compelled testimony, the Court stated that "Much might be said in favor of the view that the privilege was guaranteed against state impairment as a privilege and immunity of National citizenship, but, as has been shown, the decisions of this court have foreclosed that view." Thus the Court declined and again today declines, to appraise the relevant historical evidence of the intended scope of the first section of the Amendment. Instead it relied upon previous cases, none of which had analyzed the evidence showing that one purpose of those who framed, advocated, and adopted the Amendment had been to make the Bill of Rights applicable to the States. None of the cases relied upon by the Court today made such an analysis.

For this reason, I am attaching to this dissent, an appendix which contains a résumé, by no means complete, of the Amendment's history. In my judgment that history conclusively demonstrates that the language of the first section of the Fourteenth Amendment, taken as a whole, was thought by those responsible for its submission to the people, and by those who opposed its submission, sufficiently explicit to guarantee that thereafter no state could deprive its citizens of the privileges and protections of the Bill of Rights. Whether this Court ever will, or whether it now should, in the light of past decisions, give full effect to what the Amendment was intended to accomplish is not necessarily essential to a decision here. However that may be, our prior decisions, including *Twining*, do not prevent our carrying out that purpose, at least to the extent of making applicable to the states, not a mere part, as the Court has, but the full protection of the Fifth Amendment's provision against compelling evidence from an accused to convict him of crime. And I further contend that the "natural law" formula which the Court uses to reach its conclusion in this case should be abandoned as an incongruous excrescence on our Constitution. I believe that formula to be itself a violation of our Constitution, in that it subtly conveys to courts, at the expense of legislatures, ultimate power over public policies in fields where no specific provision of the Constitution limits legislative power. And my belief seems to be in accord with the views expressed by this Court, at least for the first two decades after the Fourteenth Amendment was adopted.

The foregoing constitutional doctrine, judicially created and adopted by expanding the previously accepted meaning of "due process," marked a complete departure from the *Slaughterhouse* philosophy of judicial tolerance of state regulation of business activities. Conversely, the new formula contracted the effectiveness of the Fourteenth Amendment as a protection from state infringement of individual liberties enumerated in the Bill of Rights. Thus the Court's second-thought interpretation of the Amendment was an about face from the *Slaughterhouse* interpretation and represented a failure to carry out the avowed purpose of the Amendment's sponsors. This reversal is dramatized by the fact that the *Hurtado* case, which had rejected the due process clause as an instrument for preserving Bill of Rights' liberties and privileges, was cited as authority for expanding the scope of that clause so as to permit this Court to invalidate all state regulatory legislation it believed to be contrary to "fundamental" principles.

The *Twining* decision, rejecting the compelled testimony clause of the Fifth Amendment, and indeed rejecting all the Bill of Rights, is the end product of one phase of this philosophy. At the same time, that decision consolidated the power of the Court assumed in past cases by laying broader foundations for the Court to invalidate state and even federal regulatory legislation. For the *Twining* decision, giving separate consideration to "due process" and "privileges or immunities," went all the way to say that the "privileges or immunities" clause of the Fourteenth Amendment "did not forbid the States to abridge the personal rights enumerated in the first eight amendments. . . ." And in order to be certain, so far as possible, to leave this Court wholly free to reject all the Bill of Rights as specific restraints upon state action, the decision declared that even if this Court should decide that the due process clause forbids the states to infringe personal liberties guaranteed by the Bill of Rights, it would do so, not "because those rights are incorporated in the first eight Amendments, but because they are of such a nature that they are included in the conception of due process of law."

At the same time that the *Twining* decision held that the states need not conform to the specific provisions of the Bill of Rights, it consolidated the power that the Court had assumed under the due process clause by laying even broader foundations for the Court to invalidate state and even federal regulatory legislation. For under the *Twining* formula, which includes non-regard for the first eight Amendments, what are "fundamental rights" and in accord with "canons of decency," as the Court said in *Twining*, and today re-affirms, is to be independently "ascertained from time to time by judicial action . . . "; "what is due process of law depends on circumstances." Thus the power of legislatures became what this Court would declare it to be at a particular time independently of the specific guarantees of the Bill of Rights such as the right to freedom of speech, religion and assembly, the right to just compensation for property taken for a public purpose, the right to jury trial or the right to be secure against unreasonable searches and seizures. Neither the contraction of the Bill of Rights safeguards nor the invalidation of regulatory laws by this Court's appraisal of "circumstances" would readily be classified as the most satisfactory contribution of this Court to the nation. In 1912, four years after the *Twining* case was decided, a book written by Mr. Charles Wallace Collins gave the history of this Court's interpretation and application of the Fourteenth Amendment up to that time. It is not necessary for one fully to agree with all he said in order to appreciate the sentiment of the following comment concerning the disappointments caused by this Court's interpretation of the Amendment:

". . . It was aimed at restraining and checking the powers of wealth and privilege. It was to be a charter of liberty for human rights against property rights. The transformation has been rapid and complete. It operates today to protect the rights of property to the detriment of the rights of man. It has become the Magna Charta of accumulated and organized capital."

That this feeling was shared, at least in part, by members of this Court is revealed by the vigorous dissents that have been written in almost every case where the *Twining* and *Hurtado* doctrines have been applied to invalidate state regulatory laws.

It seems rather plain to me why the Court today does not attempt to justify all of the broad *Twining* discussion. That opinion carries its own refutation on what may be called the factual issue the Court resolved. The opinion itself shows, without resort to the powerful argument in the dissent of Mr. Justice Harlan, that outside of Star Chamber practices and influences, the "English-speaking" peoples have for centuries abhorred and feared the practice of compelling people to convict themselves of crime. I shall not attempt to narrate the reasons. They are well known. Nor does the history of the practice of compelling testimony in this country, relied on in the *Twining* opinion, support the degraded rank which that opinion gave the Fifth Amendment's privilege against compulsory self-incrimination. I think the history here recited by the Court belies its conclusion.

The Court in *Twining* evidently was forced to resort for its degradation of the privilege to the fact that Governor Winthrop in trying Mrs. Anne Hutchinson in 1627 was evidently "not aware of any privilege against self-incrimination or conscious of any duty to respect it." Of course not. Mrs. Hutchinson was tried, if trial it can be called, for holding unorthodox religious views. People with a consuming belief that their religious convictions must be forced on others rarely ever believe that the unorthodox have any rights which should or can be rightfully respected. As a result of her trial and compelled admissions, Mrs. Hutchinson was found guilty of unorthodoxy and banished from Massachusetts. The lamentable experience of Mrs. Hutchinson and others, contributed to the overwhelming sentiment that demanded adoption of a Constitutional

Bill of Rights. The founders of this Government wanted no more such "trials" and punishments as Mrs. Hutchinson had to undergo. They wanted to erect barriers that would bar legislators from passing laws that encroached on the domain of belief, and that would, among other things, strip courts and all public officers of a power to compel people to testify against themselves.

I cannot consider the Bill of Rights to be an outworn 18th Century "strait jacket" as the *Twining* opinion did. Its provisions may be thought outdated abstractions by some. And it is true that they were designed to meet ancient evils. But they are the same kind of human evils that have emerged from century to century whenever excessive power is sought by the few at the expense of the many. In my judgment the people of no nation can lose their liberty so long as a Bill of Rights like ours survives and its basic purposes are conscientiously interpreted, enforced and respected so as to afford continuous protection against old, as well as new, devices and practices which might thwart those purposes. I fear to see the consequences of the Court's practice of substituting its own concepts of decency and fundamental justice for the language of the Bill of Rights as its point of departure in interpreting and enforcing that Bill of Rights. If the choice must be between the selective process of the *Palko* decision applying some of the Bill of Rights to the States, or the *Twining* rule applying none of them, I would choose the *Palko* selective process. But rather than accept either of these choices, I would follow what I believe was the original purpose of the Fourteenth Amendment — to extend to all the people of the nation the complete protection of the Bill of Rights. To hold that this Court can determine what, if any, provisions of the Bill of Rights will be enforced, and if so to what degree, is to frustrate the great design of a written Constitution.

SPEECH, PRESS,

RELIGION

Marsh v. *Alabama,* 326 U.S. 501 (1946)

[The liberties of free speech, free press, and free religion frequently come into jeopardy together and this has been particularly true in recent years in cases involving one religious sect, the Jehovah's Witnesses. Black has written a number of opinions involving the rights of this group and supporting their prerogative of distributing religious literature in their own way. Of these, perhaps the most controversial in the minds of many is *Marsh* v. *Alabama.*

In this case Grace Marsh, a Jehovah's Witness, distributed religious literature on the sidewalk in Chickasaw, Alabama, a company town belonging to the Gulf Shipbuilding Corporation. The company had properly notified Marsh that it did not want her on its property, its property being the town itself.

In this case Justice Black wrote the majority opinion, joined by Justices Douglas, Murphy, and Rutledge. Under earlier decisions, no ordinary town could keep a person from ordinary distribution of religious literature on its streets. The Black opinion held that there must be the same right to religious liberty in a company town as in any other kind of town, and therefore held that Marsh could not be punished. Justice Frankfurter concurred specially, Justices Reed and Burton and Chief Justice Stone dissented, and Justice Jackson took no part.]

Mr. Justice BLACK delivered the opinion of the Court.

In this case we are asked to decide whether a State, consistently with the First and Fourteenth Amendments, can impose criminal punishment on a person who undertakes to distribute religious literature on the premises of a company-owned town contrary to the wishes of the town's management. The town, a suburb of Mobile, Alabama, known as Chickasaw, is owned by the Gulf Shipbuilding Corporation. Except for that it has all the characteristics of any other American town. The property consists of residential buildings, streets, a system of sewers, a sewage disposal plant and a "business block" on which business places are situated. A deputy of the Mobile County Sheriff, paid by the company, serves as the town's policeman. Merchants and service establishments have rented the stores and business places on the business block and the United States uses one of the places as a post office from which six carriers deliver mail to the people of Chickasaw and the adjacent area. The town and the surrounding neighborhood, which cannot be distinguished from the Gulf property by anyone not familiar with the property lines, are thickly settled, and according to all indications the residents use the business block as their regular shopping center. To do so, they now, as they have for many years make use of a company-owned paved street and sidewalk located alongside the store fronts in order to enter and leave the stores and post office. Intersecting company-owned roads at each end of the business block lead into a four-lane public highway which runs parallel to the business block at a distance of thirty feet. There is nothing to stop highway traffic from coming onto the business block and upon arrival a traveler may make free use of the facilities available there. In short the town and its shopping district are accessible to and freely used by the public in general and there is nothing to distinguish them from any other town and shopping center except the fact that the title to the property belongs to a private corporation.

Had the title to Chickasaw belonged not to a private but to a municipal corporation and had appellant been arrested for violating a municipal ordinance rather than a ruling by those appointed by the corporation to manage a company town it would have been clear that appellant's conviction must be reversed. Under our decision in *Lovell* v. *Griffin* and others which have followed that case, neither a state nor a municipality can completely bar the distribution of literature containing religious or political ideas on its streets, sidewalks and public places or make the right to distribute dependent on a flat license tax or permit to be issued by an official who could deny it at will. We have also held that an ordinance completely prohibiting the dissemination of ideas on the city streets cannot be justified on the ground that the municipality holds legal title to them. And we have recognized that the preservation of a free society is so far dependent upon the right of each individual citizen to receive such literature as he himself might desire that a municipality could not, without jeopardizing that vital individual freedom, prohibit door to door distribution of literature.

From these decisions it is clear that had the people of Chickasaw owned all the homes, and all the stores, and all the streets, and all the sidewalks, all those owners together could not have set up a municipal government with sufficient power to pass an ordinance completely barring the distribution of religious literature. Our question then narrows down to this: Can those people who live in or come to Chickasaw be denied freedom of press and religion simply because a single company has legal title to all the town?

For it is the state's contention that the mere fact that all the property interests in the town are held by a single company is enough to give that company power, enforceable by a state statute, to abridge these freedoms.

We do not agree that the corporation's property interests settle the question. The State urges in effect that the corporation's right to control the inhabitants of Chickasaw is coextensive with the right of a homeowner to regulate the conduct of his guests. We cannot accept that contention. Ownership does not always mean absolute dominion. The more an owner, for his advantage, opens up his property for use by the public in general, the more do his rights become circumscribed by the statutory and constitutional rights of those who use it. Thus, the owners of privately held bridges, ferries, turnpikes and railroads may not operate them as freely as a farmer does his farm. Since these facilities are built and operated primarily to benefit the public and since their operation is essentially a public function, it is subject to state regulation. And, though the issue is not directly analogous to the one before us we do want to point out by way of illustration that such regulation may not result in any operation of these facilities, even by privately owned companies, which unconstitutionally interferes with and discriminates against interstate commerce. Had the corporation here owned the cement of the four-lane highway which runs parallel to the "business block" and operated the same under a State franchise, doubtless no one would have seriously contended that the corporation's property interest in the highway gave it power to obstruct through traffic or to discriminate against interstate commerce. And even had there been no express franchise but mere acquiescence by the State in the corporation's use of its property as a segment of the four-lane highway, operation of all the highway, including the segment owned by the corporation, would still have been performance of a public function and discrimination would certainly have been illegal.

We do not think it makes any significant constitutional difference as to the relationship between the rights of the owner and those of the public that here the State, instead of permitting the corporation to operate a highway, permitted it to use its property as a town, operate a "business block" in the town and a street and sidewalk on that business block. Whether a corporation or a municipality owns or possesses the town the public in either case has an identical interest in the functioning of the community in such manner that the channels of communication remain free. As we have heretofore stated, the town of Chickasaw does not function differently from any other town. The "business block" serves as the community shopping center and is freely accessible and open to the people in the area and those passing through. The managers appointed by the corporation cannot curtail the liberty of press and religion of these people consistently with the purposes of the Constitutional guarantees, and a state statute, as the one here involved, which enforces such action by criminally punishing those who attempt to distribute religious literature clearly violates the First and Fourteenth Amendments to the Constitution.

Many people in the United States live in company-owned towns. These people, just as residents of municipalities, are free citizens of their State and country. Just as all other citizens they must make decisions which affect the welfare of community and nation. To act as good citizens they must be informed. In order to enable them to be properly informed their information must be uncensored. There is no more reason for depriving these people of the liberties guaranteed by the First and Fourteenth Amendments than there is for curtailing these freedoms with respect to any other citizen. . . .

West Virginia State Board of Education v. Barnette, 319 U.S. 624 (1943)

[One of the best-known civil-liberty issues of the past several years has been the controversy over the power of towns and states to require that its school children repeat the oath of allegiance to the flag as a condition of attending school. The Jehovah's Witnesses contend that such a ceremony is a violation of the Biblical mandate against acknowledging images.

Justice Black had joined an earlier majority opinion holding that the requirement of the flag salute was constitutional. Fuller consideration of the question convinced him of his error, and in this case he joined in the statement that the requirement of the flag salute was incompatible with religious freedom. In this case Justice Jackson wrote the majority opinion, joined by Justices Black, Douglas, Murphy, and Rutledge and Chief Justice Stone. Justice Murphy also concurred specially. Justices Frankfurter, Roberts, and Reed dissented. In view of their former position, Justices Black and Douglas filed the following short statement.]

Mr. Justice BLACK and Mr. Justice DOUGLAS concurring:

We are substantially in agreement with the opinion just read, but since we originally joined with the Court in the *Gobitis* case, it is appropriate that we make a brief statement of reasons for our change of view.

Reluctance to make the Federal Constitution a rigid bar against state regulation of conduct thought inimical to the public welfare was the controlling influence which moved us to consent to the *Gobitis* decision. Long reflection convinced us that although the principle is sound, its application in the particular case was wrong. We believe that the statute before us fails to accord full scope to the freedom of religion secured to the appellees by the First and Fourteenth Amendments.

The statute requires the appellees to participate in a ceremony aimed at inculcating respect for the flag and for this country. The Jehovah's Witnesses, without any desire to show disrespect for either the flag or the country, interpret the Bible as commanding, at the risk of God's displeasure, that they not go through the form of a pledge of allegiance to any flag. The devoutness of their belief is evidenced by their willingness to suffer persecution and punishment, rather than make the pledge.

No well ordered society can leave to the individuals an absolute right to make final decisions, unassailable by the State, as to everything they will or will not do. The First Amendment does not go so far. Religious faiths, honestly held, do not free individuals from responsibility to conduct themselves obediently to laws which are either imperatively necessary to protect society as a whole from grave and pressingly imminent dangers or which, without any general prohibition, merely regulate time, place or manner of religious activity. Decision as to the constitutionality of particular laws which strike at the substance of religious tenets and practices must be made by this Court. The duty is a solemn one, and in meeting it we cannot say that a failure, because of religious scruples, to assume a particular physical position and to repeat the words of a patriotic formula creates a grave danger to the nation. Such a statutory exaction is a form of test oath, and the test oath has always been abhorrent in the United States.

Words uttered under coercion are proof of loyalty to nothing but self-interest. Love of country must spring from willing hearts and free minds, inspired by a fair administration of wise laws enacted by the people's elected representatives within the bounds of express constitutional prohibitions. These laws must, to be consistent with the First Amendment, permit the widest toleration of conflicting viewpoints consistent with a society of free men.

Neither our domestic tranquility in peace nor our martial effort in war depend on compelling little children to participate in a ceremony which ends in nothing for them but a fear of spiritual condemnation. If, as we think, their fears are groundless, time and reason are the proper antidotes for their errors. The ceremonial, when enforced against conscientious objectors, more likely to defeat than to serve its high purpose, is a handy implement for disguised religious persecution. As such, it is inconsistent with our Constitution's plan and purpose.

Everson v. *Board of Education of the Township of Ewing, et al.,* 330 U.S. 1 (1947)

[In the American educational system, in which public, private, and parochial schools are commonplace, exceedingly serious questions arise as to the relation of governments to parochial and private schools. It is earnestly contended by some that since taxes are collected from all, they should at least to some extent be used to aid parochial schools as well as public schools ; while others contend that any aid to parochial schools violates the principle of separation of church and state, which is part of the Bill of Rights.

In the *Everson* case Justice Black expresses himself on this issue. The immediate question was whether taxpayers' money could be used for the transportation of children to parochial as well as to public schools. Justice Black held that it could be, but at the same time made clear and explicit that more substantial or direct aid to parochial schools could not be

2. *Speech, Press, Religion*

permitted under the First Amendment. The majority opinion, written by Black, was joined by Justices Reed, Douglas, and Murphy and Chief Justice Vinson. Justices Rutledge, Frankfurter, Jackson, and Burton dissented on the general ground that not even this limited bounty was permitted by the Constitution.]

Mr. Justice BLACK delivered the opinion of the Court.

A New Jersey statute authorizes its local school districts to make rules and contracts for the transportation of children to and from schools. The appellee, a township board of education, acting pursuant to this statute authorized reimbursement to parents of money expended by them for the bus transportation of their children on regular busses operated by the public transportation system. Part of this money was for the payment of transportation of some children in the community to Catholic parochial schools. These church schools give their students, in addition to secular education, regular religious instruction conforming to the religious tenets and modes of worship of the Catholic faith. The superintendent of these schools is a Catholic priest.

The only contention here is that the State statute and the resolution, insofar as they authorized reimbursement to parents of children attending parochial schools, violate the Federal Constitution in these two respects, which to some extent, overlap. *First.* They authorize the State to take by taxation the private property of some and bestow it upon others, to be used for their own private purposes. This, it is alleged, violates the due process clause of the Fourteenth Amendment. *Second.* The statute and the resolution forced inhabitants to pay taxes to help support and maintain schools which are dedicated to, and which regularly teach, the Catholic faith. This is alleged to be a use of State power to support church schools contrary to the prohibition of the First Amendment which the Fourteenth Amendment made applicable to the states. . . .

Second. The New Jersey statute is challenged as a "law respecting the establishment of religion." The First Amendment, as made applicable to the states by the Fourteenth, commands that a state "shall make no law respecting an establishment of religion, or prohibiting the free exercises thereof." These words of the First Amendment reflected in the minds of early Americans a vivid mental picture of conditions and practices which they fervently wished to stamp out in order to preserve liberty for themselves and for their posterity. Doubtless their goal has not been entirely reached; but so far has the Nation moved toward it that the expression "law respecting the establishment of religion," probably does not so vividly remind present-day Americans of the evils, fears, and political problems that caused that expression to be written into our Bill of Rights. Whether this New Jersey law is one respecting the "establishment of religion" requires an understanding of the meaning of that language, particularly with respect to the imposition of taxes. Once again, therefore, it is not inappropriate briefly to review the background and environment of the period in which that constitutional language was fashioned and adopted.

A large proportion of the early settlers of this country came here from Europe to escape the bondage of laws which compelled them to support and attend government favored churches. The centuries immediately before and contemporaneous with the colonization of America had been filled with turmoil, civil strife, and persecutions, generated in large part by established sects determined to maintain their absolute political and religious supremacy. With the power of government supporting them, at various times and

2. *Speech, Press, Religion*

places, Catholics had persecuted Protestants, Protestants
had persecuted Catholics, Protestant sects had persecuted
other Protestant sects, Catholics of one shade of belief had
persecuted Catholics of another shade of belief, and all of
these had from time to time persecuted Jews. In efforts to
force loyalty to whatever religious group happened to be
on top and in league with the government of a particular
time and place, men and women had been fined, cast in jail,
cruelly tortured, and killed. Among the offenses for which
these punishments had been inflicted were such things as
speaking disrespectfully of the views of ministers of
government-established churches, non-attendance at those
churches, expressions of non-belief in their doctrines, and
failure to pay taxes and tithes to support them.

These practices of the old world were transplanted to and
began to thrive in the soil of the new America. The very
charters granted by the English Crown to the individuals
and companies designated to make the laws which would
control the destinies of the colonials authorized these individuals and companies to erect religious establishments
which all, whether believers or non-believers, would be required to support and attend. An exercise of this authority
was accompanied by a repetition of many of the old world
practices and persecutions. Catholics found themselves
hounded and proscribed because of their faith; Quakers
who followed their conscience went to jail; Baptists were
peculiarly obnoxious to certain dominant Protestant sects;
men and women of varied faiths who happened to be in a
minority in a particular locality were persecuted because
they steadfastly persisted in worshipping God only as their
own consciences dictated. And all of these dissenters were
compelled to pay tithes and taxes to support government-
sponsored churches whose ministers preached inflammatory
sermons designed to strengthen and consolidate the estab-

lished faith by generating a burning hatred against dissenters.

These practices became so commonplace as to shock the freedom-loving colonials into a feeling of abhorrence. The imposition of taxes to pay ministers' salaries and to build and maintain churches and church property aroused their indignation. It was these feelings which found expression in the First Amendment. No one locality and no one group throughout the Colonies can rightly be given entire credit for having aroused the sentiment that culminated in adoption of the Bill of Rights' provisions embracing religious liberty. But Virginia, where the established church had achieved a dominant influence in political affairs and where many excesses attracted wide public attention, provided a great stimulus and able leadership for the movement. The people there, as elsewhere, reached the conviction that individual religious liberty could be achieved best under a government which was stripped of all power to tax, to support, or otherwise to assist any or all religions, or to interfere with the beliefs of any religious individual or group.

The movement toward this end reached its dramatic climax in Virginia in 1785–86 when the Virginia legislative body was about to renew Virginia's tax levy for the support of the established church. Thomas Jefferson and James Madison led the fight against this tax. Madison wrote his great Memorial and Remonstrance against the law. In it, he eloquently argued that a true religion did not need the support of law; that no person, either believer or nonbeliever, should be taxed to support a religious institution of any kind; that the best interest of a society required that the minds of men always be wholly free; and that cruel persecutions were the inevitable result of government-established religions. Madison's Remonstrance received strong support throughout Virginia, and the Assembly postponed consideration of the proposed tax measure until its next session. When the proposal came up for consideration at that session, it not only died in committee, but the Assembly enacted the famous "Virginia Bill for Religious Liberty" originally written by Thomas Jefferson. The preamble to that bill stated among other things that

"Almighty God hath created the mind free; that all attempts to influence it by temporal punishments, or burthens, or by civil incapacitations, tend only to beget habits of hypocrisy and meanness, and are a departure from the plan of the Holy author of our religion who being Lord both of body and mind, yet chose not to propagate it by coercions on either . . .; that to compel a man to furnish contributions of money for the propagation of opinions which he disbelieves, is sinful and tyrannical; that even the forcing him to support this or that teacher of his own religious persuasion, is depriving him of the comfortable liberty of giving his contributions to the particular pastor, whose morals he would make his pattern. . . ."

And the statute itself enacted

"That no man shall be compelled to frequent or support any religious worship, place, or ministry whatsoever, nor shall be enforced, restrained, molested, or burthened, in his body or goods, nor shall otherwise suffer on account of his religious opinions or belief ." . . .

The "establishment of religion" clause of the First Amendment means at least this: Neither a state nor the Federal Government can set up a church. Neither can pass laws which aid one religion, aid all religions, or prefer one religion over another. Neither can force nor influence a person to go to or to remain away from church against his will or force him to profess a belief or disbelief in any religion. No person can be punished for entertaining or professing religious beliefs or disbeliefs, for church attendance or non-attendance. No tax in any amount, large or small, can be levied to support any religious activities or institutions, whatever they may be called, or whatever form they may adopt to teach or practice religion. Neither a state nor the Federal Government can, openly or secretly, participate in the affairs of any religious organizations or groups and *vice versa*. In the words of Jefferson, the clause against establishment of religion by law was intended to erect "a wall of separation between Church and State."

We must consider the New Jersey statute in accordance with the foregoing limitations imposed by the First Amendment. But we must not strike that State statute down if it is within the State's constitutional power even though it approaches the verge of that power. New Jersey cannot consistently with the "establishment of religion clause" of the First Amendment contribute tax-raised funds to the support of an institution which teaches the tenets and faith of any church. On the other hand, other language of the amendment commands that New Jersey cannot hamper its citizens in the free exercise of their own religion. Consequently, it cannot exclude individual Catholics, Lutherans, Mohammedans, Baptists, Jews, Methodists, Non-believers, Presbyterians, or the members of any other faith, *because of their faith, or lack of it*, from receiving the benefits of public welfare legislation. While we do not mean to intimate that a state could not provide transportation only to children attending public schools, we must be careful, in protecting the citizens of New Jersey against state-established churches, to be sure that we do not inadvertently prohibit New Jersey from extending its general State law benefits to all its citizens without regard to their religious belief.

Measured by these standards, we cannot say that the First Amendment prohibits New Jersey from spending tax-raised funds to pay the bus fares of parochial school pupils as a part of a general program under which it pays the fares of pupils attending public and other schools. It is undoubtedly true that children are helped to get to church schools. There is even a possibility that some of the children might not be sent to the church schools if the parents were compelled to pay their children's bus fares out of their own pockets when transportation to a public school would have been paid for by the State. The same possibility exists where the State requires a local transit company to provide reduced rates to school children including those attending parochial schools, or where a municipally owned transportation system undertakes to carry all school children free of charge. Moreover, state-paid policemen, detailed to protect children going to and from church schools from the very real hazards of traffic, would serve much the same purpose and accomplish much the same result as state provisions intended to guarantee free transportation of a kind which the state deems to be best for the school children's welfare. And parents might refuse to risk their children to the serious danger of traffic accidents going to and from parochial schools, the approaches to which were not protected by policemen. Similarly, parents might be reluctant to permit their children to attend schools which the state had cut off from such general government services, as ordinary police and fire protection, connections for sewage disposal, public highways and sidewalks. Of course, cutting off church schools from these services, so separate and so indisputably marked off from the religious function, would make it far more difficult for the schools to operate. But such is obviously not the purpose of the First Amendment. That Amendment requires the state to be a neutral in its relations with groups of religious believers and non-believers; it does not require the state to be their adversary. State power is no more to be used so as to handicap religions than it is to favor them.

This Court has said that parents may, in the discharge of their duty under state compulsory education laws, send their children to a religious rather than a public school if the school meets the secular educational requirements which the state has power to impose. It appears that these parochial schools meet New Jersey's requirements. The State contributes no money to the schools. It does not support them. Its legislation, as applied, does no more than provide a general program to help parents get their children, regardless of their religion, safely and expeditiously to and from accredited schools.

The First Amendment has erected a wall between church and state. That wall must be kept high and impregnable. We could not approve the slightest breach. New Jersey has not breached it here.

In Re Summers, 325 U.S. 561 (1945)

[In this nationalist world one of the saddest of figures is the man who cannot bring himself to love his country more than he loves his God, and who believes that duty to his God requires that he refuse to kill in the service of his country. If such a man, by virtue of sincere religious conviction, is caught between his national and his religious obligations, Black is inclined to let the religious obligation come first.

This is illustrated by various decisions, among which is the case of *Summers*. The issue here was whether the state of Illinois could bar from the practice of law in the state a man whose religious scruples forbade him to bear arms. The majority of the Court, in an opinion by Justice Reed, joined by Justices Roberts, Frankfurter, and Jackson and Chief Justice Stone, held that the man might be excluded. Justice Black wrote the following dissent, in which Justices Douglas, Murphy, and Rutledge joined.]

Mr. Justice BLACK, dissenting:

The State of Illinois has denied the petitioner the right
to practice his profession and to earn his living as a lawyer.
It has denied him a license on the ground that his present
religious beliefs disqualify him for membership in the legal
profession. The question is, therefore, whether a state which
requires a license as a prerequisite to practicing law can
deny an applicant a license solely because of his deeply-
rooted religious convictions. The fact that petitioner measures up to every other requirement for admission to the
Bar set by the State demonstrates beyond doubt that the
only reason for his rejection was his religious beliefs.

The state does not deny that petitioner possesses the following qualifications:

He is honest, moral, and intelligent, has had a college
and a law school education. He has been a law professor
and fully measures up to the high standards of legal knowledge Illinois has set as a prerequisite to admission to practice law in that State. He has never been convicted for, or
charged with, a violation of law. That he would serve his
clients faithfully and efficiently if admitted to practice is
not denied. His ideals of what a lawyer should be indicate
that his activities would not reflect discredit upon the bar,
that he would strive to make the legal system a more effective instrument of justice. Because he thinks that "Lawsuits do not bring love and brotherliness, they just create
antagonisms," he would, as a lawyer, exert himself to adjust
controversies out of court, but would vigorously press his
client's cause in court if efforts to adjust failed. Explaining
to his examiners some of the reasons why he wanted to be a
lawyer, he told them: "I think there is a lot of work to be
done in the law. . . . I think the law has a place to see
to it that every man has a chance to eat and a chance to

live equally. I think the law has a place where people can go and get justice done for themselves without paying too much, for the bulk of people that are too poor." No one contends that such a vision of the law in action is either illegal or reprehensible.

The petitioner's disqualifying religious beliefs stem chiefly from a study of the New Testament and a literal acceptance of the teachings of Christ as he understands them. Those beliefs are these:

He is opposed to the use of force for either offensive or defensive purposes. The taking of human life under any circumstances he believes to be against the Law of God and contrary to the best interest of man. He would if he could, he told his examiners, obey to the letter these precepts of Christ: "Love your Enemies; Do good to those that hate you; Even though your enemy strikes you on your right cheek, turn to him your left cheek also." The record of his evidence before us bears convincing marks of the deep sincerity of his convictions, and counsel for Illinois with commendable candor does not question the genuineness of his professions.

I cannot believe that a state statute would be consistent with our constitutional guarantee of freedom of religion if it specifically denied the right to practice law to all members of one of our great religious groups, Protestant, Catholic, or Jewish. Yet the Quakers have had a long and honorable part in the growth of our nation, and an amicus curiæ brief filed in their behalf informs us that under the test applied to this petitioner, not one of them, if true to the tenets of their faith, could qualify for the bar in Illinois. And it is obvious that the same disqualification would exist as to every conscientious objector to the use of force. For a lawyer is no more subject to call for military duty than a plumber, a highway worker, a secretary of State, or a prison chaplain.

It may be, as many people think, that Christ's Gospel of Love and submission is not suited to a world in which men still fight and kill one another. But I am not ready to say that a mere profession of belief in that Gospel is a sufficient reason to keep otherwise well qualified men out of the legal profession, or to drive law-abiding lawyers of that belief out of the profession, which would be the next logical development.

Nor am I willing to say that such a belief can be penalized through the circuitous method of prescribing an oath, and then barring an applicant on the ground that his present belief might later prompt him to do or refrain from doing something that might violate that oath. Test oaths, designed to impose civil disabilities upon men for their beliefs rather than for unlawful conduct, were an abomination to the founders of this nation. This feeling was made manifest in Article 6 of the Constitution which provides that "no religious test shall ever be required as a Qualification to any office or public Trust under the United States."

The state's denial of petitioner's application to practice law resolves itself into a holding that it is lawfully required that all lawyers take an oath to support the state constitution and that petitioner's religious convictions against the use of force make it impossible for him to observe that oath. The petitioner denies this and is willing to take the oath. The particular constitutional provision involved authorizes the legislature to draft Illinois citizens from 18 to 45 years of age for militia service. It can be assumed that the State of Illinois has the constitutional power to draft conscientious objectors for war duty and to punish them for a refusal to serve as soldiers, — powers which this Court held the United States possesses. But that is not to say that Illinois could constitutionally use the test oath it did in this case. In the *Schwimmer* and *Macintosh* Cases aliens were barred from naturalization because their then religious beliefs would bar them from bearing arms to defend the country. Dissents in both cases rested in part on the premise that religious tests are incompatible with our constitutional guarantee of freedom of thought and religion. In the *Schwimmer* Case dissent, Mr. Justice Holmes said that "if there is any principle of the Constitution that more imperatively calls for attachment than any other it is the principle of free thought — not free thought for those who agree with us but freedom for the thought that we hate. I think that we should adhere to that principle with regard to admission into, as well as to life within this country." In the *Macintosh* Case dissent, Mr. Chief Justice Hughes said, "To conclude that the general oath of office is to be interpreted as disregarding the religious scruples of these citizens and as disqualifying them for office because they could not take the oath with such an interpretation would, I believe, be generally regarded as contrary not only to the specific intent of the Congress but as repugnant to the fundamental principle of representative government." I agree with the constitutional philosophy underlying the dissents of Mr. Justice Holmes and Mr. Chief Justice Hughes.

The Illinois Constitution itself prohibits the draft of conscientious objectors except in time of war and also excepts from militia duty persons who are "exempted by the laws of the United States." It has not drafted men into the militia since 1864, and if it ever should again, no one can say that it will not, as has the Congress of the United States, exempt men who honestly entertain the views that this petitioner does. Thus the probability that Illinois would ever call the petitioner to serve in a war has little more reality than an imaginary quantity in mathematics.

I cannot agree that a state can lawfully bar from a semi-public position, a well-qualified man of good character solely because he entertains a religious belief which might prompt him at some time in the future to violate a law which has not yet been and may never be enacted. Under our Constitution men are punished for what they do or fail to do and not for what they think and believe. Freedom to think, to believe, and to worship, has too exalted a position in our country to be penalized on such an illusory basis.

I would reverse the decision of the State Supreme Court.

Bridges v. *California,*
and
The Times Mirror Company v. *Superior Court of California,* 314 U.S. 252 (1941)

[A man's belief that freedom of speech and freedom of criticism are constitutional rights is likely to diminish a little when the criticism is directed at him. Thus in many cases the issue arises whether the courts are going to permit persons to speak as freely of the courts themselves as of other institutions.

Black's answer is clear. It is yes. He believes that courts should have no greater freedom from criticism than any other institution of government, and would apply the same tests to free speech concerning any of them.

The extent of the right to criticize courts was the issue in these two cases. In the *Bridges* case the dispute arose out of a proceeding in a California state court involving an inter-union dispute. This case was heard before a California state judge named Schmidt. After the decision in that case, and while further proceedings in that matter were pending, Harry Bridges sent to the Secretary of Labor a telegram reading:

"Attempted enforcement of Schmidt decision will tie-up part of Los Angeles and involve entire Pacific coast." The California state courts held that it was contempt of court for Bridges to publicize such a statement and fined him $125.

In the second case the *Los Angeles Times* was fined $300 by a California state court for publishing an editorial concerning a pending state criminal case against two persons who had allegedly attacked non-union truck-drivers for the purpose of forcing the drivers into the union. This editorial admonished the trial court not to give the defendants probation, but to give them an "assignment to the jute mill."

The Supreme Court reversed both these orders, holding that neither expression could be punished as contempt of court. Justice Black wrote the majority opinion, joined by Justices Reed, Douglas, Murphy, and Jackson. Justice Frankfurter dissented, joined by Justices Roberts and Byrnes and Chief Justice Stone. Excerpts from the majority opinion follow.]

Mr. Justice BLACK delivered the opinion of the Court.

In brief, the state courts asserted and exercised a power to punish petitioners for publishing their views concerning cases not in all respects finally determined, upon the following chain of reasoning: California is invested with the power and duty to provide an adequate administration of justice; by virtue of this power and duty, it can take appropriate measures for providing fair judicial trials free from coercion or intimidation; included among such appropriate measures is the common law procedure of punishing certain interferences and obstructions through contempt proceedings; this particular measure, devolving upon the courts of California by reason of their creation as courts, includes the power to punish for publications made outside the court room if they tend to interfere with the fair and orderly administration of justice in a pending case; the trial court having found that the publications had such a tendency, and there being substantial evidence to support the finding, the punishments here imposed were an appropriate exercise of the state's power; insofar as these punishments constitute a restriction on liberty of expression, the public interest in that liberty was properly subordinated to the public interest in judicial impartiality and decorum.

If the inference of conflict raised by the last clause be correct, the issue before us is of the very gravest moment. For free speech and fair trials are two of the most cherished policies of our civilization, and it would be a trying task to choose between them. But even if such a conflict is not actually raised by the question before us, we are still confronted with the delicate problems entailed in passing upon the deliberations of the highest court of a state. This is not, however, solely an issue between state and nation, as it would be if we were called upon to mediate in one of those troublous situations where each claims to be the repository of a particular sovereign power. To be sure, the exercise of power here in question was by a state judge. But in deciding whether or not the sweeping constitutional mandate against any law "abridging the freedom of speech or of the press" forbids it, we are necessarily measuring a power of all American courts, both state and federal, including this one.

I

It is to be noted at once that we have no direction by the legislature of California that publications outside the court room which comment upon a pending case in a specified manner should be punishable. As we said in *Cantwell* v. *Connecticut*, such a "declaration of the State's policy would weigh heavily in any challenge of the law as infringing constitutional limitations." But as we also said there, the problem is different where "the judgment is based on a common law concept of the most general and undefined nature." For here the legislature of California has not appraised a particular kind of situation and found a specific danger sufficiently imminent to justify a restriction on a particular kind of utterance. The judgments below, therefore, do not come to us encased in the armor wrought by prior legislative deliberation. Under such circumstances, this Court has said that "it must necessarily be found, as an original question" that the specified publications involved created "such likelihood of bringing about the substantive evil as to deprive (them) of the constitutional protection."

Moreover, the likelihood, however great, that a substantive evil will result cannot alone justify a restriction upon freedom of speech or the press. The evil itself must be "substantial"; it must be "serious." And even the expression of "legislative preferences or beliefs" cannot transform minor matters of public inconvenience or annoyance into substantive evils of sufficient weight to warrant the curtailment of liberty of expression.

What finally emerges from the "clear and present danger" cases is a working principle that the substantive evil must be extremely serious and the degree of imminence extremely high before utterances can be punished. Those cases do not purport to mark the furthermost constitutional boundaries of protected expression, nor do we here. They do no more than recognize a minimum compulsion of the Bill of Rights. For the First Amendment does not speak equivocally. It prohibits any law "abridging the freedom of speech or of the press." It must be taken as a command of the broadest scope that explicit language, read in the context of a liberty-loving society, will allow.

II

Before analyzing the punished utterances and the circumstances surrounding their publication, we must consider an argument which, if valid, would destroy the relevance of the foregoing discussion to this case. In brief, this argument is that the publications here in question belong to a special category marked off by history, a category to which the criteria of constitutional immunity from punishment used where other types of utterances are concerned are not applicable. For, the argument runs, the power of judges to punish by contempt out-of-court publications tending to obstruct the orderly and fair administration of justice in a pending case was deeply rooted in English common law at the time the Constitution was adopted. That this historical contention is dubious has been persuasively argued elsewhere. In any event it need not detain us, for to assume that English common law in this field became ours is to deny the generally accepted historical belief that "one of the objects of the Revolution was to get rid of the English common law on liberty of speech and of the press."

More specifically, it is to forget the environment in which the First Amendment was ratified. In presenting the proposals which were later embodied in the Bill of Rights, James Madison, the leader in the preparation of the First Amendment, said: "Although I know whenever the great rights, the trial by jury, freedom of the press, or liberty of conscience, come in question in that body (Parliament), the invasion of them is resisted by able advocates, yet their Magna Charta does not contain any one provision for the security of those rights, respecting which the people of America are most alarmed. The freedom of the press and rights of conscience, those choicest privileges of the people, are unguarded in the British Constitution." And Madison elsewhere wrote that "the state of the press . . . under the common law, cannot . . . be the standard of its freedom in the United States."

There are no contrary implications in any part of the history of the period in which the First Amendment was framed and adopted. No purpose in ratifying the Bill of Rights was clearer than that of securing for the people of the United States much greater freedom of religion, expression, assembly, and petition than the people of Great Britain had ever enjoyed. It cannot be denied, for example, that the religious test oath or the restrictions upon assembly then prevalent in England would have been regarded as measures which the Constitution prohibited the American Congress from passing. And since the same unequivocal language is used with respect to freedom of the press, it signifies a similar enlargement of that concept as well. Ratified as it was while the memory of many oppressive English restrictions in the enumerated liberties was still fresh, the First Amendment cannot reasonably be taken as approving prevalent English practices. On the contrary, the only conclusion supported by history is that the unqualified prohibitions laid down by the framers were intended to give to liberty of the press, as to the other liberties, the broadest scope that could be countenanced in an orderly society.

III

We may appropriately begin our discussion of the judgments below by considering how much, as a practical matter, they would affect liberty of expression. It must be recognized that public interest is much more likely to be kindled by a controversial event of the day than by a generalization, however penetrating, of the historian or scientist. Since they punish utterances made during the pendency of a case, the judgments below therefore produce their restrictive results at the precise time when public interest in the matters discussed would naturally be at its height. Moreover, the ban is likely to fall not only at a crucial time but upon the most important topics of discussion. Here, for example, labor controversies were the topics of some of the publications. Experience shows that the more acute labor controversies are, the more likely it is that in some aspect they will get into court. It is therefore the controversies that command most interest that the decisions below would remove from the arena of public discussion.

No suggestion can be found in the Constitution that the freedom there guaranteed for speech and the press bears an inverse ratio to the timeliness and importance of the ideas seeking expression. Yet, it would follow as a practical result of the decisions below that anyone who might wish to give public expression to his views on a pending case involving no matter what problem of public interest, just at the time his audience would be most receptive, would be as effectively discouraged as if a deliberate statutory scheme of censorship had been adopted. Indeed, perhaps more so, because under a legislative specification of the particular kinds of expressions prohibited and the circumstances under which the prohibitions are to operate, the speaker or publisher might at least have an authoritative guide to the permissible scope of comment, instead of being compelled to act at the peril that judges might find in the utterance a "reasonable tendency" to obstruct justice in a pending case.

This unfocused threat is, to be sure, limited in time, terminating as it does upon final disposition of the case. But this does not change its censorial quality. An endless series of moratoria on public discussion, even if each were very short, could hardly be dismissed as an insignificant abridgement of freedom of expression. And to assume that each would be short is to overlook the fact that the "pendency" of a case is frequently a matter of months or even years rather than days or weeks.

For these reasons we are convinced that the judgments below result in a curtailment of expression that cannot be dismissed as insignificant. If they can be justified at all, it must be in terms of some serious substantive evil which they are designed to avert. The substantive evil here sought to be averted has been variously described below. It appears to be double: disrespect for the judiciary; and disorderly and unfair administration of justice. The assumption that respect for the judiciary can be won by shielding judges from published criticism wrongly appraises the character of American public opinion. For it is a prized American privilege to speak one's mind, although not always with perfect good taste, on all public institutions. And an enforced silence, however limited, solely in the name of preserving the dignity of the bench, would probably engender resentment, suspicion, and contempt much more than it would enhance respect.

The other evil feared, disorderly and unfair administration of Justice, is more plausibly associated with restricting publications which touch upon pending litigation. The very word "trial" connotes decisions on the evidence and arguments properly advanced in open court. Legal trials are not like elections, to be won through the use of the meeting-hall, the radio, and the newspaper. But we cannot start with the assumption that publications of the kind here involved actually do threaten to change the nature of legal trials, and that to preserve judicial impartiality, it is necessary for judges to have a contempt power by which they can close all channels of public expression to all matters which touch upon pending cases. We must therefore turn to the particular utterances here in question and the circumstances of their publication to determine to what extent the substantive evil of unfair administration of justice was a likely consequence, and whether the degree of likelihood was sufficient to justify summary punishment.

The Los Angeles Times Editorials. The Times-Mirror Company, publisher of the Los Angeles *Times*, and L. D. Hotchkiss, its managing editor, were cited for contempt for the publication of three editorials. Both found by the trial court to be responsible for one of the editorials, the company and Hotchkiss were each fined $100. The company alone was held responsible for the other two, and was fined $100 more on account of one, and $300 more on account of the other.

The $300 fine presumably marks the most serious offense. The editorial thus distinguished was entitled "Probation for Gorillas?" After vigorously denouncing two members of a labor union who had previously been found guilty of assaulting non-union truck drivers, it closes with the observation: "Judge A. A. Scott will make a serious mistake if he grants probation to Matthew Shannon and Kennan Holmes. This community needs the example of their assignment to the jute mill." Judge Scott had previously set a day (about a month after the publication) for passing upon the application of Shannon and Holmes for probation and for pronouncing sentence.

The basis for punishing the publication as contempt was by the trial court said to be its "inherent tendency" and by the Supreme Court its "reasonable tendency" to interfere with the orderly administration of justice in an action then before a court for consideration. In accordance with what we have said on the "clear and present danger" cases, neither "inherent tendency" nor "reasonable tendency" is enough to justify a restriction of free expression. But even if they were appropriate measures, we should find exaggeration in the use of those phrases to describe the facts here.

From the indications in the record of the position taken by the Los Angeles *Times* on labor controversies in the past, there could have been little doubt of its attitude toward the probation of Shannon and Holmes. In view of the paper's long-continued militancy in this field, it is inconceivable that any judge in Los Angeles would expect anything but adverse criticism from it in the event probation were granted. Yet such criticism after final disposition of the proceedings would clearly have been privileged. Hence, this editorial, given the most intimidating construction it will bear, did no more than threaten future adverse criticism which was reasonably to be expected anyway in the event of a lenient disposition of the pending case. To regard it, therefore, as in itself of substantial influence upon the course of justice would be to impute to judges a lack of firmness, wisdom, or honor, which we cannot accept as a major premise.

The Bridges Telegram. While a motion for a new trial was pending in a case involving a dispute between an A.F. of L. union and a C.I.O. union of which Bridges was an officer, he either caused to be published or acquiesced in the publication of a telegram which he had sent to the Secretary of Labor. The telegram referred to the judge's decision as "outrageous"; said that attempted enforcement of it would tie up the port of Los Angeles and involve the entire Pacific Coast; and concluded with the announcement that the C.I.O. union, representing some twelve thousand members, did "not intend to allow state courts to override the majority vote of members in choosing its officers and representatives and to override the National Labor Relations Board."

Apparently Bridges' conviction is not rested at all upon his use of the word "outrageous." The remainder of the telegram fairly construed appears to be a statement that if the court's decree should be enforced there would be a strike. It is not claimed that such a strike would have been in violation of the terms of the decree, nor that in any other way it would have run afoul of the law of California. On no construction, therefore, can the telegram be taken as a threat either by Bridges or the union to follow an illegal course of action.

Moreover, this statement of Bridges was made to the Secretary of Labor, who is charged with official duties in connection with the prevention of strikes. Whatever the cause might be, if a strike was threatened or possible the Secretary was entitled to receive all available information. Indeed, the Supreme Court of California recognized that, publication in the newspapers aside, in sending the message to the Secretary, Bridges was exercising the right of petition to a duly accredited representative of the United States government, a right protected by the First Amendment.

It must be recognized that Bridges was a prominent labor leader speaking at a time when public interest in the particular labor controversy was at its height. The observations we have previously made here upon the timeliness and importance of utterances as emphasizing rather than diminishing the value of constitutional protection, and upon the breadth and seriousness of the censorial effects of punishing publications in the manner followed below are certainly no less applicable to a leading spokesman for labor than to a powerful newspaper taking another point of view.

In looking at the reason advanced in support of the judgment of contempt, we find that here, too, the possibility of causing unfair disposition of a pending case is the major justification asserted. And here again the gist of the offense, according to the court below, is intimidation.

Let us assume that the telegram could be construed as an

announcement of Bridges' intention to call a strike, something which, it is admitted, neither the general law of California nor the court's decree prohibited. With an eye on the realities of the situation, we cannot assume that Judge Schmidt was unaware of the possibility of a strike as a consequence of his decision. If he was not intimidated by the facts themselves, we do not believe that the most explicit statement of them could have sidetracked the course of justice. Again, we find exaggeration in the conclusion that the utterance even "tended" to interfere with justice. If there was electricity in the atmosphere, it was generated by the facts; the charge added by the Bridges telegram can be dismissed as negligible. The words of Mr. Justice Holmes, spoken in reference to very different facts, seem entirely applicable here: "I confess that I cannot find in all this or in the evidence in the case anything that would have affected a mind of reasonable fortitude, and still less can I find there anything that obstructed the administration of justice in any sense that I possibly can give to those words."

Milk Wagon Drivers Union v. Meadowmoor Dairies, 312 U.S. 287 (1941)

[The most important development in the law of free speech by the New Deal Court was the unanimous determination in 1940 that picketing is a form of speech or expression, and that it is entitled to the same constitutional protection as other forms of speech or expression. On various occasions Black has expressed himself in application of this principle, and the *Meadowmoor* dissent illustrates this point of view.

The case arose in the course of a strike by Chicago milk-wagon drivers. The Illinois Supreme Court authorized an injunction against the union which restrained not only violence but also peaceful picketing. The United States Supreme Court, in an opinion written by Justice Frankfurter, and joined by Justices McReynolds, Stone, Roberts, and Murphy and Chief Justice Hughes, held that the state courts might enjoin peaceful picketing where that peaceful picketing was "enmeshed with contemporaneously violent conduct."

Justice Black, joined by Justice Douglas, dissented. His position was that of course violent picketing could be enjoined, but that peaceful picketing by individuals utterly unconnected with any possible violence could not be enjoined. Justice Reed also dissented in a separate opinion.]

Mr. Justice BLACK, dissenting:

In my belief the opinion just announced gives approval to an injunction which seriously infringes upon the constitutional rights of freedom of speech and the press. To such a result I cannot agree.

Before detailing the reasons for my disagreement, some preliminary observations will doubtless aid in clarifying the subsidiary issues. The right of the Illinois courts to enjoin violence is not denied in this case. And I agree that nothing in the federal constitution deprives them of that right. But it is claimed that Illinois — through its courts — has here sanctioned an injunction so sweeping in its terms as to deny to petitioners and others their constitutional rights freely to express their views on matters of public concern. And this is the single federal question we must decide. In their brief, petitioners state that they "have never and do not at the present time in any way condone or justify any violence by any member of the defendant union. Petitioners did not object to the issuance of an injunction restraining acts of violence. There is no contention made that the act of the Chancellor in granting such an injunction was erroneous." "Ethically, morally and legally," the petitioning union disclaims and condemns the acts of violence. And the master who conducted the hearings in the case specifically found that the union officials had instructed their pickets to refrain from violence. The record shows that the officials gave these instruction (which were obeyed), not only because they realized that resort to force and violence would be reprehensible and indefensible, but also because they recognized that such lawless conduct injures a labor union far more than it helps it. Aside from this, it cannot be doubted that attempts to persuade others by the application of physical force and violence as a substitute for persuasion by reason and peaceable argument is contrary to the first principles of our government. Nor can it be questioned that it is a prime function of courts to provide law enforcement means intended both to punish such illegal conduct and to protect against it. But this great responsibility is entrusted to courts not merely to determine the guilt or innocence of defendants, but to do so in such manner that those brought before them may enjoy a trial in which all their constitutional rights are safeguarded — including the constitutional guarantees of freedom of speech and the press.

In determining whether the injunction does deprive petitioners of their constitutional liberties, we cannot and should not lose sight of the nature and importance of the particular liberties that are at stake. And in reaching my conclusion I view the guaranties of the First Amendment as the foundation upon which our governmental structure rests and without which it could not continue to endure as conceived and planned. Freedom to speak and write about public questions is as important to the life of our government as is the heart to the human body. In fact, this privilege is the heart of our government. If that heart be weakened, the result is debilitation; if it be stilled, the result is death.

. . . *Fifth.* In my opinion the sweeping injunction here

approved is justified by neither of the rules, and is not supported by the record.

For our purposes, in order to reach a proper conclusion as to just what is the sweep of the injunction, we must necessarily turn to the complaint, the answer, the evidence, the findings, and the decision and judgment of the Illinois courts. And whether the injunction will restrain the exercise of constitutional rights depends upon the effect it will have upon the minds of those whose freedom of expression might be abridged by its mandate. This effect in turn depends upon the language appearing upon the face of the injunction. By that language we must judge it. For this injunction does not run merely against lawyers who might give it a legalistic interpretation, but against laymen as well. Our question then becomes: To what extent will the layman who might wish to write about or discuss the prohibited subjects feel that he cannot do so without subjecting himself to the possibility of a jail sentence under a summary punishment for contempt? This injunction, like a criminal statute, prohibits conduct under fear of punishment. There is every reason why we should look at the injunction as we would a statute, and if upon its face it abridges the constitutional guaranties of freedom of expression, it should be stricken down. This is especially true because we must deal only with the federal question presented, which is whether petitioners have been denied their rights under the First Amendment. The injunction, like a statute, stands as an overhanging threat of future punishment. The law of Illinois has been declared by its highest court in such manner as to infringe upon constitutional guaranties. And by this injunction that law as actually applied abridges freedom of expression. Looking at the injunction, we find that under pain of future punishment by a trial judge all of the members of the petitioning union (about six thousand) are prohibited "From interfering, hindering or otherwise discouraging or diverting, or attempting to interfere with, hinder, discourage or divert persons desirous of or contemplating purchasing milk or cream or other products aforesaid, including the use of said signs, banners or placards, and walking up and down in front of said stores as aforesaid, and further preventing the deliveries to said stores of other articles which said stores sell through retail; (or) From threatening in any manner to do the foregoing acts. . . ." It surely cannot be doubted that an act of the Illinois legislature, couched in this sweeping language, would be held invalid on its face. For this language is capable of being construed to mean that none of those enjoined can, without subjecting themselves to summary punishment, speak, write or publish anything anywhere or at any time which the Illinois court — acting without a jury in the exercise of its broad power to punish for contempt — might conclude would result in discouraging people from buying milk products of the complaining dairy. And more than that — if the language is so construed, those enjoined can be sent to jail if they even threaten to write, speak, or publish in such way as to discourage prospective milk purchasers. I find not even slight justification for an interpretation of this injunction so as to confine its prohibitions to conduct near stores dealing in respondent's milk. Neither the language of the injunction nor that of the complaint which sought the injunction indicates such a limitation. Mr. Justice Cardozo approved no such injunction as this in *Nann* v. *Raimist*. In fact, he ordered expunged from the injunction those prohibitions which impaired "defendant's indubitable right to win converts over to its fold by recourse to peaceable persuasion, and to induce them by like methods to renounce allegiance to its rival."

But the injunction approved here does not stop at closing the mouths of the members of the petitioning union. It brings within its all-embracing sweep the spoken or written words of any other person "who may . . . now . . . or hereafter . . . agree or arrange with them. . . ." So, if a newspaper should "agree or arrange" with all or some of those here enjoined to publish their side of the controversy, thereby necessarily tending to "discourage" the sale of cut-rate milk, the publishers might likewise be subject to punishment for contempt. Ordinarily the scope of the decree is co-extensive with the allegations of the bill, its supporting affidavits or findings of fact. In other words, the acts enjoined are the acts alleged in the bill as the basis for complaint. And the complaint on which the injunction here rests specifically charged that the union had caused "announcement to be made by the public press of the City of Chicago, for the purpose of intimidating the said storekeepers and causing them to cease purchasing the milk sold by said plaintiffs through fear and terror of the renewal of said conspiracy. . . ." Specific reference was made to these newspaper stories as appearing in The *Chicago Tribune* and The *Chicago Evening American*. Proof was made of these publications. And the injunction of the trial judge, set aside by the Supreme Court of Illinois, specifically saved to petitioners — as in effect did Justice Cardozo in the New York case — their right to publicize their cause by means of "advertisement or communication." But the injunction sustained here is to be issued as prayed for in the bill of complaint. And since the acts enjoined are the acts alleged in the bill as the basis for complaint, newspaper publications of the type referred to in the complaint are literally enjoined. Since the literal language of the injunction, read in the light of the complaint, the supporting evidence, and the language of the trial judge's saving clause — stricken down by action sustained here — thus unconstitutionally abridges the rights of freedom of speech and press, we cannot escape our responsibility by the simple expedient of declaring that those who might be sent to jail for violating the plain language of the injunction might eventually obtain relief by appeal to this Court. To sanction vague and undefined terminologies in dragnet clauses directly and exclusively aimed at restricting freedom of discussion upon the theory that we might later acquit those convicted for violation of such terminology amounts in my judgment to a prior censorship of views. No matter how the decree might eventually be construed, its language, viewed in the light of the whole proceedings, stands like an abstract statute with an overhanging and undefined threat to freedom of speech and the press. All this, of course, is true only as to those who argue on the side of the opponents of cut-rate distribution. No such undefined threat hangs over those who "agree or arrange" with the advocates of the cut-rate system to encourage their method of distribution.

A careful study of the entire record in this case convinces me that neither the findings nor the evidence, even viewed in the light most favorable to respondent, showed such imminent, clear and present danger as to justify an abridgement of the rights of freedom of speech and the press. The picketing, which did not begin until September, 1934, has at all times been peaceful. Usually one picket, and never more than two, walked along the street bearing a sign. These pickets never impeded traffic either on the sidewalks or in the street, nor did they disturb any passersby or customers. In fact, it is stipulated in the record that pickets "made no threats against any of these storekeepers, but peacefully picketed these stores. They made no attempt to stop any customers or to stop delivery except insofar as their situation and the signs they bore had that tendency."

There was no evidence to connect them with any kind or type of violence at any time or place. As was found by the master, this was in accordance with the instruction which was given to them by the union officials. There is no evidence and no finding that dissemination or information by pickets stimulated anyone else to commit any act of violence.

There was evidence that violence occurred — some committed by identified persons and some by unidentified persons. A strike of farmers supplying most of Chicago's milk took place in the early part of January, 1934. This strike practically stopped the inflow of milk into the city. As a result, the union drivers were ordered not to report for work on January 8 and 9, at the height of the strike. It was during this period that the larger part of the major acts of violence occurred. According to the complaint and the evidence, seven trucks were seized or damaged on the 8th and 9th of January, 1934, and one on the 6th. These are the only trucks that were ever seized or damaged, according to both the complaint and the evidence, and it was in connection with these seizures that the injuries to truck drivers, the shootings, and the threats referred to in this Court's opinion took place. Undoubtedly, some of the members of the union participated in this violence, as is shown by the fact that several were arrested, criminal prosecutions were instituted, and the cases later settled with the approval of the trial judge. It was eight months after this before any picketing occurred; four years afterward before the trial judge granted an injunction, limited to violence alone; five years before the Supreme Court of Illinois directed a more stringent injunction against peaceful persuasion; and seven years before this Court sustained the injunction.

During the period of the farmers' strike in 1934, and in

the immediately succeeding months, five stores were either bombed or burned. Three union members were tried, convicted and sentenced to the penitentiary for arson in connection with one of these burnings. All of this violence took place many months before any of the picketing occurred. In addition to these 1934 acts of violence, the evidence showed that one stench bomb was thrown into a store in 1935, one in 1936, and two in 1937. The identity of the persons throwing these stench bombs was not shown.

The only other violence alleged or testified to was the breaking of windows in cut-rate stores. Most of the testimony as to these acts of violence was given by respondent's vendors, and was extremely indefinite. The master made no findings as to specific acts of violence, nor as to the dates of their occurrence.

It is on the basis of my study of the entire record that I rest my conclusion that the forfeiture of the right to free speech effected by the injunction is not warranted. In reaching this conclusion, I fully recognize that the union members guilty of violence were subject to punishment in accordance with the principles of due process of law. And some of them have in fact been prosecuted and convicted. Punishment of lawless conduct is in accord with the necessities of government and is essential to the peace and tranquility of society. But it is going a long way to say that because of the acts of these few men, six thousand other members of their union can be denied the right to express their opinion to the extent accomplished by the sweeping injunction here sustained. Even those convicted of crime are not in this country punished by having their freedom of expression curtailed except under prison rules and regulations, and then only for the duration of their sentence.

No one doubts that Illinois can protect its storekeepers from being coerced by fear of damage to their property from window-smashing, or burnings or bombings. And to that end Illinois is free to use all its vast resources and powers, nor should this Court stand in the way so long as Illinois does not take away from its people rights guaranteed to them by the Constitution of the United States. When clear and present danger of riot disorder, interference with traffic upon the public streets, or other immediate threat to public safety, peace or order appears, the power of the Illinois courts to prevent or punish is obvious. Furthermore, this is true because a state has the power to adopt laws of general application to provide that the streets shall be used for the purpose for which they primarily exist, and because the preservation of peace and order is one of the first duties of government. But in a series of cases we have held that local laws ostensibly passed pursuant to this admittedly possessed general power could not be enforced in such a way as to amount to a prior censorship on freedom of expression, or to abridge that freedom as to those rightfully and lawfully on the streets. Illinois, like all the other states of the Union, is part of a national democratic system the continued existence of which depends upon the right of free discussion of public affairs — a right whose denial to some leads in the direction of its eventual denial to all. I am of opinion that the court's injunction strikes directly at the heart of our government, and that deprivation of these essential liberties cannot be reconciled with the rights guaranteed to the people of this Nation by their Constitution.

United Public Workers v. *Mitchell,*
330 U.S. 75 (1947)

[At the time in which these cases are edited, a new menace to civil rights is rapidly coming into being. That menace is the control of freedom by the control of employment — a man's job and thus his livelihood may be endangered if his opinions on completely unrelated matters are nonconformist.

The Hatch Act was a well-intended but none the less real step toward the use of job control as a political control. The act not only attempted to stop abuses in the civil service by hammering at the spoils system of government job distribution, but also went farther to limit, in various ways described in this opinion, the freedom of government employees to participate in political campaigns at all.

In this case, one of two decided together, the detailed facts of which are not particularly necessary to the understanding of the issue, the Court upheld the validity of the Hatch Act. Justice Reed wrote the majority opinion for Justices Frankfurter and Burton and Chief Justice Vinson, with Justice Frankfurter disagreeing with his majority colleagues on one point. Justice Douglas concurred in part and dissented in part, and Justices Murphy and Jackson did not participate. Justice Black dissented entirely, and Justice Rutledge was in substantial agreement with him.],

Mr. Justice BLACK, dissenting:

The sentence in Section 9 of the statute, here upheld, makes it unlawful for any person employed in the executive branch of the Federal Government, with minor numerical exceptions, to "take any active part in political management or in political campaigns." The punishment provided is immediate discharge and a permanent ban against re-employment in the same position. The number of federal employees thus barred from political action is approximately three million. Section 12 of the same Act affects the participation in political campaigns of many thousands of state employees. No one of all these millions of citizens can, without violating this law, "take any active part" in any campaign for a cause or for a candidate if the cause or candidate is "specifically identified with any National or State political party." Since under our common political practices most causes and candidates are espoused by political parties, the result is that, because they are paid out of the public treasury, all these citizens who engage in public work can take no really effective part in campaigns that may bring about changes in their lives, their fortunes, and their happiness.

We are not left in doubt as to how numerous and varied are the "activities" prohibited. For Section 15 sweepingly describes them as "the same activities . . . as the United States Civil Service Commission has heretofore determined are at the time this section takes effect prohibited on the part of employees in the classified civil service of the United States. . . ." Along with the vague and uncertain prior prohibitions of the Commission, are these things which the Commission had clearly prohibited: serving as an election officer; publicly expressing political views at a party caucus or political gathering for or against any candidate or cause identified with a party; soliciting votes for a party or candidate; participating in a political parade; writing for publication or publishing any letter or article, signed or unsigned, in favor of or against any political party, candidate, or faction; initiating, or canvassing for signatures on, community petitions or petitions to Congress.

In view of these prohibitions, it is little consolation to employees that the Act contradictorily says that they may "express their opinions on all political subjects and candidates." For this permission to "express their opinions," is, the Commission has rightly said, "subject to the prohibition that employees may not take any active part in . . . political campaigns." The hopeless contradiction between this privilege of an employee to talk and the prohibition against his talking stands out in the Commission's further warning to all employees that they can express their opinions publicly, but "Public expression of opinion in such way as to constitute taking an active part in political management or in political campaigns is accordingly prohibited." Thus, whatever opinions employees may dare to express, even secretly, must be at their peril. They cannot know what particular expressions may be reported to the Commission and held by it to be a sufficient political activity to cost them their jobs. Their peril is all the greater because of another warning by the Commission that "Employees are . . . accountable for political activity by persons other than themselves, including wives or husbands, if, in fact, the employees are thus accomplishing by collusion and indirection what they may not lawfully do directly and openly." Thus are the families of public employees stripped of their freedom of political action. The result is that the sum of political privilege left to government and state employees, and their families, to take part in political campaigns seems to be this: They may vote in silence; they may carefully and quietly express a political view at their peril; and they may become "spectators" (this is the Commission's word) at campaign gatherings, though it may be highly dangerous for them to "second a motion" or let it be known that they agree or disagree with a speaker.

Had this measure deprived five million farmers, or a million businessmen of all right to participate in elections, because Congress thought that federal farm or business subsidies might prompt some of them to exercise, or be susceptible to, a corrupting influence on politics or government, I would not sustain such an Act on the ground that it could be interpreted so as to apply only to some of them. Certainly laws which restrict the liberties guaranteed by the First Amendment should be narrowly drawn to meet the evil aimed at and to affect only the minimum number of people imperatively necessary to prevent a grave and imminent danger to the public. Furthermore, what federal employees can or cannot do, consistently with the various civil service regulations, rules, warnings, etc., is a matter of so great uncertainty that no person can even make an intelligent guess. This was demonstrated by the government's briefs and oral arguments in this case. I would hold that the provision here attacked is too broad, ambiguous, and uncertain in its consequences to be made the basis of removing deserving employees from their jobs.

The rights to vote and privately to express an opinion on political matters, important though they be, are but parts of the broad freedoms which our Constitution has provided as the bulwark of our free political institutions. Popular government, to be effective, must permit and encourage much wider political activity by all the people. Real popular government means "that men may speak as they think on matters vital to them and that falsehoods may be exposed through the processes of education and discussion. . . . Those who won our independence had confidence in the power of free and fearless reasoning and communication of ideas to discover and spread political and economic truth." Legislation which muzzles several million citizens threatens popular government, not only because it injures the individuals muzzled, but also because of its harmful effect on the body politic in depriving it of the political participation and interest of such a large segment of our citizens. Forcing public employees to contribute money and influence can well be proscribed in the interest of "clean politics" and public administration. But I think the Constitution prohibits legislation which prevents millions of citizens from contributing their arguments, complaints, and suggestions to the political debates which are the essence of our democracy; prevents them from engaging in organizational

activity to urge others to vote and take an interest in political affairs; bars them from performing the interested citizen's duty of insuring that his and his fellow citizens' votes
are counted. Such drastic limitations on the right of all the
people to express political opinions and take political action
would be inconsistent with the First Amendment's guaranty
of freedom of speech, press, assembly, and petition. And it
would violate, or come dangerously close to violating, Article I and the Seventeenth Amendment of the Constitution,
which protect the right of the people to vote for their Congressmen and their United States Senators and to have
their votes counted.

There is nothing about federal and state employees as a
class which justifies depriving them or society of the benefits of their participation in public affairs. They, like other
citizens, pay taxes and serve their country in peace and in
war. The taxes they pay and the wars in which they fight
are determined by the elected spokesmen of all the people.
They come from the same homes, communities, schools,
churches, and colleges as do the other citizens. I think the
Constitution guarantees to them the same right that other
groups of good citizens have to engage in activities which
decide who their elected representatives shall be.

It may be true, as contended, that if public employees
are permitted to exercise a full freedom to express their
views in political campaigns, some public officials will discharge some employees and grant promotion to others on a
political rather than on a merit basis. For the same reasons
other public officials, occupying positions of influence, may
use their influence to have their own political supporters
appointed or promoted. But here again, if the practice of
making discharges, promotions or recommendations for promotions on a political basis is so great an evil as to require
legislation, the law could punish those public officials who

308

engage in the practice. To punish millions of employees and to deprive the nation of their contribution to public affairs, in order to remove temptation from a proportionately small number of public officials, seems at the least to be a novel method of suppressing what is thought to be an evil practice.

The section of the Act here held valid reduces the constitutionally protected liberty of several million citizens to less than a shadow of its substance. It relegates millions of federal, state, and municipal employees to the role of mere spectators of events upon which hinge the safety and welfare of all the people, including public employees. It removes a sizable proportion of our electorate from full participation in affairs destined to mould the fortunes of the Nation. It makes honest participation in essential political activities an offense punishable by proscription from public employment. It endows a governmental board with the awesome power to censor the thoughts, expressions, and activities of law-abiding citizens in the field of free expression from which no person should be barred by a government which boasts that it is a government of, for, and by the people — all the people. Laudable as its purpose may be, it seems to me to hack at the roots of a Government by the people themselves; and consequently I cannot agree to sustain its validity.

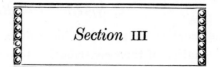

FAIR TRIAL

Chambers v. *Florida,* 309 U.S. 227 (1940)

[Some of Justice Black's best, most effective, and most valuable work as a Justice has been his contribution to the continuing effort to raise the standard of administration of criminal justice. Since his prosecutor days he has fought the third degree. On the Supreme Court he has been in a position to do something about it. At about the time Black came to the Court, it was established that a confession obtained from a prisoner by a prolonged beating could not be used; and it was then possible to move toward new horizons of decency.

If Black's work, and that of others like-minded, is effective, there will be a day when the sole method of sifting the innocent from the guilty will be by evidence, and not by beating, by prolonged and fearsome incarceration, by starvation, or by torturous grilling with bright lights shining in the victim's eyes for hours or even days at a time.

The *Chambers* case is widely regarded as the best opinion written by Black, and was warmly praised by President Roosevelt at the time of its decision. The Court held, in this unanimous opinion, that the confessions obtained as described here could not be used by the state of Florida to condemn four Negro defendants to death.]

Mr. Justice BLACK delivered the opinion of the Court.

The grave question presented by the petition for certiorari, granted in forma pauperis, is whether proceedings in

310

which confessions were utilized, and which culminated in sentences of death upon four young Negro men in the State of Florida, failed to afford the safeguard of that due process of law guaranteed by the Fourteenth Amendment.

First. The State of Florida challenges our jurisdiction to look behind the judgments below claiming that the issues of fact upon which petitioners base their claim that due process was denied them have been finally determined because passed upon by a jury. However, use by a State of an improperly obtained confession may constitute a denial of due process of law as guaranteed in the Fourteenth Amendment. Since petitioners have seasonably asserted the right under the Federal Constitution to have their guilt or innocence of a capital crime determined without reliance upon confessions obtained by means proscribed by the due process clause of the Fourteenth Amendment, we must determine independently whether petitioners' confessions were so obtained, by review of the facts upon which that issue necessarily turns. . . .

Second. The record shows —

About nine o'clock on the night of Saturday, May 13, 1933, Robert Darcy, an elderly white man, was robbed and murdered in Pompano, Florida, a small town in Broward County about twelve miles from Fort Lauderdale, the County seat. The opinion of the Supreme Court of Florida affirming petitioners' conviction for this crime stated that "It was one of those crimes that induced an enraged community . . ." And, as the dissenting judge pointed out, "The murder and robbery of the elderly Mr. Darcy . . . was a most dastardly and atrocious crime. It naturally aroused great and well justified public indignation."

Between 9:30 and 10 o'clock after the murder, petitioner Charlie Davis was arrested, and within the next twenty-four hours from twenty-five to forty Negroes living in the community, including petitioners Williamson, Chambers and Woodward, were arrested without warrants and confined in the Broward County jail, at Fort Lauderdale. On the night of the crime, attempts to trail the murderers by bloodhounds brought J. T. Williams, a convict guard, into the proceedings. From then until confessions were obtained and petitioners were sentenced, he took a prominent part. About 11 P.M. on the following Monday, May 15, the sheriff and Williams took several of the imprisoned Negroes, including Williamson and Chambers, to the Dade County jail at Miami. The sheriff testified that they were taken there because he felt a possibility of mob violence and "wanted to give protection to every prisoner . . . in jail." Evidence of petitioners was that on the way to Miami a motorcycle patrolman drew up to the car in which the men were riding and the sheriff "told the cop that he had some Negroes that he [was] . . . taking down to Miami to escape a mob." This statement was not denied by the Sheriff in his testimony and Williams did not testify at all; Williams apparently has now disappeared. Upon order of Williams, petitioner Williamson was kept in the death cell of the Dade County jail. The prisoners thus spirited to Miami were returned to the Fort Lauderdale jail the next day, Tuesday.

It is clear from the evidence of both the State and petitioners that from Sunday, May 14, to Saturday, May 20, the thirty to forty Negro suspects were subjected to questioning and cross questioning (with the exception that several of the suspects were in Dade County jail over one night). From the afternoon of Saturday, May 20, until sunrise of the 21st, petitioners and possibly one or two others underwent persistent and repeated questioning. The Supreme Court of Florida said the questioning "was in progress several days and all night before the confessions were secured" and referred to the last night as an "all night vigil." The sheriff who supervised the procedure of continued interrogation testified that he questioned the prisoners "in the day time all the week," but did not question them during any night before the all night vigil of Saturday, May 20, because after having "questioned them all day . . . (he) was tired." Other evidence of the State was "that the officers of Broward County were in that jail almost continually during the whole week questioning these boys, and other boys, in connection with this" case.

The process of repeated questioning took place in the jailer's quarters on the fourth floor of the jail. During the week following their arrests and until their confessions were finally acceptable to the State's attorney in the early dawn of Sunday, May 21st, petitioners and their fellow prisoners were led one at a time from their cells to the questioning room, quizzed, and returned to their cells to await another turn. So far as appears, the prisoners at no time during the week were permitted to see or confer with counsel or a single friend or relative. When carried singly from his cell and subjected to questioning, each found himself, a single prisoner, surrounded in a fourth floor jail room by four to ten men, the county sheriff, his deputies, a convict guard, and other white officers and citizens of the community.

The testimony is in conflict as to whether all four petitioners were continually threatened and physically maltreated until they finally, in hopeless desperation and fear of their lives, agreed to confess on Sunday morning just after daylight. Be that as it may, it is certain that by Saturday, May 20th, five days of continued questioning had elicited no confession. Admittedly, a concentration of effort — directed against a small number of prisoners including petitioners — on the part of the questioners, principally the sheriff and Williams, the convict guard, began about

3:30 that Saturday afternoon. From that hour on, with only short intervals for food and rest for the questioners — "They all stayed up all night." "They bring one of them at a time backwards and forwards . . . until they confessed." And Williams was present and participating that night, during the whole of which the jail cook served coffee and sandwiches to the men who "grilled" the prisoners.

Sometime in the early hours of Sunday, the 21st, probably about 2:30 A.M., Woodward apparently "broke" — as one of the State's witnesses put it — after a fifteen or twenty minute period of questioning by Williams, the sheriff and the constable "one right after the other." The State's attorney was awakened at his home, and called to the jail. He came, but was dissatisfied with the confession of Woodward which he took down in writing at that time, and said something like "tear this paper up, that isn't what I want, when you get something worth while call me." This same State's attorney conducted the State's case in the circuit court below and also made himself a witness, but did not testify as to why Woodward's first alleged confession was unsatisfactory to him. The sheriff did, however:

"A. No, it wasn't false, part of it was true and part of it wasn't; Mr. Maire (the State's attorney) said there wasn't enough. It wasn't clear enough.

"Q. . . . Was that voluntarily made at that time?

"A. Yes, sir.

"Q. It was voluntarily made that time.

"A. Yes, sir.

"Q. You didn't consider it sufficient?

"A. Mr. Maire.

"Q. Mr. Maire told you that it wasn't sufficient, so you kept on questioning him until the time you got him to make a free and voluntary confession of other matters that he hadn't included in the first?

314

"A. No sir, we questioned him there and we caught him in lies.

"Q. Caught all of them telling lies?

"A. Caught every one of them lying to us that night, yes, sir.

"Q. Did you tell them they were lying?

"A. Yes, sir.

"Q. Just how would you tell them that?

"A. Just like I am talking to you.

"Q. You said, 'Jack, you told me a lie'?

"A. Yes, sir.

After one week's constant denial of all guilt, petitioners "broke."

Just before sunrise, the State officials got something "worthwhile" from petitioners which the State's attorney would "want"; again he was called; he came; in the presence of those who had carried on and witnessed the all night questioning, he caused his questions and petitioners' answers to be stenographically reported. These are the confessions utilized by the State to obtain the judgments upon which petitioners were sentenced to death. No formal charges had been brought before the confessions. Two days thereafter, petitioners were indicted, were arraigned and Williamson and Woodward pleaded guilty; Chambers and Davis pleaded not guilty. Later the sheriff, accompanied by Williams, informed an attorney who presumably had been appointed to defend Davis that Davis wanted his plea of not guilty withdrawn. This was done, and Davis then pleaded guilty. When Chambers was tried, his conviction rested upon his confession and testimony of the other three confessors. The convict guard and the sheriff "were in the Court room sitting down in a seat." And from arrest until sentenced to death, petitioners were never — either in jail or in court — wholly removed from the constant observation, influence, custody and control of those whose persistent pressure brought about the sunrise confessions.

Third. The scope and operation of the Fourteenth Amendment have been fruitful sources of controversy in our constitutional history. However, in view of its historical setting and the wrongs which called it into being, the due process provision of the Fourteenth Amendment — just as that in the Fifth — has led few to doubt that it was intended to guarantee procedural standards adequate and appropriate, then and thereafter, to protect, at all times, people charged with or suspected of crime by those holding positions of power and authority. Tyrannical governments had immemorially utilized dictatorial criminal procedure and punishments to make scapegoats of the weak, or of helpless political, religious, or racial minorities and those who differed, who would not conform and who resisted tyranny. The instruments of such governments were in the main two. Conduct, innocent when engaged in, was subsequently made by fiat criminally punishable without legislation. And a liberty loving people won the principle that criminal punishments could not be inflicted save for that which proper legislative action had already by "the law of the land" forbidden when done. But even more was needed. From the popular hatred and abhorrence of illegal confinement, torture and extortion of confessions of violations of the "law of the land" evolved the fundamental idea that no man's life, liberty or property be forfeited as criminal punishment for violation of that law until there had been a charge fairly made and fairly tried in a public tribunal free of prejudice, passion, excitement and tyrannical power. Thus, as assurance against ancient evils, our country, in order to preserve "the blessings of liberty," wrote into its basic law the requirement, among others, that the forfeiture of the lives, liberties or property of people accused of crime can only follow if procedural safeguards of due process have been obeyed.

The determination to preserve an accused's right to procedural due process sprang in large part from knowledge of historical truth that the rights and liberties of people accused of crime could not be safely entrusted to secret inquisitorial processes. The testimony of centuries, in governments of varying kinds over populations of different races and beliefs, stood as proof that physical and mental torture and coercion had brought about the tragically unjust sacrifices of some who were the noblest and most useful of their generations. The rack, the thumbscrew, the wheel, solitary confinement, protracted questioning and cross questioning, and other ingenious forms of entrapment of the helpless or unpopular had left their wake of mutilated bodies and shattered minds along the way to the cross, the guillotine, the stake and the hangman's noose. And they who have suffered most from secret and dictatorial proceedings have almost always been the poor, the ignorant, the numerically weak, the friendless and the powerless.

This requirement — of conforming to fundamental standards of procedure in criminal trials — was made operative against the States by the Fourteenth Amendment. Where one of several accused had limped into the trial court as a result of admitted physical mistreatment inflicted to obtain confessions upon which a jury had returned a verdict of guilty of murder, this Court recently declared, *Brown* v. *Mississippi*, that "it would be difficult to conceive of methods more revolting to the sense of justice than those taken to procure the confessions of these petitioners, and the use of the confessions thus obtained as the basis for conviction and sentence was a clear denial of due process."

Here, the record develops a sharp conflict upon the issue of physical violence and mistreatment, but shows, without conflict, the dragnet methods of arrest on suspicion without warrant, and the protracted questioning and cross questioning of these ignorant young colored tenant farmers by State officers and other white citizens, in a fourth floor jail room, where as prisoners they were without friends, advisers or counselors, and under circumstances calculated to break the strongest nerves and the stoutest resistance. Just as our decision in *Brown* v. *Mississippi* was based upon the fact that the confessions were the result of compulsion, so in the present case, the admitted practices were such as to justify the statement that "The undisputed facts showed that compulsion was applied."

For five days petitioners were subjected to interrogations culminating in Saturday's (May 20th) all night examination. Over a period of five days they steadily refused to confess and disclaimed any guilt. The very circumstances surrounding their confinement and their questioning without any formal charges having been brought, were such as to fill petitioners with terror and frightful misgivings. Some were practical strangers in the community; three were arrested in a one-room farm tenant house which was their home; the haunting fear of mob violence was around them in an atmosphere charged with excitement and public indignation. From virtually the moment of their arrest until their eventual confessions, they never knew when just any one would be called back to the fourth floor room, and there, surrounded by his accusers and others, interrogated by men who held their very lives — so far as these ignorant petitioners could know — in the balance. The rejection of petitioner Woodward's first "confession," given in the early hours of Sunday morning, because it was found wanting, demonstrates the relentless tenacity which "broke" petitioners' will and rendered them helpless to resist their accusers further. To permit human lives to be forfeited upon confessions thus obtained would make of the constitutional requirement of due process of law a meaningless symbol.

We are not impressed by the argument that law enforcement methods such as those under review are necessary to uphold our laws. The Constitution proscribes such lawless means irrespective of the end. And this argument flouts the basic principle that all people must stand on an equality before the bar of justice in every American court. Today, as in ages past, we are not without tragic proof that the exalted power of some governments to punish manufactured crime dictatorially is the handmaid of tyranny. Under our constitutional system, courts stand against any winds that blow as havens of refuge for those who might otherwise suffer because they are helpless, weak, outnumbered, or because they are non-conforming victims of prejudice and public excitement. Due process of law, preserved for all by our Constitution, commands that no such practice as that disclosed by this record shall send any accused to his death. No higher duty, no more solemn responsibility, rests upon this Court, than that of translating into living law and maintaining this constitutional shield deliberately planned and inscribed for the benefit of every human being subject to our Constitution — of whatever race, creed or persuasion.

The Supreme Court of Florida was in error and its judgment is

Reversed.

White v. *Texas*, 310 U.S. 530 (1940)

[The *White* case is included here because it shows the application of the *Chambers* principle in a routine case. The opinion was unanimous, and is set forth here with omission of procedural details only.]

Mr. Justice BLACK delivered the opinion of the Court.

Petitioner is an illiterate farmhand who was engaged, at the time of his arrest, upon a plantation about ten miles from Livingston, Texas. On the day following the crime with which he has been charged, he was called from the field in which he was picking cotton and was taken to the house of the brother-in-law of the prosecutrix, the victim of the crime, where fifteen or sixteen Negroes of the vicinity were at the time in custody without warrants or the filing of charges. Taken to the county court house, and thence to the Polk County jail, petitioner was kept there six or seven days. According to his testimony, armed Texas Rangers on several successive nights took him handcuffed from the jail "up in the woods somewhere," whipped him, asked him each time about a confession and warned him not to speak to any one about the nightly trips to the woods. During the period of his arrest up to and including the signing of the alleged confession, petitioner had no lawyer, no charges were filed against him and he was out of touch with friends or relatives.

There were denials that petitioner was ever physically mistreated or abused. But the Rangers and a local peace officer, identified by petitioner as the officers who took him on the night trips to the woods and there whipped him, did not specifically deny that he was taken out of jail, at night, and interrogated in the woods. This local peace officer wasn't sure "how many times" the prisoner was removed from jail, and one Ranger re-stated his testimony given at the first trial that he "took him out so many times" the exact number could not be recalled. The prisoner was taken out of jail, driven "out on the road" and then "out off of the road," as this Ranger testified, in order that the officers could talk to him and because the jail was crowded. In jail, the Sheriff put petitioner by himself and "kept watching him and talking to him."

Before carrying petitioner to Beaumont, where the alleged confession was taken, the Sheriff talked about an hour and a half with him. The Rangers who had been taking petitioner to the woods at night knew the county attorney was going to Beaumont to get a statement; they, too, went there and were in and out of the eighth floor room of the jail in Beaumont, with the elevator locked, where petitioner was interrogated from approximately 11:00 P.M. to 3:00 or 3:30 A.M. The alleged confession was reduced to writing after 2 A.M. Immediately before it was taken down, the prisoner was repeatedly asked by the private prosecutor whether he was ready to confess. Petitioner then began to cry, and the typing of the confession, upon which the State's case substantially rested, was completed by the county attorney about daylight. Two citizens of Beaumont signed it as witnesses.

"Due process of law, preserved for all by our Constitution, commands that no such practice as that disclosed by this record shall send any accused to his death."

The State's petition for rehearing is denied.

Ashcraft v. *Tennessee,* 322 U.S. 143 (1944)

[The *Ashcraft* case is of interest primarily because it is not a unanimous opinion. To that extent it shows the point at which the Court begins to split in granting protection against forced confessions. Here Ashcraft was charged in a Tennessee court with the murder of his wife and was grilled under circumstances detailed in the opinion for thirty-six hours at one stretch. The opinion introduces for the first time a fairly clear-cut standard into the law of confession: the majority proclaims, by implication at least, that police may not treat a suspect any more brutally in a closed room away from the eyes of the public than a prosecuting attorney would be allowed to treat the same person in open court under the eyes of a judge.

The opinion of the Court, delivered by Justice Black, was joined by Justices Reed, Douglas, Murphy, and Rutledge and Chief Justice Stone. Justice Jackson wrote a dissent joined by Justices Roberts and Frankfurter.]

Mr. Justice BLACK delivered the opinion of the Court.

About three o'clock on the morning of Thursday, June 5, 1941, Mrs. Zelma Ida Ashcraft got in her automobile at her home in Memphis, Tennessee, and set out on a trip to visit her mother's home in Kentucky. Late in the afternoon of the same day, her car was observed a few miles out of Memphis, standing on the wrong side of a road which she would likely have taken on her journey. Just off the road, in a slough, her lifeless body was found. On her head were cut places inflicted by blows sufficient to have caused her death. Petitioner Ware, age 20, a Negro, was indicted in a state court and found guilty of her murder. Petitioner Ashcraft, age 45, a white man, husband of the deceased, charged with having hired Ware to commit the murder, was tried jointly with Ware and convicted as an accessory before the fact. Both were sentenced to ninety-nine years in the state penitentiary. The Supreme Court of Tennessee affirmed the convictions. . . .

This treatment of the confessions by the two state courts, the manner of the confessions' submission to the jury, and the emphasis upon the great weight to be given confessions make all the more important the kind of "independent examination" of petitioners' claims which, in any event, we are bound to make. Our duty to make that examination could not have been "foreclosed by the finding of a court, or the verdict of a jury, or both." We proceed therefore to consider the evidence relating to the circumstances out of which the alleged confessions came.

First, as to Ashcraft. Ashcraft was born on an Arkansas farm. At the age of eleven he left the farm and became a farm hand working for others. Years later he gravitated into construction work, finally becoming a skilled dragline and steam-shovel operator. Uncontradicted evidence in the record was that he had acquired for himself "an excellent reputation." In 1929 he married the deceased Zelma Ida Ashcraft. Childless, they accumulated, apparently through Ashcraft's earnings, a very modest amount of jointly held property including bank accounts and an equity in the home in which they lived. The Supreme Court of Tennessee found "nothing to show but what the home life of Ashcraft and the deceased was pleasant and happy." Several of Mrs. Ashcraft's friends who were guests at the Ashcraft home on the night before her tragic death testified that both husband and wife appeared to be in a happy frame of mind.

The officers first talked to Ashcraft about 6 P.M. on the day of his wife's murder as he was returning home from work. Informed by them of the tragedy, he was taken to an undertaking establishment to identify her body which previously had been identified only by a driver's license. From there he was taken to the county jail where he conferred with the officers until about 2 A.M. No clues of ultimate value came from this conference, though it did result in the officers' holding and interrogating the Ashcraft's maid and several of her friends. During the following week the officers made extensive investigations in Ashcraft's neighborhood and elsewhere and further conferred with Ashcraft himself on several occasions, but none of these

THE OPINIONS§ CIVIL RIGHTS

activities produced tangible evidence pointing to the identity of the murderer.

Then, early in the evening of Saturday, June 14, the officers came to Ashcraft's home and "took him into custody." In the words of the Tennessee Supreme Court,

"They took him to an office or room on the northwest corner of the fifth floor of the Shelby County jail. This office is equipped with all sorts of crime and detective devices such as a fingerprint outfit, cameras, high-powered lights, and such other devices as might be found in a homicide investigating office. . . . It appears that the officers placed Ashcraft at a table in this room on the fifth floor of the county jail with a light over his head and began to quiz him. They questioned him in relays until the following Monday morning, June 16, 1941, around nine-thirty or ten o'clock. It appears that Ashcraft from Saturday evening at seven o'clock until Monday morning at approximately nine-thirty never left this homicide room on the fifth floor."

Testimony of the officers shows that the reason they questioned Ashcraft "in relays" was that they became so tired they were compelled to rest. But from 7:00 Saturday evening until 9:30 Monday morning Ashcraft had no rest. One officer did say that he gave the suspect a single five minutes' respite, but except for this five minutes the procedure consisted of one continuous stream of questions.

As to what happened in the fifth-floor jail room during this thirty-six hour secret examination the testimony follows the usual pattern and is in hopeless conflict. Ashcraft swears that the first thing said to him when he was taken into custody was, "Why in hell did you kill your wife?"; that during the course of the examination he was threatened and abused in various ways; and that as the hours passed his eyes became blinded by a powerful electric light, his body became weary, and the strain on his nerves became unbearable. The officers, on the other hand, swear that throughout the questioning they were kind and considerate. They say that they did not accuse Ashcraft of the murder until four hours after he was brought to the jail building, though they freely admit that from that time on their barrage of questions was constantly directed at him on the assumption that he was the murderer. Together with other persons whom they brought in on Monday morning to witness the culmination of the thirty-six hour ordeal the officers declare that at that time Ashcraft was "cool," "calm," "collected," "normal"; that his vision was unimpaired and his eyes not bloodshot; and that he showed no outward signs of being tired or sleepy.

As to whether Ashcraft actually confessed, there is a similar conflict of testimony. Ashcraft maintains that although the officers incessantly attempted by various tactics of intimidation to entrap him into a confession, not once did he admit knowledge concerning or participation in the crime. And he specifically denies the officers' statements that he accused Ware of the crime, insisting that in response to their questions he merely gave them the name of Ware as one of several men who occasionally had ridden with him to work. The officers' version of what happened, however, is that about 11 P.M. on Sunday night, after twenty-eight hours' constant questioning, Ashcraft made a statement that Ware had overpowered him at his home and abducted the deceased, and was probably the killer. About midnight the officers found Ware and took him into custody, and, according to their testimony, Ware made a self-incriminating statement as of early Monday morning, and at 5:40 A.M. signed by mark a written confession in which appeared the statement that Ashcraft had hired him to commit the murder. This alleged confession of Ware was read to Ashcraft about six o'clock Monday morning, whereupon Ashcraft is said substantially to have admitted its truth in a detailed statement taken down by a reporter. About 9:30 Monday morning a transcript of Ashcraft's purported statement was read to him. The State's position is that he affirmed its truth but refused to sign the transcript, saying that he first wanted to consult his lawyer. As to this latter 9:30 episode the officers' testimony is reinforced by testimony of the several persons whom they brought in to witness the end of the examination.

In reaching our conclusion as to the validity of Ashcraft's confession we do not resolve any of the disputed questions of fact relating to the details of what transpired within the confession chamber of the jail or whether Ashcraft actually did confess. Such disputes, we may say, are an inescapable consequence of secret inquisitorial practices. And always evidence concerning the inner details of secret inquisitions is weighted against an accused, particularly where, as here, he is charged with a brutal crime, or where, as in many other cases, his supposed offense bears relation to an unpopular economic, political, or religious cause.

Our conclusion is that if Ashcraft made a confession it was not voluntary but compelled. We reach this conclusion from facts which are not in dispute at all. Ashcraft, a citizen of excellent reputation, was taken into custody by police officers. Ten days' examination of the Ashcrafts' maid, and of several others, in jail where they were held, had revealed nothing whatever against Ashcraft. Inquiries among his neighbors and business associates likewise had failed to unearth one single tangible clue pointing to his guilt. For thirty-six hours after Ashcraft's seizure during which period he was held incommunicado, without sleep or rest, relays of officers, experienced investigators, and highly trained lawyers questioned him without respite. From the beginning of the questioning at 7 o'clock on Saturday evening until 6 o'clock on Monday morning Ashcraft denied that he had anything to do with the murder of his wife. And at a hearing before a magistrate about 8:30 Monday morning Ashcraft pleaded not guilty to the charge of murder which the officers had sought to make him confess during the previous thirty-six hours.

We think a situation such as that here shown by uncontradicted evidence is so inherently coercive that its very existence is irreconcilable with the possession of mental freedom by a lone suspect against whom its full coercive force is brought to bear. It is inconceivable that any court of justice in the land, conducted as our courts are, open to the public, would permit prosecutors serving in relays to keep a defendant witness under continuous cross-examination for thirty-six hours without rest or sleep in an effort to extract a "voluntary" confession. Nor can we, consistently with Constitutional due process of law, hold voluntary a confession where prosecutors do the same thing away from the restraining influences of a public trial in an open court room.

The Constitution of the United States stands as a bar against the conviction of any individual in an American court by means of a coerced confession. There have been, and are now, certain foreign nations with governments dedicated to an opposite policy: governments which convict individuals with testimony obtained by police organizations possessed of an unrestrained power to seize persons suspected of crimes against the state, hold them in secret custody, and wring from them confessions by physical or mental torture. So long as the Constitution remains the basic law of our republic, America will not have that kind of government.

Betts v. *Brady,* 316 U.S. 455 (1942)

[As the foregoing cases indicate, Black has been largely successful in his efforts, as have those others with whom he has
stood, in striking at the third degree. But a trial to which a
man is forced without a lawyer may be as unfair, though the
wrong is less dramatic, as a trial in which a third-degree confession is used. Law, despite the best efforts of the reformers,
is clumsy and technical business. An ignorant poverty-
stricken farm hand like the defendant in *Betts* v. *Brady* may
be totally powerless to defend himself if no counsel is assigned
to him.

Today every defendant in federal court is entitled to a
lawyer, a right that Black's opinion in *Johnson* v. *Zerbst*
304 U.S. 458 (1938) has done much to make effective. This
is also the rule in most of the states. But in some state courts
in non-capital cases a man may be forced to trial without
legal assistance solely because of his poverty, though he plead
for help.

Black has fought that practice hard but unsuccessfully, as
the dissent of *Betts* v. *Brady* indicates. As of 1948 the *Betts*
majority view remained the law by the slim majority of 5 to
4, with Black still dissenting.

The facts of this case are set out further in the opinion be-
low. The majority opinion, holding that the defendant was
not entitled by the federal Constitution to counsel to aid him,
was written by Justice Roberts and was joined by Justices
Reed, Frankfurter, Jackson, and Byrnes and Chief Justice
Stone. Justice Black wrote the dissent, joined by Justices
Murphy and Douglas. (Justice Rutledge, since joining the
Court in place of Justice Byrnes, has taken the same view as
the dissenters here, while Justice Burton and Chief Justice
Vinson have taken the same view as Justice Roberts and
Chief Justice Stone.)]

Mr. Justice Black dissenting:

To hold that the petitioner had a constitutional right to
counsel in this case does not require us to say that "no trial

for any offense, or in any court, can be fairly conducted and justice accorded a defendant who is not represented by counsel." This case can be determined by a resolution of a narrower question: whether in view of the nature of the offense and the circumstances of his trial and conviction, this petitioner was denied the procedural protection which is his right under the Federal Constitution. I think he was.

The petitioner, a farm hand, out of a job and on relief, was indicted in a Maryland state court on a charge of robbery. He was too poor to hire a lawyer. He so informed the court and requested that counsel be appointed to defend him. His request was denied. Put to trial without a lawyer, he conducted his own defense, was found guilty, and was sentenced to eight years' imprisonment. The court below found that the petitioner had "at least an ordinary amount of intelligence." It is clear from his examination of witnesses that he was a man of little education.

If this case had come to us from a federal court, it is clear that we should have to reverse it, because the Sixth Amendment makes the right to counsel in criminal cases inviolable by the Federal Government. I believe that the Fourteenth Amendment made the Sixth applicable to the states. But this view, although often urged in dissents, has never been accepted by a majority of this Court and is not accepted today. A statement of the grounds supporting it is, therefore, unnecessary at this time. I believe, however, that, under the prevailing view of due process, as reflected in the opinion just announced, a view which gives this Court such vast supervisory powers that I am not prepared to accept it without grave doubts, the judgment below should be reversed.

This Court has just declared that due process of law is denied if a trial is conducted in such manner that it is "shocking to the universal sense of justice" or "offensive to the common and fundamental ideas of fairness and right." On another occasion, this Court has recognized that whatever is "implicit in the concept of ordered liberty" and "essential to the substance of a hearing" is within the procedural protection afforded by the constitutional guaranty of due process.

The right to counsel in a criminal proceeding is "fundamental." It is guarded from invasion by the Sixth Amendment, adopted to raise an effective barrier against arbitrary or unjust deprivation of liberty by the Federal Government.

An historical evaluation of the right to a full hearing in criminal cases, and the dangers of denying it, were set out in the *Powell* case, where this Court said: "What . . . does a hearing include? Historically and in practice, in our own country at least, it has always included the right to the aid of counsel when desired and provided by the person asserting the right. . . . Even the intelligent and educated layman . . . lacks both the skill and knowledge adequately to prepare his defense, even though he have a perfect one. He requires the guiding hand of counsel in every step in the proceedings against him. Without it, though he be not guilty, he faces the danger of conviction because he does not know how to establish his innocence."

A practice cannot be reconciled with "common and fundamental ideas of fairness and right," which subjects innocent men to increased dangers of conviction merely because of their poverty. Whether a man is innocent cannot be determined from a trial in which, as here, denial of counsel has made it impossible to conclude, with any satisfactory degree of certainty, that the defendant's case was adequately presented. No one questions that due process requires a hearing before conviction and sentence for the serious crime of robbery. As the Supreme Court of Wisconsin said, in 1859, ". . . would it not be a little like mockery to secure to a pauper these solemn constitutional guaranties for a fair and full trial of the matters with which he was charged, and yet say to him when on trial, that he must employ his own counsel, who could alone render these guaranties of any real permanent value to him. . . . Why this great solicitude to secure him a fair trial if he cannot have the benefit of counsel?"

Denial to the poor of the request for counsel in proceedings based on charges of serious crime has long been regarded as shocking to the "universal sense of justice" throughout this country. In 1854, for example, the Supreme Court of Indiana said: "It is not to be thought of, in a civilized community, for a moment, that any citizen put in jeopardy of life or liberty should be debarred of counsel because he was too poor to employ such aid. No Court could be respected, or respect itself, to sit and hear such a trial. The defense of the poor, in such cases, is a duty resting somewhere, which will be at once conceded as essential to the accused, to the Court, and to the public." And most of the other states have shown their agreement by constitutional provisions, statutes, or established practice judicially approved, which assure that no man shall be deprived of counsel merely because of his poverty. Any other practice seems to me to defeat the promise of our democratic society to provide equal justice under the law.

Smith v. *Texas,* 311 U.S. 128 (1940)

[A trial cannot be fair unless the jury is fairly chosen. It has been an accepted constitutional doctrine since the Civil War that this principle requires that Negroes not be excluded from juries. Yet it has been the practice in many areas, by many devices, to keep them off.

Because the Constitutional principle is so clear, those seeking to avoid it have used devices of at least slight subtlety. The rules do not openly state that Negroes will never be chosen for duty, and the discrimination is left to administration.

In this case the Court in a unanimous opinion by Justice Black struck down such a pattern of discrimination. In a later case Black wrote even more bluntly, establishing a presumption that when in an area in which Negroes live there have been none on juries for many years, it will be assumed unless the state can prove otherwise that there has been discrimination, and the conviction will be voided. In the *Smith* case a conviction obtained by such a discriminatory device was set aside.]

Mr. Justice BLACK delivered the opinion of the Court.

In Harris County, Texas, where petitioner, a Negro, was indicted and convicted of rape, Negroes constitute over 20% of the population, and almost 10% of the poll-tax payers; a minimum of from three to six thousand of them measure up to the qualifications prescribed by Texas statutes for grand jury service. The court clerk, called as a state witness and testifying from court records covering the years 1931 through 1938, showed that only 5 of the 384 grand jurors who served during that period were Negroes; that of 512 persons summoned for grand jury duty, only 18 were Negroes; that of these 18, the names of 13 appeared as the last name on the 16 man jury list, the custom being to select the 12 man grand jury in the order that the names appeared on the list; that of the 5 Negroes summoned for grand jury service who were not given the number 16, 4 were given numbers between 13 and 16, and 1 was number 6; that the result of this numbering was that of the 18 Negroes summoned, only 5 ever served, whereas

379 of the 494 white men summoned actually served; that of 32 grand juries empanelled, only 5 had Negro members, while 27 had none; that of these 5, the same individual served 3 times, so that only 3 individual Negroes served at all; that there had been no Negroes on any of the grand juries in 1938, the year petitioner was indicted; that there had been none on any of the grand juries in 1937; that the service of Negroes by years had been: 1931, 1; 1932, 2; 1933, 1; 1934, 1; 1935, none; 1936, 1; 1937, none; 1938, none.

It is petitioner's contention that his conviction was based on an indictment obtained in violation of the provision of the Fourteenth Amendment that "No state shall . . . deny to any person within its jurisdiction the equal protection of the laws." And the contention that equal protection was denied him rests on a charge that Negroes were in 1938 and long prior thereto intentionally and systematically excluded from grand jury service solely on account of their race and color. That a conviction based upon an indictment returned by a jury so selected is a denial of equal protection is well settled, and is not challenged by the state. But both the trial court and the Texas Court of Criminal Appeals were of opinion that the evidence failed to support the charge of racial discrimination. For that reason the Appellate Court approved the trial court's action in denying petitioner's timely motion to quash the indictment. But the question decided rested upon a charge of denial of equal protection, a basic right protected by the Federal Constitution. And it is therefore our responsibility to appraise the evidence as it relates to this constitutional right.

It is part of the established tradition in the use of juries as instruments of public justice that the jury be a body truly representative of the community. For racial discrimination to result in the exclusion from jury service of otherwise qualified groups not only violates our Constitution and the laws enacted under it but is at war with our basic concepts of a democratic society and a representative government. We must consider this record in the light of these important principles. The fact that the written words of a state's laws hold out a promise that no such discrimination will be practiced is not enough. The Fourteenth Amendment requires that equal protection to all must be given — not merely promised.

Here, the Texas statutory scheme is not in itself unfair; it is capable of being carried out with no racial discrimination whatsoever. But by reason of the wide discretion permissible in the various steps of the plan, it is equally capable of being applied in such a manner as practically to proscribe any group thought by the law's administrators to be undesirable. And from the record before us the conclusion is inescapable that it is the latter application that has prevailed in Harris County. Chance and accident alone could hardly have brought about the listing for grand jury service of so few Negroes from among the thousands shown by the undisputed evidence to possess the legal qualifications for jury service. Nor could chance and accident have been responsible for the combination of circumstances under which a Negro's name, when listed at all, almost invariably appeared as number 16, and under which number 16 was never called for service unless it proved impossible to obtain the required jurors from the first 15 names on the list.

The state argues that the testimony of the commissioners themselves shows that there was no arbitrary or systematic exclusion. And it is true that two of the three commissioners who drew the September, 1938, panel testified to that effect. Both of them admitted that they did not select any Negroes, although the subject was discussed, but both categorically denied that they intentionally, arbitrarily or systematically discriminated against Negro jurors as such. One said that their failure to select Negroes was because they did not know the names of any who were qualified and the other said that he was not personally acquainted with any member of the Negro race. This is, at best, the testimony of two individuals who participated in drawing 1 out of the 32 jury panels discussed in the record. But even if their testimony were given the greatest possible effect, and their situation considered typical of that of the 94 commissioners who did not testify, we would still feel compelled to reverse the decision below. What the Fourteenth Amendment prohibits is racial discrimination in the selection of grand juries. Where jury commissioners limit those from whom grand juries are selected to their own personal acquaintance, discrimination can arise from commissioners who know no Negroes as well as from commissioners who know but eliminate them. If there has been discrimination, whether accomplished ingeniously or ingenuously, the conviction cannot stand.

Duncan v. *Kahanamoku,* 327 U.S. 304 (1946)

[Larger than any of the foregoing questions of fair trial by courts is the question of whether courts may be ousted of their jurisdiction altogether, and their functions transferred to other branches of the government. In war-time the military is prone to grasp for authority to try persons by military commissions rather than by the constitutional method of judge, jury, counsel, confrontation of witnesses, and so on through the guaranties of Anglo-American justice. The foremost single bulwark of our law against such military invasion of civil rights is the Civil War decision of ex parte *Milligan,* a Civil War opinion that Black lauded as a Senator and has applied as a judge. In the *Duncan* case Black wrote the opinion invalidating the military trial of civilians in Hawaii during the recent war.

This opinion involves two criminal proceedings. Harry White, a Honolulu stockbroker, was charged with embezzlement and was arrested in Honolulu in August 1942, about eight months after Pearl Harbor. Duncan, a civilian shipfitter, was arrested in Honolulu for brawling with two marine sentries on February 24, 1944.

Immediately following Pearl Harbor, the Governor of Hawaii declared martial law in Hawaii, suspended the operation of the civil courts, and authorized trials by military commissions for all offenses. He purported to act under the Organic Act, or basic congressional statute governing Hawaii. As a result both White and Duncan were tried, as were hundreds of other persons in Hawaii during the war, by military courts rather than by civil courts, and without numerous of the constitutional protections normally placed around persons accused of crime.

The issue here was whether convictions and sentences imposed by the military on Duncan and White could be carried out. Justice Black wrote the majority opinion, invalidating the sentences. This opinion was joined by Justices Reed, Douglas, Murphy, and Rutledge. Justice Murphy also concurred specially, as did Chief Justice Stone. Justices Burton and Frankfurter dissented, and Justice Jackson took no part.]

Mr. Justice BLACK delivered the opinion of the court.

Did the Organic Act during the period of martial law give the armed forces power to supplant all civilian laws and to substitute military for judicial trials under the conditions that existed in Hawaii at the time these petitioners were tried? The relevant conditions, for our purposes, were the same when both petitioners were tried. The answer to the question depends on a correct interpretation of the Act. But we need not construe the Act, insofar as the power of the military might be used to meet other and different conditions and situations. The boundaries of the

situation with reference to which we do interpret the scope
of the Act can be more sharply defined by stating at this
point some different conditions which either would or might
conceivably have affected to a greater or lesser extent the
scope of the authorized military power. We note first that
at the time the alleged offenses were committed the dangers
apprehended by the military were not sufficiently imminent
to cause them to require civilians to evacuate the area or
even to evacuate any of the buildings necessary to carry on
the business of the courts. In fact, the buildings had long
been open and actually in use for certain kinds of trials.
Our question does not involve the well-established power of
the military to exercise jurisdiction over members of the
armed forces, those directly connected with such forces, or
enemy belligerents, prisoners of war, or others charged with
violating the laws of war. We are not concerned with the
recognized power of the military to try civilians in tribunals established as a part of a temporary military government over occupied enemy territory or territory regained
from an enemy where civilian government cannot and does
not function. For Hawaii since annexation has been held by
and loyal to the United States. Nor need we here consider
the power of the military simply to arrest and detain civilians interfering with a necessary military function at a time
of turbulence and danger from insurrection or war. And
finally, there was no specialized effort of the military, here,
to enforce orders which related only to military functions,
such as, for illustration, curfew rules or blackouts. For
these petitioners were tried before tribunals set up under a
military program which took over all government and su-
perseded all civil laws and courts. If the Organic Act,
properly interpreted, did not give the armed forces this
awesome power, both petitioners are entitled to their freedom.

I

In interpreting the Act we must first look to its language. Section 67 makes it plain that Congress did intend the Governor of Hawaii, with the approval of the President, to invoke military aid under certain circumstances. But Congress did not specifically state to what extent the army could be used or what power it could exercise. It certainly did not explicitly declare that the Governor in conjunction with the military could for days, months or years close all the courts and supplant them with military tribunals. If a power thus to obliterate the judicial system of Hawaii can be found at all in the Organic Act, it must be inferred from Section 67's provision for placing the Territory under "martial law." But the term "martial law" carries no precise meaning. The Constitution does not refer to "martial law" at all and no Act of Congress had defined the term. It has been employed in various ways by different people and at different times. By some it has been identified as "military law" limited to members of, and those connected with, the armed forces. Others have said that the term does not imply a system of established rules but denotes simply some kind of day to day expression of a General's will dictated by what he considers the imperious necessity of the moment. In 1857 the confusion as to the meaning of the phrase was so great that the Attorney General in an official opinion had this to say about it: "The Common Law authorities and commentators afford no clue to what martial law as understood in England really is. . . . In this country it is still worse." What was true in 1857 remains true today. The language of Section 67 thus fails to define adequately the scope of the power given to the military and to show whether the Organic Act provides that courts of law be supplanted by military tribunals.

III

Since both the language of the Organic Act and its legislative history fail to indicate that the scope of "martial law" in Hawaii includes the supplanting of courts by military tribunals, we must look to other sources in order to interpret that term. We think the answer may be found in the birth, development and growth of our governmental institutions up to the time Congress passed the Organic Act. Have the principles and practices developed during the birth and growth of our political institutions been such as to persuade us that Congress intended that loyal civilians in loyal territory should have their daily conduct governed by military orders substituted for criminal laws, and that such civilians should be tried and punished by military tribunals? Let us examine what those principles and practices have been, with respect to the position of civilian government and the courts and compare that with the standing of military tribunals throughout our history.

People of many ages and countries have feared and unflinchingly opposed the kind of subordination of executive, legislative and judicial authorities to complete military rule which according to the government Congress has authorized here. In this country that fear has become part of our cultural and political institutions. The story of that development is well known and we see no need to retell it all. But we might mention a few pertinent incidents. As early as the 17th Century our British ancestors took political action against aggressive military rule. When James I and Charles I authorized martial law for purposes of speedily punishing all types of crimes committed by civilians the protest led to the historic Petition of Right which in uncompromising terms objected to this arbitrary procedure and prayed that it be stopped and never repeated. When later the American colonies declared their independence one of the grievances listed by Jefferson was that the King had endeavored to render the military superior to the civil power. The executive and military officials who later found it necessary to utilize the armed forces to keep order in a young and turbulent nation, did not lose sight of the philosophy embodied in the Petition of Rights and the Declaration of Independence, that existing civilian government and especially the courts were not to be interfered with by the exercise of military power. In 1787, the year in which the Constitution was formulated, the Governor of Massachusetts colony used the militia to cope with Shays's rebellion. In his instructions to the Commander of the troops the Governor listed the "great objects" of the mission. The troops were to "protect the judicial courts . . . ," "to assist the civil magistrates in executing the laws . . . ," and to "aid them in apprehending the disturbers of the public peace. . . ." The Commander was to consider himself "constantly as under the direction of the civil officer, saving where any armed force shall appear and oppose . . . [his] marching to execute these orders." President Washington's instructions to the Commander of the troops sent into Pennsylvania to suppress the Whiskey Rebellion of 1794 were to see to it that the laws were enforced and were to deliver the leaders of armed insurgents to the regular courts for trial. The President admonished the Commanding General "that the judge can not be controlled in his functions." In the many instances of the use of troops to control the activities of civilians that followed, the troops were generally again employed merely to aid and not to supplant the civilian authorities. The last noteworthy incident before the enactment of the Organic Act was the rioting that occurred in the Spring of 1899 at the Coeur-d'Alene mines of Shoshone County, Idaho. The President ordered the regular troops to report to the Governor for instructions and to support the civil authorities in preserving the peace. Later the State Auditor as agent of the Governor, and not the Commanding General, ordered the troops to detain citizens without trial and to aid the Auditor in doing all he thought necessary to stop the riot. Once more, the military authorities did not undertake to supplant the courts and to establish military tribunals to try and punish ordinary civilian offenders.

Courts and their procedural safeguards are indispensable to our system of government. They were set up by our founders to protect the liberties they valued. Our system of government clearly is the antithesis of total military rule and the founders of this country are not likely to have contemplated complete military dominance within the limits of a Territory made part of this country and not recently taken from an enemy. They were opposed to governments that placed in the hands of one man the power to make, interpret and enforce the laws. Their philosophy has been the people's throughout our history. For that reason we have maintained legislatures chosen by citizens or their representatives and courts and juries to try those who violate legislative enactments. We have always been especially concerned about the potential evils of summary criminal trials and have guarded against them by provisions embodied in the Constitution itself. Legislatures and courts are not merely cherished American institutions; they are indispensable to our government.

Military tribunals have no such standing. For as this Court has said before: ". . . the military should always be kept in subjection to the laws of the country to which it belongs, and that he is no friend to the Republic who advocates the contrary. The established principle of every free people is, that the law shall alone govern; and to it the

military must always yield." Congress prior to the time of
the enactment of the Organic Act had only once authorized
the supplanting of the courts by military tribunals. Legislation to that effect was enacted immediately after the
South's unsuccessful attempt to secede from the Union. Insofar as that legislation applied to the Southern States
after the war was at an end it was challenged by a series of
Presidential vetoes as vigorous as any in the country's history. And in order to prevent this Court from passing on
the constitutionality of this legislation Congress found it
necessary to curtail our appellate jurisdiction. Indeed,
prior to the Organic Act, the only time this Court had ever
discussed the supplanting of courts by military tribunals
in a situation other than that involving the establishment of
a military government over recently occupied enemy territory, it had emphatically declared that "civil liberty and
this kind of martial law cannot endure together; the an-
tagonism is irreconcilable; and, in the conflict, one or the
other must perish."

We believe that when Congress passed the Hawaiian Organic Act and authorized the establishment of "martial
law" it had in mind and did not wish to exceed the boundaries between military and civilian power, in which our
people have always believed, which responsible military and
executive officers had heeded, and which had become part of
our political philosophy and institutions prior to the time
Congress passed the Organic Act. The phrase "martial law"
as employed in that Act, therefore, while intended to authorize the military to act vigorously for the maintenance
of an orderly civil government and for the defense of the
Islands against actual or threatened rebellion or invasion,
was not intended to authorize the supplanting of courts by
military tribunals. Yet the government seeks to justify the
punishment of both White and Duncan on the ground of

such supposed Congressional authorization. We hold that both petitioners are now entitled to be released from custody.

United States v. *Lovett,* 328 U.S. 303 (1946)

[The first four cases in this section illustrate abuses in trial by courts, and the Hawaiian cases illustrate abuses in trials by the executive department. The *Lovett* case is included because it involves what was substantially a trial by the remaining branch of the federal government, the Congress. As the opinion shows, a man may be deprived of his rights by any of the three branches of the government, and it is the duty of the Supreme Court to protect against all three.

Here the Dies, or Un-American, Committee of the House of Representatives presented charges against a number of government employees. This Un-American Committee was thus prosecutor, while a second House committee was judge, and the full Congress was executioner of a sentence that after a certain date no salary could be paid to three government employees, Messrs. Watson, Dodd, and Lovett.

President Roosevelt declared that he considered this action by Congress unconstitutional, but he was compelled to sign the bill that contained it because it also contained vital war appropriations. The three employees were kept on government rolls after the date fixed, and then they sued for their salaries on the ground that the statute was unconstitutional.

The Court, in an opinion by Justice Black, held the provision denying payment to these men unconstitutional. This opinion was joined by Justices Douglas, Murphy, Rutledge, and Burton. Justices Frankfurter and Reed concurred in the result on other grounds, and Justice Jackson did not participate.]

Mr. Justice BLACK delivered the opinion of the Court.

In the background of the statute here challenged lies the House of Representatives' feeling in the late thirties that many "subversives" were occupying influential positions in the Government and elsewhere and their influence must not remain unchallenged. As part of its program against "subversive" activities the House in May 1938 created a Committee on Un-American Activities, which became known as the Dies Committee after its Chairman, Congressman Martin Dies. This Committee conducted a series of investigations and made lists of people and organizations it thought "subversive." The creation of the Dies Committee was followed by provisions such as § 9A of the Hatch Act and 17 (b) of the Emergency Relief Appropriations Act of 1941, which forbade the holding of a federal job by anyone who was a member of a political party or organization that advocated the overthrow of our Constitutional form of Government in the United States. It became the practice to include a similar prohibition in all appropriations acts, together with criminal penalties for its violation. Under these provisions the Federal Bureau of Investigation began wholesale investigations of federal employees, which investigations were financed by special Congressional appropriations. Thousands were investigated.

While all this was happening Mr. Dies on February 1, 1943, in a long speech on the floor of the House attacked thirty-nine named Government employees as "irresponsible, unrepresentative, crackpot, radical bureaucrats" and affiliates of "communist front organizations." Among these named individuals were the three respondents. Congressman Dies told the House that respondents, as well as the other thirty-six individuals he named, were, because of their beliefs and past associations unfit to "hold a government position" and urged Congress to refuse "to appropriate money for their salaries." In this connection he proposed that the Committee on Appropriations "take immediate and vigorous steps to eliminate these people from public office." Four days later an amendment was offered to the Treasury-Post Office Appropriation Bill which provided that "no part of any appropriation contained in this Act shall be used to pay the compensation of" the thirty-nine individuals Dies had attacked. The Congressional Record shows that this amendment precipitated a debate that continued for several days. All of those participating agreed that the "charges" against the thirty-nine individuals were serious. Some wanted to accept Congressman Dies' statements as sufficient proof of "guilt," while others referred to such proposed action as "legislative lynching," smacking "of the procedure in the French Chamber of Deputies, during the Reign of Terror." The Dies charges were referred to as "indictments," and many claimed this made it necessary that the named federal employees be given a hearing and a chance to prove themselves innocent. Congressman Dies then suggested that the Appropriations Committee "weigh the evidence and . . . take immediate steps to dismiss these people from the federal service." Eventually a resolution was proposed to defer action until the Appropriations Committee could investigate, so that accused federal employees would get a chance to prove themselves "innocent" of communism or disloyalty, and so that each "man would have his day in court," and "There would be no star chamber proceedings." . . .

The Senate Appropriations Committee eliminated Section 304 and its action was sustained by the Senate. After the first conference report which left the matter still in disagreement the Senate voted 69 to 0 against the conference report which left § 304 in the bill. The House however insisted on the amendment and indicated that it would not approve any appropriation bill without § 304. Finally after the fifth conference report showed that the House would not yield the Senate adopted § 304. When the President signed the bill he stated: "The Senate yielded, as I have been forced to yield, to avoid delaying our conduct of the war. But I cannot so yield without placing on record my view that this provision is not only unwise and discriminatory, but unconstitutional." . . .

We hold that § 304 falls precisely within the category of Congressional actions which the Constitution barred by providing that "No Bill of Attainder or Ex Post Facto Law shall be passed." In *Cummings* v. *Missouri,* this Court said, "A bill of attainder is a legislative Act which inflicts punishment without a judicial trial. If the punishment be less than death, the act is termed a bill of pains and penalties. Within the meaning of the Constitution, bills of attainder include bills of pains and penalties." The *Cummings* decision involved a provision of the Missouri Reconstruction Constitution which required persons to take an Oath of Loyalty as a prerequisite to practicing a profession. Cummings, a Catholic Priest, was convicted for teaching and preaching as a minister without taking the oath. The oath required an applicant to affirm that he had never given aid or comfort to persons engaged in hostility to the United States and had never "been a member of or connected with any order, society, or organization inimical to the government of the United States. . . ." In an illuminating opinion which gave the historical background of the Constitutional prohibition against bills of attainder, this Court invalidated the Missouri Constitutional provision both because it constituted a bill of attainder and because it had an ex post facto operation. On the same day the *Cummings* Case was decided, the Court, in Ex parte *Garland,* also held invalid on the same grounds an Act of Congress which required attorneys practicing before this Court to take a similar oath. Neither of these cases has ever been overruled. They stand for the proposition that legislative acts, no matter what their form, that apply either to named individuals or to easily ascertainable members of a group in such a way as to inflict punishment on them without a judicial trial are bills of attainder prohibited by the Constitution. Adherence to this principle requires invalidation of § 304. We do adhere to it.

Section 304 was designed to apply to particular individuals. Just as the statute in the two cases mentioned it "operates as a legislative decree of perpetual exclusion" from a chosen vocation. This permanent proscription from any opportunity to serve the Government is punishment, and of a most severe type. It is a type of punishment which Congress has only invoked for special types of odious and dangerous crimes, such as treason, acceptance of bribes by members of Congress, or by other governmental officials, and interference with elections by Army and Navy officers.

Section 304, thus, clearly accomplishes the punishment of named individuals without a judicial trial. The fact that the punishment is inflicted through the instrumentality of an Act specifically cutting off the pay of certain named individuals found guilty of disloyalty, makes it no less galling or effective than if it had been done by an Act which designated the conduct as criminal. No one would think that Congress could have passed a valid law, stating that after investigation it had found Lovett, Dodd, and Watson "guilty" of the crime of engaging in "subversive activities," defined that term for the first time, and sentenced them to perpetual exclusion from any government employment. Section 304, while it does not use that language, accomplishes that result. The effect was to inflict punishment without the safeguards of a judicial trial and "determined by no previous law or fixed rule." The Constitution declares that that cannot be done either by a state or by the United States.

Those who wrote our Constitution well knew the danger inherent in special legislative acts which take away the life, liberty, or property of particular named persons, because the legislature thinks them guilty of conduct which deserves punishment. They intended to safeguard the people of this country from punishment without trial by duly constituted courts. And even the courts to which this important function was entrusted were commanded to stay their hands until and unless certain tested safeguards were observed. An accused in court must be tried by an impartial jury, has a right to be represented by counsel, he must be clearly informed of the charge against him, the law which he is charged with violating must have been passed before he committed the act charged, he must be confronted by the witnesses against him, he must not be compelled to incriminate himself, he cannot twice be put in jeopardy for the same offense, and even after conviction no cruel and unusual punishment can be inflicted upon him. When our Constitution and Bill of Rights were written, our ancestors had ample reason to know that legislative trials and punishments were too dangerous to liberty to exist in the nation of free men they envisioned. And so they proscribed bills of attainder. Section 304 is one. Much as we regret to declare that an Act of Congress violates the Constitution, we have no alternative here.

Section 304 therefore does not stand as an obstacle to payment of compensation to Lovett, Watson, and Dodd. The judgment in their favor is affirmed.

Section IV

MARRIAGE AND

DIVORCE

Williams v. *North Carolina,* 325 U.S. 226 (1945)

[The *Williams* case scarcely fits any of the categories into which these materials have been divided. It is included because of the earnestness with which Black expressed the feeling that the law should struggle to avoid situations in which a man may have a legitimate divorce in one part of the country and be a bigamist in another. Perhaps a man should have a "civil right" to know whether or not he is married.

Mr. Williams and Mrs. Hendrix, each of whom had previously been married in North Carolina, went to Nevada in 1940 and obtained divorces. Thereupon Mr. Williams and Mrs. Hendrix were married in Nevada and returned to North Carolina to live. The first Mrs. Williams and Mr. Hendrix had stayed at home in North Carolina while their spouses took up residence in Nevada for the purpose of obtaining the divorces.

The state of North Carolina brought a criminal action against Williams and his second wife charging bigamy. The essential issue was whether the Nevada divorces were valid. The couple were convicted in North Carolina. In 1942 the Supreme Court, in an opinion by Justice Douglas, reversed the conviction, saying that North Carolina, under the Constitution, was required to give "full faith and credit" to the Nevada divorce decrees and had not done so. The Supreme Court, however, reserved the question of whether North Carolina would have to recognize the Nevada divorces if North Carolina found that the "residence" in Nevada was "fraudulent."

Thereupon North Carolina tried Williams and Mrs. Hendrix again, this time finding that the residence had been "fraudulent." In a second appeal to the Supreme Court that Court this time sustained the conviction in an opinion by Justice Frankfurter, joined by Justices Roberts, Reed, Murphy, and Jackson and Chief Justice Stone. Justice Murphy also concurred specially, joined by Justice Jackson and Chief Justice Stone. Justice Rutledge dissented. Justice Black dissented in an opinion with which Justice Douglas concurred and from which the following excerpts are taken.]

Mr. Justice BLACK dissenting:

Anglo-American law has, until today, steadfastly maintained the principle that before an accused can be convicted of crime, he must be proven guilty beyond a reasonable doubt. These petitioners have been sentenced to prison because they were unable to prove their innocence to the satisfaction of the State of North Carolina. They have been convicted under a statute so uncertain in its application that not even the most learned member of the bar could have advised them in advance as to whether their conduct would violate the law. In reality the petitioners are being deprived of their freedom because the State of Nevada, through its legislature and courts, follows a liberal policy in granting divorces. They had Nevada divorce decrees which authorized them to remarry. Without charge or proof of fraud in obtaining these decrees, and without holding the decrees invalid under Nevada law, this Court affirms a conviction of petitioners, for living together as husband and wife. I cannot reconcile this with the Full Faith and Credit Clause and with congressional legislation passed pursuant to it. . . .

The fact that two people will be deprived of their constitutional rights impels me to protest as vigorously as I can

4. *Marriage and Divorce*

against affirmance of these convictions. Even more, the Court's opinion today will cast a cloud over the lives of countless numbers of the multitude of divorced persons in the United States. The importance of the issues prompts me to set out my views in some detail.

Statistics indicate that approximately five million divorced persons are scattered throughout the forty-eight states. More than 85% of these divorces were granted in uncontested proceedings. . . .

Today's opinion undermines and makes uncertain the validity of every uncontested divorce decree. It wipes out every semblance of their finality and decisiveness. It achieves what the Court terms the "desirable effect" of providing the "same" quality to every divorce decree, "wherever the question arises" — it endows them all alike with the "same" instability and precariousness. The result is to classify divorced persons in a distinctive and invidious category. A year ago, a majority of this Court in a workmen's compensation case declared the Full Faith and Credit clause of the Constitution was a "nationally unifying force"; today, as to divorce decrees, that clause, coupled with a new content recently added to the Due Process Clause, has become a nationally disruptive force. Uncontested divorce decrees are thus so degraded that a person who marries in reliance upon them can be sent to jail. . . .

The petitioners were married in Nevada. North Carolina has sentenced them to prison for living together as husband and wife in North Carolina. This Court today affirms those sentences without a determination that the Nevada marriage was invalid under that State's laws. This holding can be supported, if at all, only on one of two grounds: (1) North Carolina has extra-territorial boundaries, or, (2) North Carolina can punish people who live together in that state as husband and wife even though they have been validly married in Nevada. A holding based on either of these two grounds encroaches upon the general principle recognized by this Court that a marriage validly consummated under one state's laws is valid in every other state. If the Court is today abandoning that principle, it takes away from the states a large part of their hitherto plenary control over the institution of marriage. A further consequence is to subject people to criminal prosecutions for adultery and bigamy merely because they exercise their constitutional right to pass from a state in which they were validly married into another state which refuses to recognize their marriage. . . .

The Court permits North Carolina to disregard the decrees on the following line of reasoning. No state need give full faith and credit to a "void" decree. A decree rendered by a court without "jurisdiction" is "void." No state court has "jurisdiction" to grant a divorce unless one of the parties is "domiciled" in Nevada. Therefore, the Nevada court had no "jurisdiction," the decrees are "void," and North Carolina need not give them faith or credit. The solution to all these problems depends in turn upon the question common to all of them — does State law or Federal law apply?

The Constitution provides that "Full Faith and Credit shall be given in each State to the public Acts, Records, and judicial Proceedings of every other State. And the Congress may by general Laws prescribe the Manner in which such Acts, Records and Proceedings shall be proved, and the *Effect thereof.*" (Emphasis added.) Acting pursuant to this constitutional authority, Congress in 1790 declared what law should govern and what "Effect" should be given the judgments of state courts. That statute is still the law. Its command is that they "shall have such faith and credit given to them . . . as they have by law or usage in the courts of the State from which they are taken." If, as the Court today implies, divorce decrees should be given less effect than other court judgments, Congress alone has the constitutional power to say so. We should not attempt to solve the "divorce problem" by constitutional interpretation. At least, until Congress had commanded a different "Effect" for divorces granted on a short sojourn within a state, we should stay our hands. A proper respect for the Constitution and the Congress would seem to me to require that we leave this problem where the Constitution did. If we follow that course, North Carolina cannot be permitted to disregard the Nevada decrees without passing upon the "faith and credit" which Nevada itself would give to them under its own "law or usage." The Court has decided the matter as though it were a purely *federal* question; Congress and the Constitution declared it to be a *state* question. The logic of the Court does not persuade me that we should ignore these mandates of the Congress and the Constitution. Nevada's decrees purported to grant petitioners an absolute divorce with a right to remarry. No "law or usage" of Nevada has been pointed out to us which would indicate that Nevada would, under any circumstances, consider its decrees so "void" as to warrant imprisoning those who have remarried in reliance upon such existing and unannulled decrees. . . .

Implicit in the majority of the opinions rendered by this and other courts, which, whether designedly or not, have set up obstacles to the procurement of divorces, is the assumption that divorces are an unmitigated evil, and that the law can and should force unwilling persons to live with each other. Others approach the problem as one which can best be met by moral, ethical and religious teachings. Which viewpoint is correct is not our concern. I am confident, however, that today's decision will no more aid in the solu-

tion of the problem than the Dred Scott decision aided in
settling controversies over slavery. This decision, I think,
takes the wrong road. Federal courts should have less, not
more, to do with divorces. Only when one state refuses to
give that faith and credit to a divorce decree which Congress and the Constitution command, should we enter this
field. . . .

ALIENS

Ex parte Kawato, 317 U.S. 69 (1942)

[Kawato was a Japanese alien who had lived in the United States since 1905. In 1941 he brought an action to collect wages due him as a fisherman and to recover compensation for injuries suffered in the course of his work. The defendant interposed an objection in 1942, before the matter had been tried, claiming that Kawato could not sue in an American court because of the war between the United States and Japan. The essence of the argument was that an enemy alien has "no right to prosecute any action in any court of the United States during the pendency" of the war.

The opinion of the Court was delivered by Justice Black. In a portion of the opinion not included here, the Court analyzed the relevant federal statutes and concluded that no statute barred Kawato from proceeding.]

Mr. Justice BLACK delivered the opinion of the Court.

"Alien enemy" as applied to petitioner is at present but the legal definition of his status because he was born in Japan with which we are at war. Nothing in this record indicates, and we cannot assume, that he came to America for any purpose different from that which prompted millions of others to seek our shores — a chance to make his home and work in a free country, governed by just laws, which promise equal protection to all who abide by them.

His suit invokes the protection of those laws through our courts both to obtain payment of wages alleged to have been promised him by American citizens for lawful work and reimbursement on account of damages suffered while working for those citizens.

There doubtless was a time when the common law of England would have supported dismissal of petitioner's action, but that time has long since passed. A number of early English decisions, based on a group concept which made little difference between friends and enemies barred all aliens from the courts. This rule was gradually relaxed as to friendly aliens until finally in *Wells* v. *Williams,* the Court put the necessities of trade ahead of whatever advantages had been imagined to exist in the old rule, and held that enemy aliens in England under license from the Crown might proceed in the courts. As applied ever since, alien enemies residing in England have been permitted to maintain actions, while those in the land of the enemy were not; and this modern, humane principle has been applied even when the alien was interned as is petitioner here.

The original English common law rule, long ago abandoned there, was, from the beginning, objectionable here. The policy of severity toward alien enemies was clearly impossible for a country whose life blood came from an immigrant stream. In the war of 1812, for example, many persons born in England fought on the American side. Harshness toward immigrants was inconsistent with that national knowledge, present then as now, of the contributions made in peace and war by the millions of immigrants who have learned to love the country of their adoption more than the country of their birth. Hence, in 1813 Chief Justice Kent, in *Clarke* v. *Morey,* set the legal pattern which, with sporadic exceptions, has since been followed. The core of that decision he put in these words: "A lawful residence implies protection, and a capacity to sue and be sued. A contrary doctrine would be repugnant to sound policy, no less than to justice and humanity." Thus the courts aligned their policy with that enjoined upon the President by Congress in 1812 when it directed him to administer the laws controlling aliens in a manner that would be "consistent with the public safety, and according to the dictates of humanity and national hospitality."

In asking that the rights of resident aliens be abrogated in their behalf, private litigants in effect seek to stand in the position of government. But only the government, and not the private individual, is vested with the power to protect all the people, including loyal aliens, from possible injury from disloyal aliens. If the public welfare demands that this alien shall not receive compensation for his work or payment for his injuries received in the course of his employment, the government can make the decision without allowing a windfall to these claimants. Even if petitioner were a non-resident enemy alien, it might be more appropriate to release the amount of his claim to the Alien Property Custodian rather than to the claimants; and this is precisely what was done in *Birge-Forbes Co.* v. *Heye,* in which this Court said that the sole objection to giving judgment for an alien enemy "goes only so far as it would give aid and comfort to the other side." The ancient rule against suits by resident alien enemies has survived only so far as necessary to prevent use of the courts to accomplish a purpose which might hamper our own war efforts or give aid to the enemy. This may be taken as the sound principle of the common law today.

INDEX

INDEX

A NOTE ON THE TYPE USED IN THIS BOOK

The text of this book was set on the Linotype in *Scotch,* a
type-face that has been in continuous service for more than
one hundred years. It is usually considered that the style of
"modern face" followed in our present-day cuttings of Scotch
was developed in the foundry of Alexander Wilson and Sons
of Glasgow early in the nineteenth century. The new Wilson
patterns were made to meet the requirements of the new fashion in printing that had been set going at the beginning of the
century by the "modern" types of Didot in France and of Bo-
doni in Italy. It is to be observed that the *modern* in these
matters is a modernity of A.D. 1800, not of today. The "mod-
ernist" type-faces of today are quite another story.

The book was manufactured by The Plimpton Press, Nor-
wood, Massachusetts. Typography and binding based on original designs by W. A. Dwiggins.